M000211637

CAPABILITIES, POWER, AND INSTITUTIONS

EDITED BY
STEPHEN L. ESQUITH AND FRED GIFFORD

CAPABILITIES, POWER, AND INSTITUTIONS

Toward a More Critical Development Ethics

The Pennsylvania State University Press
University Park, Pennsylvania

Library of Congress
Cataloging-in-Publication Data

Capabilities, power, and institutions : toward a more
critical development ethics /
edited by Stephen L. Esquith and Fred Gifford.
p.   cm.
Includes bibliographical references and index.
Summary: "A collection of essays that extend, criticize,
and reformulate the capability approach to human
development, originally formulated by Amartya Sen
and Martha Nussbaum, in order to better understand the
importance of power, especially institutional power"
—Provided by publisher.
ISBN 978-0-271-03661-8 (cloth : alk. paper)
1. Political ethics.
2. Social ethics.
3. Social justice.
4. Distributive justice.
5. Welfare economics.
I. Esquith, Stephen L. (Stephen Lawrence), 1949– .
II. Gifford, Fred.

JA79.C253 2010
172—dc22
2009038283

Copyright © 2010
The Pennsylvania State University
All rights reserved
Printed in the United States of America
Published by
The Pennsylvania State University Press,
University Park, PA 16802-1003

The Pennsylvania State University Press is a
member of the Association of
American University Presses.

It is the policy of The Pennsylvania State
University Press to use acid-free paper.
Publications on uncoated stock satisfy
the minimum requirements of American
National Standard for Information
Sciences—Permanence of Paper for Printed
Library Material, ANSI Z39.48–1992.

This book is printed on Natures Natural,
which contains 50% post-consumer waste.

Contents

CONTENTS

Acknowledgments

The original impetus for this volume came from a three-day conference on ethics and development held at Michigan State University in April 2005, cosponsored by the International Development Ethics Association (IDEA); several international programs at MSU, including the Center for Advanced Study of International Development; and the Department of Philosophy. The contributions to this volume build on the conversations held during that conference and subsequent work by our contributors in many other venues and fora.

The growing field of ethics and development has spawned new journals, meetings, and programs throughout the world over the past decade, perhaps most notably the *Journal of Human Development and Capabilities* and the *Journal of Global Ethics*. At MSU since 2005, building on existing faculty and programmatic resources in agricultural ethics and bioethics, we have created an interdisciplinary doctoral program in ethics and development. The contributions to this volume reflect the breadth and depth of this new interdisciplinary field. We are grateful to our colleagues in organizations such as IDEA and the Human Capability Development Association, and in institutions such as our own who recognize the need for addressing the challenges and problems in and of development from an ethically informed perspective.

There are many individuals we should thank—in addition to the contributors to this volume, conference conveners, and editors—who have made possible this particular critical collection of essays on the human capability approach to development. Their names recur frequently in these essays. Several people, however, have been just as important behind the scenes. David Wiley, former longtime director of the African Studies Center at MSU; Karen Klomparens, dean of the Graduate School at MSU; John Staatz of the Department of Agricultural, Food, and Resource Economics; and Scott Whiteford, former director of the Center for Latin American and Caribbean Studies at MSU (now director of the Center for Latin American Studies, University of Arizona), provided substantial institutional and intellectual support. Sandy Thatcher, former director of the Pennsylvania State University Press, provided critical encouragement throughout the editorial process. His acute comments and constructive suggestions, as well as those of our reviewers, have helped us craft a volume that is more focused and critical. Carol Cole in the Residential College in the Arts and Humanities at MSU and Nicholas Taylor, copyeditor for Pennsylvania State University Press, have been ideal copyeditors, moving us through several drafts, one contributor at a time. The careful work done by our former graduate student Kwangsu Mok in constructing the index for this volume was indispensable. We thank them all with pleasure for their encouragement and hard work.

Stephen L. Esquith
Fred Gifford

Introduction:
Institutions and Urgency

Stephen L. Esquith

The essays in this collection extend, criticize, and reformulate the capability approach to human development to better understand the importance of power, especially institutional power. As originally formulated by Amartya Sen and Martha Nussbaum, the capability approach has certainly been concerned with institutions. In *Development as Freedom* (1999), Sen writes, "Individuals live and operate in a world of institutions. Our opportunities and prospects depend crucially on what institutions exist and how they function. Not only do institutions contribute to our freedoms, their roles can be sensibly evaluated in the light of their contributions to our freedom. To see development as freedom provides a perspective in which institutional assessment can systematically occur" (142). The organizing question of this volume is: Has the capability approach been concerned with institutions *enough*? Despite his recent critique of "transcendental institutionalism" (Sen 2010, 24), there are clear signs that Sen has taken institutions seriously,[1] including his 2005 review of Paul Farmer's *Pathologies of Power* (Sen 2005, xi–xvii).[2]

We begin with a relatively friendly answer: not quite enough. We then move through a series of essays that take the capability approach more heavily to task. Each of the essays maps out new territory, some closer to home and some

I wish to thank Fred Gifford, John Staatz, Shelley Feldman, Sabina Alkire, and Al Schmid for their comments on earlier drafts of this introduction, as well as the anonymous reviewers for the Pennsylvania State University Press.

well beyond the boundaries of Sen's and Nussbaum's capability approach to development. In every case, however, the arguments presented take the capability approach as an important point of departure or object of contestation. Whatever its shortcomings, the capability approach is the most ambitious theory of development we have; it must be addressed critically to move human development further along a more ethical path.

As Mahbub ul Haq put it in 1995 during the early days of the capability approach: "It is fair to say that the human development paradigm is the most holistic development model that exists today. It embraces every development issue, including economic growth, social investment, people's empowerment, provision of basic needs and social safety nets, political and cultural freedoms, and all other aspects of people's lives. It is neither narrowly technocratic nor overly philosophical. It is a practical reflection of life itself" (Haq 2003, 21). The essays in this collection share this ambition; they take up issues in economics, anthropology, politics, and society without being narrowly technocratic, and they raise philosophical questions about moral assumptions and goals without being overly philosophical. In the process, they sometimes extend the original capability approach, but more often they criticize its treatment of power and institutions precisely because these contributors also share with the capability approach a certain sense of urgency. This urgency stems from the fact that problems and dilemmas faced by poor countries and the poor residents of richer countries are not theirs alone. Whether we call it globalization or neoliberal globalization,[3] we increasingly share a common fate and should not remain "coolly accustomed" to these problems and dilemmas.[4] This is as true for the effects of poverty and civil war on regional stability as it is for the effects of transgenic crops on biodiversity.[5] These are not problems and dilemmas that can be exported, quarantined, or ignored with impunity.

Another way to think of this sense of urgency is to recognize, as Nigel Dower argues in the final contribution to this volume, that ethics itself is becoming a global necessity, if not yet a global reality. Not only are the ethical problems and issues of today global in structure and scope, but the development of principles of ethical reasoning and the norms of ethical life are becoming more widely debated. According to Dower (Chapter 9, this volume), the globalization of ethics is a "process whereby certain values come to be accepted by all or almost all people across the world." This may overstate how far along this process has moved, but not how widely shared the sense of urgency is that such an ethic be found. It is with this sense of urgency that our contributors take on the promise as well as the limitations of the capability approach.

The Fragmentary Development of Development Ethics

How, beyond their shared sense of urgency, should we describe ethical theories of development in general? One way is to try to piece together the problems and dilemmas that have been discussed. Development ethics has struggled with issues such as cultural relativism, technological determinism, and the meaning of human flourishing in the context of globalization (Gasper 2004). These theories have only begun to come to terms with the question of who is responsible for the uneven and sometimes paradoxical developments wrought by the policies of privatization, liberalization, and deregulation that have steered globalization.[6] Further, the theoretical picture is fragmentary because of the uneven effect of globalization around the world.

Globalization has created hierarchies within developed countries as well as hierarchical relationships between developed and less developed countries (Sharma 2008). Neoliberal globalization also has not touched down uniformly around the world. Global transactions, campaigns, and investments occur intensely in some locales with a variety of results, and hardly at all in others. To use James Ferguson's apt metaphor, neoliberal globalization hops from place to place, sometimes leaving the poorest countries worse off than they were before, sometimes skipping over them entirely. Where it has touched down in Africa, for example, globalization often has meant the extraction of natural resources without a significant investment in local human capital, or it has meant the establishment of armed enclaves and private security forces at the expense of local popular governance (Ferguson 2006).

Despite this mixed record, many advocates of neoliberal development policies remain optimistic about the future of globalization. They continue to believe that market-oriented development policies and strategies, "humanely augmented," will rid the world of hunger, poverty, and war once and for all. They tell us that we just have to get the development technology right (Easterly 2001; Lipton 1998; but see Rodrik 2001).

Jeffrey D. Sachs, economist, Nobel laureate, special adviser to UN secretary-general Kofi Annan on the Millennium Development Goals, and a surprising critic of some market strategies to solve the problems of extreme poverty, still shares this basic article of faith with his trade liberalization opponents. For Sachs, the single most important reason why prosperity has spread in some regions such as India, and why it has begun to spread in others such as China and Brazil, is "the transmission of technologies and the ideas underlying them"

(2005, 41). To end poverty, he argues, basic appropriate technologies must be brought on a country-by-country, "clinical" basis to the one billion people, or almost one-sixth of humanity, who live in extreme poverty. The causes of extreme poverty vary because physical geographies vary, but the solutions have a common characteristic: the poor are trapped in extreme poverty and cannot extricate themselves from it without help, primarily in the form of technological know-how (56–57).

Are the poor getting this kind of help through neoliberal globalization policies? Another Nobel laureate and former chief economist of the World Bank, Joseph E. Stiglitz, worries that they are not: "Globalization today is not working for many of the world's poor. It is not working for much of the environment. It is not working for the stability of the global economy. The transition from communism to a market economy has been so badly managed that, with the exception of China, Vietnam, and a few Eastern European countries, poverty has soared as incomes have plummeted" (2002, 214). Sachs and Stiglitz are not alone in criticizing the current direction of neoliberal globalization.[7] Platitudes such as the inevitable trade-off between growth and equity are being shelved by the United Nations, which recognizes that increasing levels of inequality within and across national boundaries are not just intrinsically abhorrent, but are also obstacles to economic growth.[8]

There are many competing reasons why inequality is increasing, undercutting growth, and thereby leaving the fruits of globalization beyond the reach of so many. According to the United Nations, the poorest countries are moving away from, not toward, the 2015 Millennium Development Goals (halving poverty, hunger, and human suffering) because public-sector domestic investment and foreign aid have failed to provide the foundations and infrastructure for private investment and growth in the poorest parts of the world, especially sub-Saharan Africa.[9] Others also recognize the link between poverty and inequality but argue that in some cases the absence of institutional infrastructure itself may be the product of certain kinds of foreign aid. Just as some forms of economic aid have had unintended negative economic consequences (for example, the so-called Dutch disease, in which some forms of aid negatively affect exchange rates), other forms of aid have also weakened rather than strengthened political institutions by replacing the connections between tax-paying citizens and the tax-collecting government with a government-donor relationship (Moss, Pettersson, and Van de Walle 2006).

Despite these reservations and concerns, optimists like Sachs and Stiglitz still believe that carefully targeted foreign aid is a necessary, if not sufficient, condition for escaping the traps of extreme poverty. Economic skeptics reject Sachs's program for reaching the Millennium Development Goals as just a remake of earlier "Big Push" approaches of the 1950s and 1960s. These critics warn that large amounts of aid, even emergency food aid, can adversely affect local markets, driving local producers off their land and creating a larger urban poor population with no means to purchase food. While the supply of food goes up, the effective demand for it declines and people go hungry. Famines, they argue, have not been the result of food shortages but of lost wages leading to declining purchasing power, especially among the urban poor. William Easterly has argued that Sachs, despite his claims to the contrary, substitutes administrative top-down initiatives for better information and stronger incentives to promote piecemeal and bottom-up reforms that avoid these unwanted, unintended consequences (Easterly 2006a, 2006b).

Political skeptics have been more stridently opposed to both small, bottom-up pulls as well as big, top-down pushes. They argue that richer and more democratic industrialized countries cannot afford economic development that is not tied directly to their military-security interests. The metaphors and symbols these political skeptics have used ("clash of civilizations" and "ethnic pandemonium," for example) have lent support to politicians willing to exploit a politics of fear rather than a politics of humanitarian aid and development (Pieterse 2004). The resulting shifts in policy and spending priorities have been significant. Most notably, U.S. development policies have been dramatically affected by the perception that the war in Iraq is only one part of a larger, longer worldwide war against terrorism. According to Stiglitz and Linda J. Bilmes (2008), as of March 2008 cost estimates for the United States for the war in Iraq were at three trillion dollars.

Under attack by economic and political skeptics and benignly ignored by optimists, development ethics has emerged in fragments. Against these skeptics anthropologists, sociologists, geographers, and philosophers have joined institutional economists in trying to piece together a body of development ethics literature, and while there are signs of fruitful communication across these academic disciplinary lines, there is still nothing like a "holistic" theory of development ethics or even agreement on which problems facing development ethics are the most important.

Instead, what we have is ethical fragmentation to match the fragmentation at the policy level. Between the fall of the Berlin Wall in 1989 and the terrorist attacks of September 11, 2001, globalization was characterized as a complex system or network of high-speed communication. Some commentators were more effusive than others, but all shared a common belief in the integrated nature of this emerging network. Ethics was a matter of keeping things in balance and distributing development's bounty humanely and fairly.[10]

As particular ethical arguments have been introduced to cope with problems such as the use of transgenic crops in agriculture, intellectual property rights, and the use of stem cells for medical research, development ethics has become more fragmented. As case law and rules of thumb are produced to deal with such problems, the model of a global network or system seems more simplistic, and metaphors that permit more local variations ("landscapes," "plateaus") have come into play. In the somewhat elusive words of one critic of global meta-narratives, "Particular assemblages of technology and politics not only create their own spaces, but also give diverse values to the practices and actors thus connected to each other" (Ong 2005, 338). Development ethics has become an array of different technology-specific language games, not a single discourse.

What are the fragments of development ethics that are now in play? (Gasper 2007).

1. *Basic Needs.* For some who think of development in terms of meeting basic human needs, security—whether military and political security or food and water security—must come first. For them, human rights are primarily the rights to have these basic needs met. To meet these needs, transportation, communication, and financial institutions must be built. That means roads, dams, airports, and high-speed Internet connections. Only then, they believe, will people have the opportunities and the wherewithal to bring their goods to market, participate in development decisions, send their children to school, work more productively, and save for the future. Basic needs require the creation of a sustainable development path, and this requires food and water security and health security, not just military security (Reader 2006).

2. *Capabilities.* Others, who recognize the goal of meeting basic human needs, argue that there is a danger of universalizing this concept. Needs vary considerably from culture to culture. Instead, these authors stress capacity building and human capabilities, especially in the areas of health and education. Capabilities can be measured in terms of skills and abilities, opportunities and control over resources, and even moral virtues like care and concern for others. These are the critical levers for development and security (Sen 1999; and Nussbaum 2000).

3. *Participation.* Still others stress participatory development in local political institutions as well as participation in economic institutions like growers' cooperatives and community schools. They believe that the most important

human right is the right to participate in development decisions. This is how we learn about our capabilities and choose among them. This is how needs become more concrete. Development decisions will be better if more stake-holders participate, and development policies will be more effective with this kind of buy-in (Crocker 2008).

The essays in this volume place capabilities at the center of development ethics, closely flanked by basic needs on one side and informed participation on the other. At the same time, many of the authors raise critical questions from the perspectives of human needs and participation about the adequacy of the capability approach to come to terms with both the exercise of power and the weight of institutions.

Locating Capabilities Within Development Ethics

Almost all scholars and practitioners in the field of development are now familiar with the work of Amartya Sen, Martha Nussbaum, and other social scientists and philosophers identified with the capability approach. Journals that relish breaking new interdisciplinary ground have opened their pages to vigorous debate over this line of thought.[11] Even philosophers, relatively slow to get their views out in print, have entered the fray (Symposium 2006).

Sen and Nussbaum, more than anyone, have forced social scientists and policymakers to take seriously the ethical issues and questions embedded in the study and processes of development. One might even say that Sen and Nussbaum, sometimes in tandem and sometimes separately, have been the catalysts for this new, albeit still fragmentary, interdisciplinary field of development ethics.

Any attempt to characterize the capability approach in general is bound to be misleading to some degree. The command of ancient and modern literary texts, Western and Eastern, that Sen and Nussbaum enjoy, as well as their knowledge of law and social science, inform and enrich their philosophical work. Having said this, it is unavoidable that we begin this volume, so much of which is indebted to their thought, with a brief statement of just what we take to be the main ideas behind the capability approach and its place within development ethics.

At one level, the capability approach offers an alternative to the dominant indices such as per capita income for measuring the success of development policies. In their introduction to the contemporary normative ferment in social science, David B. Grusky and Ravi Kanbur say that "there is a growing consensus among academics, policy makers, and even politicians that poverty and inequality should no longer be treated as soft social issues that can safely be subordinated to more important and fundamental interests in maximizing total economic output" (2006, 1). They primarily have Sen's and Nussbaum's work in mind. Rather than merely replacing one yardstick with another, the capability approach has sought to expand our understanding of what should count as good development, not just how to measure it. It incorporates a range of indices and measures of development rather than reducing development to one measure, however robust it may be in some cases.

One theoretical point of comparison is between the capability approach and contractualist approaches such as John Rawls's theory of justice, which focuses on the distribution of resources (in Rawls, "primary goods") as the lever for development. The advantage contractualism has over the capability approach, at least thus far, is that it offers a justification for explicit public principles of justice. That is, if we think about contractualism from the point of view of actual parties rather than the agents in a Rawlsian hypothetical original position, contractualism enables us to talk about how reasonable persons might debate and reach compromises on development priorities. This is what is meant by public reason and deliberative democracy. On the other hand, contractualism falters in extending its deliberative principles globally, whereas the capability approach strives to reach across national borders.[12]

A more common way to think about the relative theoretical virtues of the capability approach is to compare it to utilitarianism. While classical utilitarianism is easily ridiculed for substituting revealed preferences for real human needs, economists today are well aware of the difference and therefore stress the fundamental importance of basic needs. For example, Sachs does not hesitate; on his count there are six basic needs: primary education, nutrition, access to antimalarial bed nets, access to safe drinking water and sanitation, one-half kilometer of paved roads for every thousand of population, and access to safe cooking fuels and stoves (2005, 292–93). One might object to the vagueness of the term "access," but Sachs believes unconditionally that these needs can be met: "The single most important reason why prosperity spread, and why it continues to spread, is the transmission of technologies and the ideas underlying them" (41). Institutional explanations, he contends, are overrated (Sachs 2003, 38–41).

How do we measure this poverty? For Sachs it is a matter of determining how far short people fall from satisfying their fundamental needs for food, clean water, reading and writing skills adequate for employment, comparable technical skills, and generally a reasonably long life expectancy in good health. Sachs's need-based utilitarianism has very little room for moral concepts such as human rights, dignity, or flourishing. To the extent that morality may play a role in development, he suggests, it will be to motivate people to contribute to the satisfaction of the needs of those who are trapped, through no fault of their own, in poverty. Rights talk may not be nonsense on stilts, as Bentham put it, but it is only rhetoric—useful rhetoric, to be sure, but rhetoric nonetheless.[13]

In contrast, exponents of the capability approach have sought to give their theory a stronger moral foundation without dismissing the utilitarian emphasis on the satisfaction of basic needs. While also critical of "revealed preferences," the capability approach still takes seriously—perhaps above all else—that development should be about giving people more choices to realize those things that they believe make them human—their material needs and also their higher aspirations. In an essay originally presented at a training course preceding the Third International Conference on the Capabilities Approach in Pavia, Italy, on September 6, 2004, Ingrid Robeyns made this point: "Well-being and development should be discussed in terms of people's capabilities to function, that is, on their *effective opportunities* to undertake the actions and activities that they want to engage in, and be whom they want to be."[14]

Freedom to choose how we wish to live our lives among a large set of human capabilities, according to Sen, is the key moral value of the capability approach; it is the essence of justice (Sen 2008). For Nussbaum, human capabilities, in the plural, constitute human flourishing as forms of acting and being in the world, not just possessing or wanting certain things. Denied access to these ways of being, a person is in effect denied her or his human dignity. In this sense, respect for human dignity, not the pursuit of mutual advantage, is what is needed for everyone, not just family, friends, and compatriots, to have an effective opportunity to flourish (Nussbaum 2006, 68–85). Nussbaum concludes that the capability approach is therefore one species of a human rights approach. Without endorsing any one particular list of human capabilities, Sen fleshes this out by describing human rights as ethical demands for certain freedoms that are important and socially determinable. He argues that freedom to choose our capabilities in an informed and uncoerced way describes, at least in large part, what it means to possess human rights. He admits, however, that human rights cannot be reduced to capabilities. The qualification is worth quoting at length because it reflects both the open-minded way the advocates of the capability approach have proceeded and their wariness of reductionism:

"Although the idea of capability has considerable merit in the assessment of the opportunity aspect of freedom, it cannot possibly deal adequately with the process aspect of freedom, since capabilities are characteristics of individual advantages, and they fall short of telling us enough about the fairness or equality of the processes involved, or about the freedom of citizens to invoke and utilize procedures that are equitable" (Sen 2004a, 336). It is this theoretical limit of the capability approach that has led Sen and others such as David A. Crocker to ask what a democratic and participatory development process that respects human capabilities would be like. In their revised 2002 edition of *India: Development and Participation*, Jean Drèze and Sen stress several ways in which democratic participation has been and could be more effective as a means to avoid famine and long-term hunger.

Matters of process, our authors argue, are inherently tied to power and institutional structure, and many of the arguments that Drèze and Sen make are also about institutions. Is there a difference between what capabilities theorists have outlined and what the authors of this collection mean by power and institutions? Sen has been concerned about effective opportunities to choose the capabilities we wish to develop and how they depend on forms of property, the rules of contract, and fixed political boundaries. He has been concerned that institutional structures not be imposed through top-down development, although they often are. Since its adoption as a central, if not the dominant normative framework for the United Nations *Human Development Reports* since 1990, it has been clear that the capability approach is a theory that can make a difference in practice. Where, then, does the difference lie?

Criticizing the Capability Approach

All ethical theories are about how human beings should live their lives. One answer to this question is that they should live their lives freely because freedoms are good things to have in themselves, and because they are important instruments for achieving other moral ends. That is, freedoms are means to other good things that people value and ought to value. But it is not always easy to put this idea of instrumental freedom into practice. Sabina Alkire (2005), who has applied the capability approach to particular local cases, asks how we decide what instrumental freedoms to cultivate. What trade-offs do they force? What capabilities do they expand?[15] These are difficult empirical *and* normative questions, but perhaps even they may underestimate the ethical issues that development confronts. Are they at the heart of the matter when we ask what should be the purpose of an ethical theory of development, or is ethics about even more disturbing matters than how we should operationalize instrumental values such as freedom? Should an ethical theory of development make those in more developed countries uncomfortable—really squirm, as Allan Schmid phrases it—and not just puzzled by problems of implementation? Where would this squirm come from? As Schmid has discussed elsewhere, it comes with the recognition that to realize human capabilities for the many poor, basic institutional changes must occur and the poor must have a say in them.[16]

Another challenge for any ethical theory of development, but especially the capability approach, is the matter of geography. Even if the capability approach can make us squirm, are we really in any position to overcome the enormous differences in endowments provided by the environmental natural lottery? Is it really possible for those who have been left out to achieve the kind of development that they would like to have? One answer is that it may depend quite a bit on where you happen to be, as Jared Diamond (1999) and Sachs (2005) have argued. Or, as Schmid asks, are there institutional preconditions to development just as important as any natural lottery? Consistent with Schmid's perspective, Daniel Little maintains that among the most important factors are the systems of landholding and political power sharing, which usually do not depend on geography.[17] According to Little, an approach to development sensitive to the ways in which institutions such as these shape capabilities and meet human needs is much more likely to succeed.

Yet another challenge to the capability approach is that it does not go deep enough—that is, it fails to challenge conventional views about human nature. This is most evident in debates over the meaning of human security. The capability approach most recently has had to address whether welfare, well-being, and security can and should be integrated within a single comprehensive ethical theory. In his Report to the United Nations General Assembly on March 21, 2005, Secretary-General Annan summarized this interdependency, or "larger freedom": "Not only are development, security and human rights all imperative; they also reinforce each other. This relationship has only been strengthened in our era of rapid technological advances, increasing economic interdependence, globalization, and dramatic geopolitical change. While poverty and denial of human rights may not be said to 'cause' civil war, terrorism, or organized crime, they all greatly increase the risk of instability and violence." What is the most appropriate conception of moral identity that should ground theories of vulnerability (security) and capability? Here one should be open to non-Western theories of the self and also to feminist theories of care that, according to Des Gasper and Thanh-Dam Truong, connect vulnerability and capability, rather than presenting these as competing alternative moral values in the way that some postdevelopment theorists have suggested (Rahnema 1997, 400).

Nussbaum has argued that there are compelling arguments in favor of moral universalism, especially as they apply to the well-being of women.[18] Listening to these myriad and sometimes dissonant voices to identify their common humanity is a central task of the capability approach. But the more abstract the idea of the person, Shelley Feldman argues, the greater the danger that persons are caught up in and constituted by structures of power that differentially shape their room to maneuver. She argues that neoliberal development policies and institutional reforms represent one such structure of power that is not adequately addressed by the capability approach. According to Feldman, the capability approach has taken for granted the nation-state system characterized by uneven development within a global structure of capitalism. This danger for the capability approach, argues Asunción St. Clair, goes beyond the issues of moral and cultural relativism. The capability approach as it has been applied by multi-lateral institutions has lost its pragmatic orientation. It tacitly assumes an international normative order conforming to what Sen (2001) has called the "Ten Truths of Globalization," and that Nigel Dower worries has silently biased debates over ethics and development.

There are alternative, existing normative orders, argues David Barkin. In particular, we ought to be mindful of the epistemologies of indigenous peoples when critically considering the reach and purchase of any theory of development ethics. Capabilities are indeed important, but their locus of development can also be situated through the inherited knowledge of developing communities. In response to these strong criticisms by Feldman, St. Clair, and Barkin, Paul B. Thompson asks us to be patient despite the urgent need for ethical development and the attractiveness of indigenous perspectives. Development is too serious a business to be driven by unreflective value judgments, regardless of how intuitively appealing they may be. Thompson argues that the philosophical basis for our sense of urgency—its faith in a consequence-driven conception of ethical justification—ought to be called into question. The development of human capabilities, whether they are grounded locally in indigenous values or universally in global values, must eventually be justified pragmatically. What would this mean in practice?

Participation and Experimentation

Twentieth-century development theories began with a focus on economic growth, and much of the work in ethics and development, including the capability approach, has been organized to expand this focus without neglecting the important contributions that economic analysis can still make. Development, we know all too well, must proceed on several tracks. Strategies for economic growth, however they are organized, will fail unless they are connected to social, educational, and political institutions. This involves the level of control that civil society groups as well as local city and village governments have in development planning and implementation. No one openly advocates top-down development anymore, not even Sachs, but getting things right from the bottom up and from side to side means understanding, as Crocker (2008) and David Ellerman (2005) have forcefully argued elsewhere, the interaction of local and global networks of power in a process of participatory development. Perhaps what is needed is a "globalization of ethics" that values local institutional experimentation.

A global commitment to economically subsidizing and politically supporting local experimentation in developing countries inevitably will cut across existing political boundaries and jeopardize existing relative comparative advantages in trade. This is what Roberto Mangiabera Unger calls "radical pragmatism." It is consistent with the goals of the capability approach but much more cognizant of the inertia of existing institutions and the power of new local institutions to contest this inertial force.[19]

Experimentation can begin with economic processes of production, but it must reach the political level if it is to be effective in practice. Experiments in regional government and forms of federalism will be necessary if the false necessities of existing trade and strategic advantages that block human development are to be dislodged. But the most basic change, according to Unger, may involve our ability to distinguish between urgency and crisis. Economic and political institutional experiments can be driven by a sense of urgency— I would argue that they have to be. They will not occur, however, in an atmosphere of crisis such as the current financial meltdown or as a response to an unforeseen calamity, as opportune as this may first appear. In Unger's words: "A calamity—often in the form of an economic collapse or armed conflict—can break any order. . . . To render politics experimental is to dispense with the need for this ally" (2007b, 42–43). The essays in this volume reflect this sense of urgency in their call for participatory development and pragmatic experimentation across existing political boundaries.

NOTES

1. For contrasting views on this question, see Deneulin (2006) and Alkire (2006).

2. Sen (2005) defends Farmer's case study approach to "structural violence" by likening Farmer's account of this phenomenon to Wittgenstein's concepts of ostension and family resemblance.

3. "Neoliberal globalization" and neoliberalism generally are often polemical terms that are not adequately distinguished from liberal globalization policies and liberalism. As Jan Nederveen Pieterse has argued, however, one can usefully group under this heading certain market-oriented government policies after 1989, from trade liberalization to the so-called Washington Consensus. See Pieterse (2004) and Scholte (2005).

4. I borrow this disheartening phrase from Drèze and Sen: "The fact that so many people continue to die each year from famines, and that many millions more go on perishing from persistent deprivation on a regular basis, is a calamity to which the world has, somewhat incredibly, got coolly accustomed" (1999, 275–76).

5. Seeds travel promiscuously across political borders, and while refugees and internally displaced persons do not travel as easily, the global networks of remittances spawned by poverty and civil wars have expanded considerably. See IMF (2005) and OECD (2005).

6. For an overview of this process, see Scholte (2000, 2006). For a discussion of responsibility in this context, see Kuper (2005). My own views on global responsibilities can be found in *The Political Responsibilities of Everyday Bystanders* (2010, forthcoming).

7. For example, see the 2005 WIDER Lecture by Nancy Birdsall, president of the Center for Global Development (Birdsall 2005).

8. According to the UNDP: "Extreme inequality is not just bad for poverty reduction—it is bad for growth. Long run efficiency and greater equity can be complementary. Poor people remain poor partly because they cannot borrow against future earnings to invest in production, the education of their children, and assets to reduce their vulnerability. Insecure land rights and limited access to justice can create further barriers to investment" (2005, 53). Also, now from the World Bank: "If inequality falls during a growth spell, poverty generally falls by more than if inequality had not changed [and] higher income inequality reduces the effectiveness of future economic growth in reducing absolute income poverty" (2005, 76).

9. According to the UN Millennium Project: "The primary responsibility for development lies with countries themselves. As an indispensable condition for defeating poverty, each country must recommit to pursuing the national institutions and policies conducive to dynamic and sustainable economic growth. But many low-income countries, including fairly well-governed ones, cannot afford the public investments in basic infrastructure, human capital, and public administration that are foundations for private sector growth and economic development. Many Least Developed Countries, especially in sub-Saharan Africa, are stuck with low or negative growth. Why? Because their savings rates are too low to offset population growth and depreciation, and they are unable to attract the needed investments from abroad" (2005, 50).

10. For example, Friedman (2000) and Castells (2001).

11. For example, *Political Geography* 23, no. 7 (2004); *Economics and Philosophy* 17, no. 1 (2001); and *Feminist Economics* 9, nos. 2–3 (2003).

12. For a critique of the capability approach from this perspective, see Pogge (2002); for counterarguments, see Nussbaum (2006).

13. For a harsher view of rights-based humanitarianism, arguing that it has unwittingly become part of a militarized foreign policy regime, see Chandler (2001).

14. Emphasis added. Sen makes a similar point about "effective freedom" in his 1984 Dewey Lectures (1985). I am indebted to Sabina Alkire for this reference.

15. For further readings on these and related questions, see Comim, Qizilbash, and Alkire (2008).

16. See, for example, Schmid (2004).

17. I am indebted to John Staatz for this point. In personal correspondence he writes: "In what sense does Finland have a better natural endowment than the Democratic Republic of the Congo? Even if one talks about a country that has few resources, the definition of the country itself is a function of institutional rules. For example, Nevada probably has no more natural resources than Mauritania, but the institutional rules link Nevada into a larger country that has more resources on which it can draw, while Mauritania is 'separate' as a result of lines drawn on a map by Europeans in the nineteenth century."

18. The relationship between the capability approach as a theory of global distributive justice and multicultural theories of identity politics is complex and cannot be done justice here. This was the subject of the United Nations *Human Development Report, 2004*, written explicitly from the perspective of the capability approach and stressing the freedom to choose one's cultural identity ("cultural liberty"), rather than the preservation of group cultural identity, as one of the basic freedoms. See, for example, Sen (2004b).

19. See Unger (2007a, 2007b); also Rodrik (2007).

REFERENCES

Alkire, Sabina. 2005. *Valuing Freedoms: Sen's Capabilities Approach and Poverty Reduction.* New York: Oxford University Press.

———. 2006. Structural Injustice and Democratic Practice: The Trajectory in Sen's Writings. In *Transforming Unjust Structures: The Capability Approach*, ed. Séverine Deneulin, Mathias Nebel, and Nicholas Sagovsky, 47–62. Dordrecht, the Netherlands: Springer.

Annan, Kofi. 2005. *In Larger Freedom: Towards Development, Security, and Human Rights for All.* United Nations General Assembly, 59th sess., March 21, par. 16.

Birdsall, Nancy. 2005. Why Inequality Matters in a Globalizing World. 2005 World Institute for Development Economics Research (WIDER) Lecture. Helsinki, October 26. http://www.cgdev.org/content/opinion/detail/4793/.

Castells, Manuel. 2001. *The Internet Galaxy: Reflections on the Internet, Business, and Society.* New York: Oxford University Press.

Chandler, David. 2001. The Road to Military Humanitarianism: How the Human Rights NGOs Shaped a New Humanitarian Agenda. *Human Rights Quarterly* 23 (3): 678–700.

Comim, Flavio, Mozaffar Qizilbash, and Sabina Alkire. 2008. *The Capability Approach: Concepts, Measures, and Applications.* Cambridge: Cambridge University Press.

Crocker, David A. 2008. *Ethics of Global Development: Agency, Capability, and Deliberative Democracy.* Cambridge: Cambridge University Press.

Deneulin, Séverine. 2006. "Necessary Thickening": Ricoeur's Ethic of Justice as a Complement to Sen's Capability Approach. In *Transforming Unjust Structures: The Capability Approach*, ed. Séverine Deneulin, Mathias Nebel, and Nicholas Sagovsky, 27–46. Dordrecht, the Netherlands: Springer.

Diamond, Jared. 1999. *Guns, Germs, and Steel: The Fates of Human Societies.* New York: Norton.

Drèze, Jean, and Amartya Sen. 1999. *Hunger and Public Action.* In *The Amartya Sen and Jean Drèze Omnibus.* New York: Oxford University Press.

———. 2002. *India: Development and Participation.* 2nd ed. Oxford: Oxford University Press.

Easterly, William. 2001. *The Elusive Quest for Growth.* Cambridge: MIT Press.

———. 2006a. The Big Push Déjà Vu: A Review of Jeffrey Sachs's *The End of Poverty: Economic Possibilities for Our Time. Journal of Economic Literature* 44 (1): 96–105.

————. 2006b. *The White Man's Burden: Why the West's Efforts to Aid the Rest Have Done So Much Ill and So Little Good.* New York: Penguin.

Ellerman, David. 2005. *Helping People Help Themselves.* New York: World Bank.

Esquith, Stephen L. 2010. *The Political Responsibilities of Everyday Bystanders.* University Park: Pennsylvania State University Press, forthcoming.

Ferguson, James. 2006. *Global Shadows: Africa in a Neoliberal World Order.* Durham: Duke University Press.

Friedman, Thomas L. 2000. *The Lexus and the Olive Tree: Understanding Globalization.* New York: Anchor Books.

Gasper, Des. 2004. *The Ethics of Development: From Economism to Human Development.* Edinburgh: Edinburgh University Press.

————. 2007. Human Rights, Human Needs, Human Development, Human Security: Relationships Between Four International "Human" Discourses. Working Paper 445, Institute of Social Studies. http://biblio.iss.nl/opac/uploads/wp/wp445.pdf.

Grusky, David B., and Ravi Kanbur. 2006. Introduction: The Conceptual Foundations of Poverty and Inequality Measurement. In *Poverty and Inequality*, ed. David B. Grusky and Ravi Kanbur, 1–29. Stanford: Stanford University Press.

Haq, Mahbub ul. 2003. The Human Development Paradigm. In *Readings in Human Development: Concepts, Measures, and Policies for a Development Paradigm*, ed. Sakiko Fukuda-Parr and A. K. Shiva Kumar, 2nd ed., 17–34. New York: Oxford University Press.

IMF. 2005. *World Economic Outlook: Globalization and External Imbalances.* Washington, D.C.: World Bank.

Kuper, Andrew, ed. 2005. *Global Responsibilities: Who Must Deliver on Human Rights?* New York: Routledge.

Lipton, Michael. 1998. *Successes in Anti-poverty.* Geneva: International Labor Organization.

Moss, Todd, Gunilla Pettersson, and Nicolas Van de Walle. 2006. An Aid-Institutions Paradox? A Review Essay on Aid Dependency and State Building in Sub-Saharan Africa. Working Paper 74, Center for Global Development. http://www.cgdev.org/content/publications/detail/5646.

Nussbaum, Martha C. 2000. *Women and Human Development.* Cambridge: Cambridge University Press.

————. 2006. *Frontiers of Justice: Disability, Nationality, Species Membership.* Cambridge: Harvard University Press.

OECD. 2005. *Migration, Remittances, and Development.* Paris: OECD.

Ong, Aihwa. 2005. Ecologies of Expertise: Assembling Flows. In *Global Assemblages: Technology, Politics, and Ethics as Anthropological Problems*, ed. Aihwa Ong and Stephen J. Collier, 337–53. Malden, Mass.: Blackwell.

Pieterse, Jan Nederveen. 2004. *Globalization or Empire.* New York: Routledge.

Pogge, Thomas. 2002. Can the Capability Approach Be Justified? *Philosophical Topics* 30 (2): 167–228. Special issue, "Global Inequities," ed. Martha Nussbaum and Chad Flanders.

Rahnema, Majid. 1997. Afterword: Towards Post-development: Searching for Signposts, a New Language, and New Paradigms. In *The Post-development Reader*, ed. Majid Rahnema with Victoria Bawtree, 377–404. London: Zed Books.

Reader, Soran, ed. 2006. *The Philosophy of Need.* New York: Cambridge University Press.

Rodrik, Dani. 2001. *The Global Governance of Trade: As if Development Really Mattered.* New York: United Nations Development Programme.

————. 2007. *One Economics, Many Recipes: Globalization, Institutions, and Economic Growth.* Princeton: Princeton University Press.

Sachs, Jeffrey D. 2003. Institutions Matter, But Not for Everything. *Finance and Development*, June.

———. 2005. *The End of Poverty: Economic Possibilities for Our Time*. New York: Penguin.

Schmid, A. Allan. 2004. *Conflict and Cooperation: Institutional and Behavioral Economics*. New York: Wiley-Blackwell.

Scholte, Jan Aart. 2000. *Globalization: A Critical Introduction*. Basingstoke, UK: Palgrave.

———. 2005. The Sources of Neoliberal Globalization. United Nations Institute for Social Development Programme Paper, no. 8, October.

———. 2006. Political Struggles Will Determine Better Globalisation. *Global Policy Forum*, March 15.

Sen, Amartya. 1985. Well-Being, Agency, and Freedom: The Dewey Lectures, 1984. *Journal of Philosophy* 82 (4): 169–221.

———. 1999. *Development as Freedom*. New York: Knopf.

———. 2001. Dix verités sur la mondialisation. *Le Monde*, September 18.

———. 2004a. Elements of a Theory of Human Rights. *Philosophy and Public Affairs* 32 (4): 315–56.

———. 2004b. How Does Culture Matter? In *Culture and Public Action: A Cross-Disciplinary Dialogue on Development Policy*, ed. Vijayendra Rao and Michael Walton, 37–58. Stanford: Stanford University Press.

———. 2005. Forward to *Pathologies of Power: Health, Human Rights, and the New War on the Poor*, by Paul Farmer. Berkeley and Los Angeles: University of California Press.

———. 2008. The Idea of Justice. *Journal of Human Development* 9 (3): 331–42.

———. 2010. *The Idea of Justice*. Cambridge, MA: Harvard University Press.

Sharma, Shalendra D. 2008. The Many Faces of Today's Globalization: A Survey of Recent Literature. *New Global Studies* 2 (2): 1–27.

Stiglitz, Joseph E. 2002. *Globalization and Its Discontents*. New York: Norton.

Stiglitz, Joseph E., and Linda J. Bilmes. 2008. *The Three Trillion Dollar War: The True Cost of the Iraq Conflict*. New York: Norton.

Symposium on Capabilities. 2006. *Journal of Political Philosophy* 14 (3).

UNDP (United Nations Development Programme). 2005. *Human Development Report, 2005: International Development at a Crossroads: Aid, Trade, and Security in an Unequal World*. New York: UNDP.

Unger, Roberto Mangiabera. 2007a. *The Free Market Reimagined: The World Division of Labor and the Method of Economics*. Princeton: Princeton University Press.

———. 2007b. *The Self Awakened: Pragmatism Unbound*. Cambridge: Harvard University Press.

UN Millennium Project. 2005. *Investing in Development: A Practical Plan to Achieve the Millennium Development Goals*. New York: UNDP.

World Bank. 2005. *World Development Report, 2006: World Equity and Development*. New York: World Bank and Oxford University Press

1

Instrumental Freedoms and Human Capabilities

Sabina Alkire

This chapter poses a question: To what extent can instrumental freedoms—with which the greater part of human development and indeed the enterprise of many countries is concerned—be linked to the "ends" of development, if these are conceived as human capabilities?

If Afghanistan, through its turmoil and struggles, succeeds in containing conflict and drug trade, and cultivates a sound vibrant economy through such concrete measures as opening new markets, improving contract enforcement, extending the rule of law, and building access roads, this will rightly merit praise and admiration. If the Afghani people also attain freedom from undernourishment—a continuing threat as food prices rise[1]—this will also undoubtedly generate warm acclaim. The question is how these freedoms—for both may be called that—relate to one another. How do the intrinsically valued human freedoms—being nourished, being educated, being loved, being healthy, doing good work—relate to instrumental freedoms such as financial transparency, economic opportunity, political freedom, and protective security?

This is a central question to human development, for human development aims to shift the objective of development from instrumentally valued variables such as income or human capital to a set of intrinsically valued ends related to human freedom. Yet much of development is more visibly linked with the expansion of instrumental freedoms than with the expansion of individual capabilities.[2] It is not a question that belongs entirely within development ethics, for many of the connections require empirical scrutiny. Indeed, the question of the relationship between development activities and final ends requires a response of the same broad form as a production function in economics, which maps the relationships between inputs (instrumental freedoms in our case) and outputs (capabilities and other central outcomes).

While we may be able to measure the carbon particles in the atmosphere or the depth of the ozone layer, and while we may be able to relate this directly to an instrumental freedom such as ecological security,[3] we cannot cash out directly the value of carbon emissions regulations in terms of expanded human capabilities. There are many familiar barriers to a neat conversion factor. The people affected may continue to be born for centuries; the chain of causality may run through fish, vegetables, water, or other parts of the ecosystem; the functionings that would expand for different people vary, as would the people's evaluation of them; and of course the dizzying task of generating an accurate prediction may seem like child's play in comparison with the hurtling challenge of proscribing the counterfactual.

Similar disjunctions pertain to changes in the global economy. What and whose human capabilities are expanded or undermined by the setting up of a hedge fund? By raising interest rates? By reducing the days it takes to register a new business? By a tax law reform? By undertaking fundamental research on genetics or nanotechnology?

It is because these links are so vexing and difficult to make at more than a superficial level—and perhaps cannot be comprehensively made without seeming excessively contrived and artificial—that many have found Sen's capability approach to add scant value thus far when it comes to issues of the environment, macroeconomics, technology and basic scientific research, institution building and long-range planning, and so on. Further, much of the literature on the capability approach has focused on capability measurement rather than on investigating the links between instrumental freedoms and capabilities.[4] The practical value of the capability approach—and indeed of other avenues of development ethics—rests, at least in part, on the degree to which these links can be strengthened.

Moreover, humans act not only for economic and social advancement but also, at times, to satisfy their moral sentiments. Indeed, some seek to enhance others' human development. Yet it is difficult to gauge what "effective" freedom we have to expand others' capabilities. A clearer assessment of the extent to which expanding concrete instrumental freedoms advances others' lives may thus be of personal interest to those who wish to act (as hedge fund managers, central bank advisers, institutional economists, philanthropists, or ethicists, for example) to expand others' freedoms. It could also be of analytical value to those interested in linking responsibility to effective power.[5]

A leopard that has eaten on the previous day but is restless this afternoon may stalk far more deer than it intends to attack, hence creating broad havoc without downing any prey. So too this chapter will cavalierly scare up many more questions than it will capture and address. The intent, however, is to challenge others to improve on present techniques for orienting development processes to advance the freedoms people value, for there are interesting questions that could be addressed, perhaps for the first time, because of our ability to work across disciplines, to draw on participatory processes, and to access and process a far greater range of empirical data.

Terms

The capability approach is a normative proposition. The proposition is this: that social arrangements should be primarily evaluated according to the extent of freedom people have to promote or achieve functionings they value. Put simply, progress (or development, or poverty reduction) occurs when people have greater freedom.

The capability approach has evolved, and its terminology has done likewise. In Sen's *Development as Freedom* (1999), capabilities are sometimes called real freedoms or, simply, freedoms. What does Sen mean by capability or real freedom? Sen's definition of capability has two parts: *freedom*, and valuable beings and doings (*functionings*). I begin with the latter.

Functionings is an overarching term for the activities and situations people recognize to be constitutive of well-being, such as a running habit, sitting down to a hearty meal, having a loving family, or working at a meaningful job. Functionings are of intrinsic importance, although they may also be instrumentally useful. Which functionings are centrally important varies across time and place and among different people. Also, the functionings that are relevant in a particular situation depend on many factors, such as the institutions, sectors, or groups involved; whether the discussion focuses on planning, evaluation, or comparison; and so on. Thus Sen argues that the set of focal functionings will have to be set and reset again and again in different ways; one list will not do.

Capability "refers to the alternative combinations of functionings that are feasible for her to achieve. Capability is thus a kind of freedom: the substantive freedom to achieve alternative functioning combinations (or, less formally put, the freedom to achieve various lifestyles)" (Sen 1999, 75). Another way of describing capability is "opportunity freedom," a term Sen also uses. This kind of freedom resembles that described by T. H. Green, who wrote, "We do not mean merely freedom from restraint or compulsion. . . . When we speak of freedom as something to be so highly prized, we mean a *positive power or capacity* of doing or enjoying something worth doing or enjoying" (Green 1881, 370; emphasis added).

Sen takes care to distinguish the ends and the means of development, pointing out that they have often been jumbled together in misleading ways. This is partly because many aspects of human development have intrinsic and instrumental value at the same time. For example, education is both valuable in itself and a wonderful means by which to advance worker productivity, child spacing, family health and nutrition, and the education of the next generation. But it is important to acknowledge ends and means independently from one another, because policies that focus only on advancing a capability in an instrumental sense may be quite insufficient (Sen 1997a, 2002).

Instrumental freedoms are a class of freedoms that in addition to forming part of the objective or "end" of development are also "crucially effective means." Sen argues that these means can be identified empirically: "This acknowledgment [of freedom as a crucially effective means] can be based on empirical analysis of the consequences of—and the interconnections between—freedoms of distinct kinds, and on extensive empirical evidence that indicates that freedoms of different types typically help to sustain each other" (Sen 2004b).[6]

In *Development as Freedom* (1999), Sen identifies five instrumental freedoms that he claims "tend to contribute to the general capability of a person to live more freely":

1. *Political freedoms*, for example, democracy, the freedoms to scrutinize and criticize authorities, and to enjoy a free press and multiparty elections.
2. *Economic facilities*, for example, people's opportunity to have and use economic resources or entitlements.
3. *Social opportunities*, for example, people's ability to have health care, to be educated, and to live in a society where others likewise enjoy these goods.
4. *Transparency guarantees*, for example, the ability to trust others and to know that the information one receives is clear and honestly disclosed.
5. *Protective security*, for example, social protections for vulnerable people that prevent abject deprivation. (38–40)

Sen claims that these freedoms "tend to contribute to the general capability of a person to live more freely." It is this claim I would like to probe more fully, and in particular the avenues by which this and similar claims can be sustained, elaborated, or challenged.

These definitions should have clarified the central proposition with which we began: that social arrangements (including development policies, economic institutions, social protection systems, and so on) should be evaluated primarily according to the extent of capabilities or intrinsically valued freedoms that people enjoy in them. In other words, the value of various instrumental freedoms should depend on the expansion of capabilities they create and sustain.

To reorient development away from income or even instrumental freedoms and toward human well-being and real freedoms might seem an elementary conceptual move. Indeed, the *Human Development Reports*, which have been published since 1990, have made this pattern of thought seem a natural and convenient perspective from which to analyze a number of applied policy topics ranging from gender and the environment to technology, globalization, and cultural liberty. It is easy to convey to the public the point that the economy should promote human freedom, rather than human lives merely promoting a healthy economy. The task of compiling and analyzing even existing information, however, is complex and often overlooked.

Capability Comparison and Consequential Analysis

As is apparent from the description thus far, Sen's capability approach has changed the terms of the utilitarian calculus while retaining its underlying consequentialism. Sen (2000) defines consequentialism as a "discipline of responsible choice based on the chooser's evaluation of states of affairs, including consideration of all the relevant consequences viewed in light of the exact circumstances of that choice" (477).

To oversimplify this position somewhat, part of what is required to put the capability approach into practice is to switch from an income/utility-maximizing metric to a capability-expanding metric. In this case, the task is to identify the marginal human capabilities that are expanded—or undermined—by alternative courses of action. If a single action can be identified that yields the richest field of capability expansion—the largest capability "budget set" if you will (Sen and Foster 1998)—it will dominate the alternative courses of action. The course of action might be identified by what Stewart (1985) called a meta-production function or by another set of planning tools such as an extended variation of cost-benefit analysis. Of course, there will be much incompleteness and partial ordering of actions, and the incommensurability between alternative capability sets is expected to be quite substantial. But penetrating analyses may be advanced and debated even given these constraints.

That conception is very telegraphic and incomplete, but not so distorted as to be unrecognizable. When Sen addresses evaluative reasoning at length, the framework advanced is a nuanced and even meticulous form of consequentialist reasoning—which can among other things incorporate human rights (1984, 1996), situated responsibility (1996, 2000), imperfect obligations (2000, 2004a), and other ethical considerations. The consequential framework is intended to reflect interconnections between variables and communicate the uncertainty or ambiguity of many analyses. Further, it includes information on processes and thus builds up a picture not only of "'culmination outcomes' (that is, only final outcomes without taking any note of the process of getting there, including the exercise of freedom)," but also of "'comprehensive outcomes' (taking note of the processes through which the culmination outcomes come about)" (1999, 27).

The logic of human development as the maximization of human freedoms consequent to development policies and activities, suitably qualified by other considerations, emerges clearly as the ethical shape of Sen's approach. In practice, while a consequential framework may be unable to identify one "best" alternative, it will rule out one or more alternatives as undesirable: "Maximization does not . . . demand that all alternatives be comparable, and does not even require that a best alternative be identifiable. It only requires that we do not choose an alternative that is worse than another that can be chosen instead" (Sen 2000).[7] Note that in this framework the value of instrumental freedoms is tethered to their connection to and impact on intrinsically valued human freedoms: they cannot be evaluated in isolation from these connections.

Identifying Instrumental Freedoms

The five freedoms presented in *Development as Freedom* are quite interesting, for they presume that consequential reasoning is feasible. Indeed, Sen's work seems steeped in this conviction. Still, the empirical evidence that justifies the five freedoms is rather patchy and not systematically presented. This is not inappropriate in a popular book, but it does suggest that further research is needed to explore in depth these empirical interconnections.

The need for stronger empirical foundations is important, for if *Development as Freedom*'s five freedoms are advanced as representing the capability approach in practice—as indeed they are—they may be advanced on the basis of prestige, authority, imitation, or haste. The opportunity to enrich or challenge the empirically suggested connections may be overlooked. Further, the list of instrumental freedoms leaves many other questions unanswered; for example, different kinds of social opportunities or protective security have distinct impacts on human freedoms, and we would wish to identify which instrumental freedoms are most effective in creating and sustaining capabilities.

I would argue, therefore, for a more vigorous, more bumptious, more insistent engagement of development ethics in trying to make a comprehensive consequential reasoning practicable. One could do worse than to start by reexamining the rationale for advancing Sen's five instrumental freedoms—or indeed other freedoms. This will entail empirical as well as ethical insights. It could be accomplished by research that synthesizes existing studies and data related to a concrete problem, and analyzes it using the normative framework of the capability approach. Indeed, this might open a rich field of research. As is usually the case, this is by no means unworked ground; what is needed is for the literature related to capabilities to be connected with the other literatures.

The basic-needs literature, in this context, is a useful starting point because it addresses technical planning issues and political discussions as well as issues of measurement. For example, Frances Stewart's book *Planning to Meet Basic Needs* (1985) is primarily concerned with the "translation of a simple human objective into plans and policies" (1). Recall that like the capability approach, the basic-needs approach focuses on human beings as "ends"—its objective is to meet the basic needs of all people. Stewart writes, "It is helpful to be clear, right from the start, that the BN-approach is concerned with the objectives rather than the mechanisms of development" (2). Having established that objective, however, it immediately begins to work upstream to identify the threshold or cut-off point for each need, a time or duration period for basic needs, and also some account of how or whether to value achievements that are unrelated to basic needs. Stewart also identifies the need for a standard production function that includes institutions and organizations, and analyzes intrafamily relationships that may block or facilitate meeting basic needs. Important for our purposes, she also introduces the concept of meta-production function—which, she observes, "is not a normal part of economic planning" (5). The meta-production function aims to trace relationships between inputs and intermediate outputs (basic goods and services), and human outcomes (in the form of what Stewart calls the full life objective, or, in our case, expanded capabilities).

The meta-production function still has been studied "much less" than other issues, in part because the connections may or may not be possible to trace, but certainly are challenging. The remainder of the chapter sketches some of these challenges.

Interconnections

The first is the obvious—but not therefore simple—challenge of tracing the consequences of changes in instrumental freedoms on human capabilities. What capabilities expand, and whose, and do they set off further positive or negative production cycles? As Sen points out, human freedoms are not like ripe plums that are visible from afar and come racing down as soon as you nudge a tree of instrumental freedoms, almost begging to be gathered, sorted, and weighed (1997b, sec. 4). When consequential reasoning is difficult, how should the investment manager, the deputy secretary of a developing country transport industry, or the software technician of a statistics bureau identify the capability expansions that will be unveiled by alternative courses of action open to them, and thus make ethical choices? If in fact it is not possible to identify the consequences of expanded instrumental freedoms on capabilities, then, sharply put, the capability approach does not add value because it cannot be applied.

Another challenge is time and the need for a dynamic evaluative framework. To map capability expansions requires one to extrapolate capability expansion not only across people and capabilities but also down through time. This is trying enough with respect to income and net present value; with respect to a plural vector of capabilities the challenge deepens.

A third challenge is the need to impute uncertainty and (separately) measurement error—to keep track of these and other ambiguities and not try to be more precise than the evidence permits. This is a principle Sen does not tire of commending. Again, however, the technicalities of aggregating uncertainty coefficients and measurement errors in complex multidimensional analyses are quite deep. Of course, there are many other challenges.

If we prove unable to map the net human capability consequences of actions, then, for very good reasons, prospective analyses may turn on sharpening the instrumental freedoms within their own terms of efficiency and output. In most cases this reasoning is useful and may be sufficient: a transport industry that builds and maintains roads seems obviously superior to a corrupt transport industry of absentee workers who must walk to their secondary place of employment because the roads are so terrible. In other situations, however, this reasoning, which Sen refers to as technical or engineering reasoning, may fall short. Many will recall that Sen describes one who only engages in this form of reasoning as "a decision expert whose response to seeing a man engaged in slicing his toes with a blunt knife is to rush to advise him that he should use a sharper knife to better serve his evident objective" (1995, 16). Unfortunately, the situations in which technical reasoning is misguided are not invariably so apparent as the toe-slicing example might suggest.

An example of this challenge is the poverty impacts of alternative macroeconomic policies. Interest rate and exchange rate regimes are not so far removed as one might think from the lived experience of the wage laborer or the small farmer, but the grounds on which they are most commonly fixed focus on financial or technical criteria precisely because the poverty impacts are difficult and tedious to trace. This is a challenge to which, I would suggest, development ethics should contribute, by tracing the connections and identifying some particularly salient relationships.

Valued Capabilities

Thus far we have examined the challenge of cashing out the human consequences of alternative development policies or activities—of shaking down the red-ripe plums, or developing the meta-production function. As useful as that metaphor may be, it is now time to expand it because the image suggests that the consequences, the plums, the capabilities of interest, are visible from afar and easily recognized. This is decidedly not the case, for yet another reason.

Recall that Sen defines capabilities as *valuable* beings and doings. He does so while also pointing out that people are diverse and reasonably consider different beings and doings to be of value, and that the social or political choice of which capabilities to pursue must negotiate in some manner this diversity of values and priorities. Sen argues that public debate should influence the capabilities on which to focus, the distribution of capabilities across a population, and the selection of other principles by which to evaluate comprehensive outcomes. He writes: "Public participation in these valuational debates—in explicit or implicit forms—is a crucial part of the exercise of democracy and responsible social choice. . . . In a freedom-oriented approach, the participatory freedoms cannot but be central to public policy analysis" (Sen 1999, 110).

This complicates the picture in a number of different ways, of which I will mention two. First, there is the evident analytical complication. It is challenging enough if one is trying to maximize income. It is difficult to estimate shadow prices, to set the social discount ranges, and to identify and price indirect effects. But at least one thing is clear: the maximand. In the human development framework, the maximand itself is and should be a separate topic for discussion; it should be a creative and moving target.

Second, there is the difficulty of implementation: even if public deliberation and participation seems very sound as a method for making value judgments, practical questions quickly emerge: How are these discussions to be convened, and how often? Who is to be present? And what grounds are there for expecting value judgments to be based on participants' values, rather than being a function of their knowledge, interests, and power? As Dasgupta, Sen, and Marglin (1972) write regarding a similar issue, "We are roughly in the position of the mice of Aesop's fable who found their ingenious plan of putting a bell on the cat to warn them of his presence foiled by the lack of a suitable means of implementing the plan. Who is to 'bell the cat?'" (247).[8]

A number of authors and practitioners have detailed the extensive connections between the intention of deliberative democracy and Sen's capability approach. But Richardson and others argue that the challenges of creating deep deliberative moments that affect public policy are not to be underestimated (Richardson 1994, 2006; Crocker 2006, 2008). One challenge is to identify the alternative capability sets; another is to communicate feasible alternatives in a way that is interesting and accessible to diverse publics; another is to manage the power differentials between different geographical regions, between men and women, young and old, rich and poor, and across ethnic, racial, cultural, and religious groups within the same public; another is to forge working agreements across conflicts of interests and values that will be politically feasible to implement.

So the capability approach is a two-ring rather than a one-ring circus. The first ring concerns the comprehensive evaluation of alternative courses of action—the link between instrumental freedoms and human outcomes on which this chapter focuses. In this ring various alternative situations, or courses of action, might be evaluated by multiple judges and technical advisers, according to multiple categories, and thus their potential links to human freedoms—their capability production functions—are clarified. In the second ring people discuss their own values and priorities, and argue, modify, and improve their articulation of capabilities and their priority. On the basis of this discussion they either select a course of action or, at the very least, give input into the categories of evaluation. The two rings thus are interlinked, not independent one from the other.

Cost-Benefit Reconsidered

Thus far the measurements advanced all focus on honing our ability to track expansions in human freedoms. Yet the measurement of human freedom is not the only area in which we have improved or—arguably—should improve the scope of measurement.

Consider, for example, the tasks of "capacity building." In many development activities, capacity building is viewed as an objective, an outcome, or an end (and rightly, in my view). Yet from the capability perspective, this is conceptually incomplete because it sees the people whose capacity has been expanded merely as instruments for some other cause (instead of ends in themselves). Even if we were to take such a view, the value of building people's own capacity as workers and leaders depends in part on the increased contribution that they are able to make to expanding others' human capabilities. Yet it is difficult to isolate and predict the stream of capability expansions that might ensue from, for example, teaching a local community-based organization how to keep accounts, how to save, how to set up a central revolving fund, and so on. The attention precisely to this connection is, I argue, not as insistent as perhaps it might be, and is one concrete example of the problems that require attention.

What is needed, analytically, to connect instrumental interventions to build institutional capacity at the micro, local, national, and global levels with human capabilities is not hard to see. Its difficulties are likewise clear. Comparisons need to be set up—whether as randomized experiments or as activities that are matched in other ways—and the impact of a range of capacity-building exercises on present and future capability expansion tracked and aggregated over time and at different levels: individual, local-institution, NGO, and wider. Concurrent to these comparisons, interacting with them and informed by them, need to be the deliberative processes by which people identify the freedoms they value and wish to advance at each point in time.

Social cost benefit analysis was a 1970s fad concurrent with integrated rural development. It foundered precisely because of the difficulty of tracing the direct and indirect externalities, of imputing uncertainty, and of aggregating the core variables as well as the uncertainty coefficients. Its own incompetence discredited its findings, and the practice became more or less extinct. If we take seriously the logic of Sen's capability approach, however, to put it into practice will require precisely the development of careful, full, comparative, consequentialist studies, using sophisticated computing techniques and multilevel, multidisciplinary research methods. Such an undertaking would have more than one role for development ethics; in fact, it may be that this undertaking could describe one legitimate branch of development ethics.

Prospective Analysis

The concerns raised above shape to a great extent the channels by which the capability approach can be put into practice. Elsewhere I have tried to observe how the capability approach is seen by some as an evaluative framework and by others as a framework for prospective analysis (Alkire 2008).

When considered as an evaluative framework, the capability approach constitutes a framework for hearing and assessing various putatively enriching connections between instrumental freedoms and capabilities. Thus the tracing of claimed connections between actions (often to increase instrumental freedoms) and human freedoms, and the active comparison of one set of claims with alternative claims, constitute the capability approach in practice. This is a key point to grasp. It leaves the capability approach in many cases serenely above the fray, in the seat of judge, not barrister.

But the evaluative perspective is incomplete, for people do not only seek ethical grounds by which to judge development to be more humane, they actually wish for development to become more humane. Indeed, the assessment of the capability approach in practice appears to turn on whether it can identify and promote alternatives that turn out to be more effective and equitable means of expanding a range of fundamental capabilities. The identification *and advocacy* of such alternatives has in fact been the aim of the *Human Development Reports* each year.

What many seek from Sen's capability approach is a set of alternative policies that will generate a more humane economy with greater human freedoms. Indeed, the interest in the five instrumental freedoms reflects this interest. The alternative policies will take the form of production functions that link instrumental freedoms—which policies can influence directly—with capability outcomes.

Development as it is already practiced trades on particularly pivotal connections between instrumental freedoms and human freedoms (which may in practice be articulated as capabilities or in very different ways). Development policies change when it becomes apparent that a new set of instrumental freedoms is relatively more efficient in creating the desired outcomes than the previous set. For example, building on the work of Hayek and Milton Friedman,

Thatcherite economics advanced privatization and liberalization policies. The Washington Consensus argued that similar highly leveraged policies, taken together, best advanced their desired objective: economic growth. Robert Putnam and others argued that social capital has a high marginal rate of return and hence should be cultivated as an instrumental freedom. New Growth theorists inserted human capital into the growth equations. Hernando de Soto (2001) advocated the establishment of property rights on the basis of the diverse values that accrue to the poor who enjoy them.[9] Antiglobalization protesters argued that the demolition of the World Bank and International Monetary Fund would halt the decay of human freedoms and promote equity. Right or wrong, alternative schools of development compete by advertising different connections between the instrumental freedoms that policies can affect directly, and the outcomes that they consider to be ends.

This chapter has tried to describe and commend the second, vitally important kind of analysis that complements evaluative analysis, which I have called prospective analysis. It may seem an odd focus for development ethics, given that prospective analyses cannot be undertaken without vigorous engagement with a significant range of vexing and intricate empirical issues. Yet the contribution of a trained and clear mind, and its ability to avoid muddle and keep track of the final objective while at the same time considering regressions, historical precedents, and institutional patterns, is not to be underestimated.

NOTES

1. Thirty percent of Afghanis reportedly were undernourished in 2005 (*National Risk* 2007). The report cited the percentage of the national population below minimum levels of dietary energy consumption adjusted by age and gender. The figure was considered an underestimate; 61 percent of Afghanis were found to have low dietary diversity and poor food consumption (68).

2. Of course, economics is not only concerned with normative issues: description and prediction are also part of its methodology, and the accuracy of descriptive and predictive matters will influence the normative exercise; see Sen (1989).

3. Anantha Duraiappah (2004) adds this instrumental freedom to Sen's list.

4. I have referred to these as "prospective analyses" (Alkire 2008).

5. Sen discussed effective power in the Dewey Lectures (1985) and has elaborated a preliminary account of the linkage between responsibility and effective power (2007).

6. The footnote to this passage in the original text reads, "The evidence is discussed in Amartya Sen, *Development as Freedom.*"

7. See also Sen (1997b).

8. See also Dasgupta, Sen, and Marglin (1972, 135–53).

9. According to Soto: "The poor have accumulated trillions of dollars of real estate during the past forty years. What the poor lack is easy access to the property mechanisms that could legally fix the economic potential of their assets so that they could be used to produce, secure,

or guarantee greater value in the expanded market" (2001, under "Hidden Conversion Process of the West").

REFERENCES

Alkire, Sabina. 2008. Using the Capability Approach: Prospective and Evaluative Analyses. In *The Capability Approach: Concepts, Measures, and Applications*, ed. Flavio Comim, Mozaffar Qizilbash, and Sabina Alkire, 26–50. Cambridge: Cambridge University Press.

Crocker, David. 2006. Ethics of Global Development: Agency, Capability, and Deliberative Democracy: An Introduction. *Philosophy and Public Policy Quarterly* 26 (1–2): 21–27.

———. 2008. *Ethics of Global Development: Agency, Capability, and Deliberative Democracy.* Cambridge: Cambridge University Press.

Dasgupta, Partha, Amartya Kumar Sen, and Stephen A. Marglin. 1972. *Guidelines for Project Evaluation.* United Nations Industrial Development Organization. New York: United Nations.

Duraiappah, Anantha Kumar. 2004. *Exploring the Links: Human Well-Being, Poverty, and Ecosystem Services.* United Nations Environment Programme. Winnipeg, Canada: International Institute for Sustainable Development.

Green, T. H. 1881. Liberal Legislation and Freedom of Contract. In *Works of Thomas Hill Green*, ed. R. L. Nettleship, 3:365–86. London: Longmans, Green. Quoted in Sen (2002, 587).

National Risk and Vulnerability Assessment 2005. 2006. Kabul, Afghanistan: Ministry of Rehabilitation and Development and Central Statistics Office http://www.nss-afghanistan.com/documents/Market.prices.final0306.pdf.

Richardson, H. S. 1994. *Practical Reasoning About Final Ends.* Cambridge: Cambridge University Press.

———. 2006. *Democratic Autonomy: Public Reasoning About the Ends of Policy.* Oxford: Oxford University Press.

Sen, Amartya. 1984. Rights and Capabilities. In *Resources, Values, and Development*, 307–24. Cambridge: Harvard University Press.

———. 1985. Well-Being, Agency, and Freedom: The Dewey Lectures, 1984. *Journal of Philosophy* 82 (4): 169–221.

———. 1989. Economic Methodology: Heterogeneity and Relevance. *Social Research* 56 (Summer): 299–329.

———. 1995. Rationality and Social Choice. *American Economic Review* 85 (1): 1–24.

———. 1996. Legal Rights and Moral Rights: Old Questions and New Problems. *Ratio Juris* 9 (2): 153–67.

———. 1997a. Human Capital and Human Capability (editorial). *World Development* 25 (12): 1959–61.

———. 1997b. Maximization and the Act of Choice. *Econometrica* 65 (4): 745–80.

———. 1999. *Development as Freedom.* New York: Knopf.

———. 2000. Consequential Evaluation and Practical Reason. *Journal of Philosophy* 97 (9): 477–502.

———. 2002. To Build a Country, Build a Schoolhouse. *New York Times*, May 27.

———. 2004a. Elements of a Theory of Human Rights. *Philosophy and Public Affairs* 32 (4): 315–56.

———. 2004b. Reanalyzing the Relationship Between Ethics and Development. Speech delivered at the Inter-American Development Bank, January 16, Washington, D.C.

———. 2007. The Idea of Justice. Mahbub ul Haq Memorial Lecture on Human Development, September 19, New School for Social Research, New York.

Sen, Amartya K., and James E. Foster. 1998. *On Economic Inequality.* Oxford: Oxford University Press.

Soto, Hernando de. 2001. The Mystery of Capital. *Finance and Development*, March 1. http://www.imf.org/external/pubs/ft/fandd/2001/03/desoto.htm.

Stewart, Frances. 1985. *Planning to Meet Basic Needs.* London: Macmillan.

2

The Missing Squirm Factor in Amartya Sen's Capability Approach

A. Allan Schmid

Did you have breakfast this morning?

Did you make an ethical decision?

If you are like most people, you did not think about it. But you know that there are hungry people in the world, yes, even right in your hometown. You exercised an option within your opportunity (capability) set without much thought justifying why it was in your set and not in others'. I am not a philosopher, but to me an ethical decision involves a choice wherein if one person gets her first choice, then someone else does not. Whenever people are interdependent, there are necessarily ethical decisions to be made.

In 2005 the Michigan State University student newspaper ran several stories that are interrelated and relevant to ethics and development. An editorial affirmed the university's recent decision to serve fair trade coffee in all MSU dining halls (MSU Brew 2005). A small group of students had successfully lobbied the University Housing food service coordinator to buy coffee certified as being produced by farmers receiving a fair wage and produced in an environmentally sustainable manner. The change would increase the cost of coffee in the dormitories by fifteen thousand dollars per year. Was this a move toward freedom as choice for Brazilian farmers and future generations? Well, yes— especially if you ignore the nonfreedom of the students who will pay more but don't give a hang for Brazilian farmers. They might prefer other good causes or just another beer! Does their freedom count?

The second story was titled "MSU Joins Group for Worker's Rights" (Davis 2005). Our MSU president, Lou Anna K. Simon, recommended that the university join the Worker Rights Consortium, which certifies that makers of clothing bearing the university's logo have not violated human rights. The president was reported to have reservations, however, with respect to a clause providing maternity leave benefits for women workers, as no cost estimates were given. The third headline that caught my attention was "University Apts., Dorm Rates Could Increase" (Vanhulle 2005). The Board of Trustees was asked to approve new rates for the following year, said to be necessary to cover the increased cost of fuel and natural gas. No mention of coffee costs. There were no cross-references among these three stories. No one asked or volunteered to rank and prioritize Brazilian farmers and garment workers around the world.

These stories illustrate that ethical decisions are implicit every day in our lives. I personally applaud these activist students, though they and the campus journalists have not begun to connect the dots. Still, I wonder if they also feel they pay enough for their McDonald's hamburgers, bananas, copper plumbing, and cotton tops, without worrying whether their dorm staff (many of whom are minorities) earn a living wage. These stories of trade-offs in relative opportunity sets can be placed alongside the story that Amartya Sen (1999, 54) uses to illustrate his conception of freedom and foundations of justice. Annapurna needs some yard work done and can only give it to one of three job seekers (she is only aware of three, although there are probably more). All are poor, but one is poorer than the others. One is more unhappy (the others are used to their predicament), and the other could use the money to help cure a terrible disease. Sen would have Annapurna (and us) agonize over how to rank these "freedoms as opportunities." But note that none of these choices costs Annapurna anything, except perhaps the good feeling of doing the right thing. Contrast her choices to those of the students above, who apparently felt they could not justify continuing to make choices within their large opportunity sets when others had smaller ones. "Interpersonal welfare comparison" language is quite abstract and bloodless. Sen's approach tends to point to the ranking of projects such as education and health care rather than how the costs of Alpha's opportunities are born by Beta. Arguing over a list of what constitutes the good life has little ethical bite—little blood. Nothing like asking if Alpha can justify opportunities incompatible with Beta's choices. The United Nations Development Programme (UNDP 2004) does something useful in charting "development" over time and making comparisons among countries. But the elites will not squirm over publication of new annual indicators. They might squirm a bit if their favorite project (perhaps highway expansion in Mumbai) is not funded because of a low capability improvement index, but nothing like when the question is raised of whose preferences count when freedoms conflict. If there is no cause for unease (squirm), have we really uncovered the deep ethical issues?

The Missing Squirm Factor

Let me suggest some specific decisions of the kind that unavoidably pit opportunities of one group against another and demand an ethical choice:

1. Should U.S. cotton farmers' prices be protected by denying markets to farmers in Africa or Brazil?
2. Should France prohibit head scarves in schools?
3. Should abortion be permitted?
4. Should the minimum wage be increased?
5. Should Wal-Mart be able to close a store if workers try to unionize?
6. Should an aggrieved worker have to prove intent of the employer to discriminate by age or gender?
7. Should old electric power plants continue to discharge high levels of mercury and other toxic materials?
8. Should the income tax be more progressive?

All these questions have a high squirm factor. They involve a trade-off among freedoms of different people with different situations and interests. They have more bite than a bunch of analysts or citizens arguing over weights to be assigned to income, or education status, or self-realization, or whatever in an expanded benefit-cost analysis or UNDP report. Des Gasper (2004, 229) suggests that development ethics "uncovers the issue of costs and who bears them." Thomas Pogge (2002, 57) says that "we must ask whether proposed compensation rules achieve equity among their beneficiaries with their diverse special needs, and equity among their contributors." Sen's language occupies the moral high ground since it is hard to argue against freedom, but it avoids the question of freedom for whom. Opportunity to choose health, education, friends, sex, and so forth is too general to identify the particular interdependencies and rights that determine who counts when different people's desired freedoms conflict. *Whose freedom* is the moral question we all understand but often are afraid to ask.

Weights and Public Choice

"There is thus a strong methodological case for emphasizing the need to assign explicitly evaluative weights to different components of quality of life (or well-being) and then to place the chosen weights for open public discussion and critical scrutiny," says Sen (1999, 81). There are both conceptual and practical problems here. Consider applying weights to the income of the poor but not the rich. How can citizens or their political representatives make an informed choice without knowing how much the tax bill will be and who pays it? (Schmid 1989). Debate over assigning weights to a year of life expectancy versus a dollar of income versus a year of education is not meaningful to most people; anyone who ever did an actual cost-benefit study or tried to engage the public in such weighting exercises knows the problem.

Public choices are made in particular contexts. For example, do students want to pay twenty-five cents more for fair trade coffee, and must all students in the dorms pay? Debate over how that question got to the top of the agenda over twelve other causes is seldom explicit (and given bounded rationality cannot be). The practical question is never how to weight a dollar to a Brazilian grower, or the weight of the grower's dignity, or the sustainability of the land and water (and whether we should note the material washed away into the streams when the beans are pulped). My observation is that the U.S. Congress (or the World Bank) seldom allocates funds to projects based on real-income measures. Sen might applaud, but the "explicitly evaluative weights" that Sen suggests are not used either. In practice, supporters of a particular project will be pleased if such measures make their favorite look good, but they are perfectly willing to spend their political capital to get the necessary votes if it does not. If the project also saves lives, provides jobs to the unemployed, and so forth, so much the better, even if there are ten other unfunded projects that provide more of these benefits.

It is not that "freedom as capability" makes no sense. But does it help uncover the causes of poverty as Sen claims? Perhaps we should forget the freedom framework and look instead for the interdependencies in the economy and society. A problem of the poor is that their interests are seldom a cost of others' actions. It is not enough to be for more freedom and capabilities; one has to go point by point, interdependence by interdependence, and ask the justification (justice) for each present allocation of those opportunities—that is, who has the right and who the exposure and nonright. We can all feel good in supporting land reform and rejecting child labor and women being prohibited from working. But how many of us squirm when enjoying the appreciation in the value of our house or apartment from the general growth of the city and its infrastructure improvements? Does development as freedom cause us to ask, "Why do land owners have the right to the economic rents created by a new metro stop or a highway interchange?" Or, "Why do many of the benefits of technological change go to landlords and not tenants?" There are dozens of these interdependencies where the poor are on the short end of the stick. Sen directs our attention to choices among health, education, participation, and the like. Surely, a sick person has few choices, but is the answer subsidized health care, or in looking at the rights that produced so little income that the poor can't pay for health care or have it included in job benefits in the first place?

Capabilities Versus Resources

The philosophical literature is full of debate about capabilities versus resources approaches to devising a measure by which to judge conditions and policies relating to poverty and inequality (Pogge 2002). The resource approach argues that inequality should be defined as bundles of resources needed by humans in general, while the capability approach argues that the measure should take account of "personal characteristics that govern the conversion of primary goods into the person's ability to promote her ends" (Sen 1999, 74). Pogge argues that if the disfavored are to be compensated according to their capabilities, it follows that "such compensation is to be levied on the naturally favored in proportion to how favored they are relative to the same set of valuable capabilities" (2002, 61). This is administratively unworkable compared to resourcist measures. In 1998, 47 percent of humankind earned less than two dollars per day and commanded only 1 percent of global income. Pogge argues that this resourcist measure does more to provide clear and workable criteria and how to achieve it than can capability measures. We who constitute a much smaller percentage of the population but a large percentage of global income cannot avoid the squirm factor here.

Markets

Markets as institutions are addressed by Sen (1999, chap. 5), who argues that they are not the bugaboo some claim or the salvation promised by others. His suggestions for improvement are significant and indicative of his perspective. He wants markets supplemented by basic education, medical facilities, and availability of resources (land). He says the market is fine, but that people are not prepared to make good use of it and avoid asymmetrical access to information. He does not emphasize that markets begin when there is a distribution of rights (freedoms and accompanying exposures); therefore he does not call attention to why some come to the market with so few rights to trade. Surely, markets are efficient. But if you change who has what rights, you change what is efficient (Schmid 2004). Efficiency is not a prior single thing to be achieved, but rather a derivative and a working out of the values implicit in the antecedent rights that are then to be traded. The ethical issue is the choice of Efficiency 1 versus Efficiency 2. There is no such thing as free trade; all trade begins with an allocation of freedoms and opportunities.

Conclusion

Human beings are the subject of development. Sen's argument that human welfare can't be fully measured in monetary income is unexceptional, but is "development as freedom" necessary to reach this conclusion? Sen uses freedom to modify consequentialism to include some process dimensions as consequences.[1] He uses freedom options to provide a common language (metric?) for utilitarian and libertarian (procedural) values. Why not just speak of prized experiences? What does the freedom language add? In short, I am not convinced that the capability perspective adds much or helps identify the sources of poverty. Any argument about freedom (space) that does not explicitly ask *whose freedom* misses the heart of ethical choice.[2] Sen's capability approach and input to the Human Development Index in the UNDP's annual *Human Development Reports* enable us to feel ethically righteous without having to justify our particular advantages; I can embrace land reform in South America while taking for granted cotton subsidies and the appreciation of my house. *If the construction of ethical choices does not make us squirm, it is not well constructed.*

NOTES

1. I thank Paul Thompson for stimulating my thinking here.
2. Sen (1999, 65) does note that "liberties of different people are interlinked," but he does not make much of it.

REFERENCES

Davis, Amy. 2005. MSU Joins Group for Workers' Rights. *State News* (East Lansing, Mich.), April 5.

Gasper, Des. 2004. *The Ethics of Development.* Edinburgh: Edinburgh University Press.

MSU Brew (editorial). 2005. *State News* (East Lansing, Mich.), April 5.

Pogge, Thomas. 2002. Can the Capability Approach Be Justified? *Philosophical Topics* 30 (2): 167–228.

Schmid, A. Allan. 1989. *Benefit-Cost Analysis: A Political Economy Approach.* Boulder, Colo.: Westview.

———. 2004. *Conflict and Cooperation: Institutional and Behavioral Economics.* Oxford: Blackwell.

Sen, Amartya. 1999. *Development as Freedom.* New York: Knopf.

UNDP (United Nations Development Programme). 2004. *Human Development Report, 2004: Cultural Liberty in Today's Diverse World.* New York: Oxford University Press. http://hdr.undp.org/en/media/hdr04_complete.pdf.

Vanhulle, Lindsay. 2005. University Apts., Dorm Rates Could Increase. *State News* (East Lansing, Mich.), April 5.

3

Institutions, Inequality, and Well-Being: Distributive Determinants of Capabilities Realization

Daniel Little

This volume is focused on the moral importance of capabilities as the touchstone to ethical theories of economic development.[1] I believe that this perspective is correct, and that the greatest moral insight and the greatest human progress result from sustained efforts to align economic development policies with the goal of increasing the realization of human capabilities across the whole of society (Little 2003). But I also believe that our ability to achieve this goal is highly sensitive to the distributive structures and property systems that exist in poor countries. Accordingly, this chapter is concerned with the distributional characteristics of developing countries and the profound impact that different property systems can have on the full human development of the poor. Poor people in developing countries usually measure their ability to fulfill their most basic human capabilities by their position within the domestic property system: their access to land and credit, to the components of human capital (health, clean water, education), and to employment. I will maintain that the chief determinants of the outcomes for human well-being among poor people in developing countries are the property relations and political arrangements through which development proceeds (the economic structure of the developing country). As a result, ethically desirable human development goals are difficult to attain within any social system in which the antecedent property relations are highly stratified and in which political power is largely in the hands of the existing elites.

This approach thus combines another of Amartya Sen's important contributions to development thinking—his emphasis on the centrality of the entitlement bundle (Sen 1981, 1983)—with some of the insights of Marx's political sociology of wealth and poverty (Marx 1977; Marx and Engels 1976). Strikingly, the central viewpoint of this chapter is one that was well understood two or three decades ago, when development scholars across a broad swath of academic and policy circles were calling for both entitlement reform and land reform (Adelman and Morris 1973; Chenery and Syrquin 1975; Herring 1983).[2] This perspective has been eclipsed in the past two decades by neoliberalism, and we need once more to pay attention to these crucial factors of agrarian life.

Agrarian Relations, Capabilities, and Entitlements

Creating an economy in which all persons can fulfill their human capabilities as fully as possible is the ultimate moral good of economic development. This is the central point of the capability approach. This goal requires a social system in which people have adequate access to life's necessities—food, clothing, shelter, clean water, health care—and to the necessities that permit the flourishing of their human talents—education, employment opportunity, and freedom. So far, so good. But what must be achieved to create such a social order? The central thrust of the arguments presented here is that structural inequalities, entrenched through property systems that systematically limit the material resources controlled by the poor and through legal-political systems that systematically reduce the voice of the poor to a whisper, are the greatest obstacle to even limited realization of this goal. So a central objective within economic development policies in the developing world must be a renewed attention to property reform and grassroots democracy. Absent attention to reforming the basic social-property institutions that govern the poor, there is likely to be only limited progress in facilitating the full development of the human capabilities of this impoverished population.

The central premises of my argument are these:

1. Improving the quality of life and degree of human development (the realization of human capabilities) of all members of society is the primary goal of economic development (and the central thesis of the capability approach).
2. Low household income causes low levels of development of the human capabilities of household members. A central determinant of human development of poor households is, precisely, their poverty: the level of income that the household is able to generate throughout the year. Low income causes household inability to purchase essentials of life (food, clothing, shelter); to pay for

rudimentary health care; to pay school tuition (and release their children from farm labor so they may attend school); and to gain the human-capital skills that would permit employment in higher-income positions. These are exactly the social goods needed to cultivate a central core of human capabilities (for example, health and literacy) (the "poverty" premise).[3]

3. Household income in developing societies is determined in large measure by the structure of the social-property system within which householders find themselves: land ownership, access to credit, access to employment, and access to markets for inputs and products. Small farmers face one set of social-property limitations; landless workers face another set; and urban poor face yet another configuration. In each instance, however, the social-property system creates systematic limitations for persons in those social positions to increase their incomes significantly and consistently (the "institutions" premise).

4. The specifics of the social-property system are intimately related to powerful economic and political interests in developing societies; these groups commonly possess extensive political power, and reform of these institutions in favor of the poor is consequently very difficult (the "power and politics" premise).

5. Therefore—

   a. The structure of the social-property system in most developing societies confers substantial inequalities of capabilities realization and human development on different categories of people in society.

   b. A concern for the realization of human capabilities to the highest level feasible must focus on the nature of the social-property institutions within which poor people exist.

I do not suggest that Sen and other advocates of the capability approach are insensitive to these premises. But I do maintain that there is a tendency within the broad spectrum of contemporary development thinking, including the capability approach, to look to aggregate measures of human development at the national level—for example, the Human Development Index (HDI)—which obscures the very extensive inequalities of attainment of human capabilities that exist in many countries for many subpopulations. And I maintain that the capability approach has been less attentive than it needs to be to the social and political mechanisms that create these intranational and intrasocietal inequalities. So this chapter is a plea for returning to a more structural and institutional analysis of the mechanisms through which poverty and low human development are reproduced in many developing countries (and many developed countries as well).

Two types of conclusions follow from this line of thought. First is a recognition of the causal role that the social-property system has in the processes through which people in poor countries are enabled to more fully develop their human capabilities and experience higher quality of life. The specific institutions and social relations through which people earn their livings matter, and these institutions are the outcome of long and intense struggles among powerful players in society. We need to understand those institutions in detail, and in many instances those institutions need to be reformed to ameliorate their bias against the poor.

The second insight is the recognition that it is important to disaggregate data describing a population's quality of life across several socially relevant forms of difference: urban-rural, property status, region, occupational groups, gender, and ethnic group, for example. Efforts to measure progress in terms of rising quality of life that depend on national data erase the direction and pace of change for different social groups. Indices such as the HDI (UNDP 2000) or the Physical Quality of Life Index (Morris 1979) are valuable but limited in that they depend on countrywide data and therefore do not permit us to measure more socially differentiated processes of change in important variables associated with quality of life. Several examples of studies of quality of life at the subnational level illustrate the importance of this sort of disaggregation. One is Walther Aschmoneit's county-level study in China (Aschmoneit 1990), in which he documents very extensive and growing inequalities of quality of life in different regions of the country. Another is V. K. Ramachandran's study of infant mortality in West Bengal (Ramachandran 1991), in which he demonstrates that the health status of different social groups—landless workers versus more affluent social groups—reflects substantial inequalities. Both studies document very substantial intracountry variation in quality of life across occupational groups, region, and urban-rural status. These intra- and interregional differences in the attainment of a population's human development plainly reflect the workings of underlying social mechanisms, and central among these mechanisms are the workings of the social-property system.

Who Benefits from Agricultural Modernization?

Let us begin with an important empirical example of economic development without commensurate gain for the poor of the region: the effects of the Green Revolution in the rice-growing regions of Malaysia. James Scott provides a careful survey of the development process in Malaysia in *Weapons of the Weak*

(1985). The chief innovations were a government-financed irrigation project making double cropping possible; the advent of modern-variety rice strains; and the introduction of machine harvesting, replacing hired labor. Scott considers as relevant parameters the distribution of landholdings, the forms of land tenure in use, the availability of credit, the political parties on the scene, and the state's interests in development.

Scott's chief finding is that double cropping and irrigation substantially increased revenues in the Muda region, but that these increases were very unequally distributed. Much of the increase flowed to the small circle of managerial farmers, credit institutions, and outside capitalists who provided equipment, fertilizers, and transport. Finally, Scott finds that the lowest stratum—perhaps 40 percent—has been substantially marginalized in the village economy. Landlessness has increased sharply as managerial farms absorb peasant plots; a substantial part of the rural population is now altogether cut off from access to land. And mechanized harvesting substantially decreases the demand for wage labor. This group is dependent on wage labor, either on the managerial farms or through migration to the cities. The income flowing to this group is more unstable than the subsistence generated by peasant farming; and with fluctuating consumption goods prices, it may or may not suffice to purchase the levels of food and other necessities this group produced for itself before development. These circumstances have immediate consequences for the ability of poor households to achieve the development of their human capabilities. Their nutritional status, health, literacy, and mobility are all directly impaired by their low and unstable household income. Finally, both the state and the urban sector benefit substantially, as the increased revenues created by high-yield rice cultivation generate profits and tax revenues that can be directed toward urban development.

Scott draws this conclusion:

> The gulf separating the large, capitalist farmers who market most of the region's rice and the mass of small peasants is now nearly an abyss, with the added (and related) humiliation that the former need seldom even hire the latter to help grow their crops. Taking 1966 as a point of comparison, it is still the case that a majority of Muda's households are more prosperous than before. It is also the case that the distribution of income has worsened appreciably and that a substantial minority—perhaps 35–40 percent—have been left behind with very low incomes which, if they are not worse than a decade ago, are not appreciably better. Given the limited absorptive capacity of the wider economy, given the loss of

wages to machines, and given the small plots cultivated by the poor strata, there is little likelihood that anything short of land reform could reverse their fortunes. (1985, 81)

This example well illustrates the problems of distribution and equity that are unavoidable in the process of rural development. The process described here is one route to "modernization of agriculture" in that it involves substitution of new seed varieties for old, replacement of traditional technologies with new ones, integration into the global economy, and leads to a sharp increase in the productivity of agriculture. Malaysia is in effect one of the great successes of the Green Revolution. At the same time it creates a sharp division between winners and losers: peasants and the rural poor largely lose income, security, and autonomy; while rural elites, urban elites, and the state gain through the increased revenues generated by the modern farming sector.

Property Relations, Political Power, and Distribution of Income

How do people earn their livings? The economic institutions of the given society (property relations and market institutions, for example) determine the answer to this question. An economy represents a set of social positions for the men and women who make it up. These persons have a set of human needs—nutrition, education, health care, housing, clothing, and so forth. And they need access to the opportunities that exist in society—opportunities for employment and education, for example. The various positions that exist within the economy in turn define the entitlements that persons have—wages, profits, access to food subsidies, rights of participation, and the like. The material well-being of a person—the "standard of living"—is chiefly determined by the degree to which his "entitlements" through these various sources of income provide the basis for acquiring enough goods in all the crucial categories to permit the individual to flourish (Sen 1981). If wages are low, the consumption bundle that this income will afford is very limited. If crop prices are low, peasants will have low incomes. If business taxes are low, business owners may retain more business income in the form of profits, which will support larger consumption bundles and larger savings. There is thus a degree of conflict of interest among the agents within the economic system; the institutions of distribution may favor workers, lenders, farmers, business owners, or the state, depending on their design.

Central in this schematic account are the institutions and social relations through which economic processes take place. This complex includes, first, the property system. The property system defines how individuals and corporations acquire and retain physical and nonphysical assets. What rights does the property owner possess? How is land owned? Is there a mix of private and public property (for example, public ownership of utilities and roads)? Are there restrictions on the use and disposal of private property? What are the legal conditions of wage labor? Second, the institutions of the state—regulation, fiscal policy, property and contract law—set the context of economic activity. Third are the specific forms that labor takes in a given economy—farm labor, industrial labor, service labor; skilled versus unskilled labor; and so forth. Finally, there are the many ways in which self-seeking individuals can take advantage of existing institutional arrangements, leading to the possibility of corruption, both private and public.

A substantial shortcoming of current approaches to development theory is that insufficient attention is paid to the institutional determinants of income distribution (Taylor 1983, 1990). Analysis of these institutional arrangements is mandatory if we are to have an informed basis for designing poverty-alleviating strategies of development. Local institutional arrangements—the property system, the institutions of credit, the characteristics of labor markets, and the circumstances of political power—decisively influence the distribution of the benefits of economic growth in existing rural economies. A chief determinant of the distribution and character of poverty in a given economy is the system of entitlements that the economy creates for its population: the means through which persons gain income through wages, interest and rent, sales of products, state-funded subsidies, and the like, as well as the distribution of ownership rights in productive assets. It is therefore essential to consider the institutional framework that determines the generation of income.[4]

The Distributive Features of Neoliberal Development Schemes

The distributive characteristics of economic development schemes are largely determined by the specifics of the institutional arrangements through which they work, including chiefly the form of land ownership and the distribution of political power. This perspective works within a framework of analysis that identifies the social relations of production and the system of surplus extraction that they represent as the fundamental determinant of the distribution of income, wealth, and political power.[5]

We may distinguish broadly between two families of development strategies: those that funnel development through existing property relations and political power alignments, and those that involve a redistribution of property and political power in favor of the dispossessed. In many parts of the less-developed world, the existing property relations define an agrarian class structure based on both highly stratified land ownership and existing political institutions that are highly responsive to the political organizations of the elite. We may say that neoliberal strategies of development are those that aim at diffusing technology, new investment funds, expertise, and so forth through these existing private property arrangements and then let the distributive chips fall where they may. Redistributive strategies undertake to alter these fundamental institutional arrangements in such a way as to confer more power, autonomy, and welfare on the least-well-off stratum of rural society.[6]

In addition to analysis of the property relations defining economic activity and interests, it is also important to provide an analysis of political power at the local and national level. Given that different strategies affect local interests differently, and given that the strategy chosen will result from a complex political process involving various affected parties, it is crucial to know what players will be most able to influence the goals and implementation of the development plan. In what is otherwise a sustained denial of the claim that the Green Revolution has exacerbated inequalities, Hayami and Ruttan write, "It is a common observation that, in a society characterized by extreme bias in economic and political resources, it is difficult to bring about institutional reforms that are biased against those who possess substantial economic and political resources. A disproportional share of institutional credit and subsidized inputs will, in such situations, be directed into the hands of the larger farmers. . . . It is extremely difficult to implement institutional changes that are neutral or biased toward the poor in a society characterized by extreme inequality in economic resources and political power" (1985, 360).[7]

Rural development that flows through existing private property relations has a built-in structural tendency toward favoring the interests of the rich over the poor—large landowners over small, owners over tenants, and managerial farmers over hired hands. Such schemes do not do very well at improving the welfare of the lowest stratum of rural society, and they work to extend rather than narrow rural inequalities. (See an effort to model these effects in Little 2003, 82–86.)

These conclusions rest on several converging lines of argument. First is a political point: development strategies are the object of intense political activity within the developing country, and the extreme inequalities in political powers between large landowners and peasants guarantee that the former will have the preponderant voice in this political struggle. As a result, we should expect that development strategies will emerge that are biased toward the interests of the landowner.

Second, there is a structural tendency stemming from the character of stratified property holdings themselves that leads to deepening inequalities between landowners and landless workers. Excluding tax revenues, incomes are generated through two basic sources—income on property (rent, profit, interest) and income from wages. The effect of rural development is to increase the productivity of rural farming systems—ultimately, to increase the yields on land. These increased yields are then converted into increased earnings for the owners of land and other capital resources. Wages increase only if the demand for labor rises; but to the extent that mechanization is part of the package of technological changes that are introduced, the opposite is more likely. Thus there is a tendency for the larger share of the gains through innovation to flow to the owners of land and capital.[8]

Another important feature of rural inequality is that between large and small owners (managerial farmers and landlords on the one hand and subsistence peasant farmers on the other). How does rural development affect the micro-farmer? There is much debate on this question in the literature, but several factors appear fairly clear. The very small farmer faces serious barriers to successful implementation of technical innovations of the Green Revolution. First, his plot is very small—often too small to fully satisfy subsistence needs. He has little access to credit, since he has little collateral or political influence. His current cultivation is frequently a food crop, whereas the available spectrum of innovations is oriented toward riskier market crops. And many—though not all—of the available innovations are indivisible, requiring a minimum acreage to be used efficiently. This is particularly true of mechanized innovations (tractors, harvesters, etc.). Finally, the small farmer is frequently heavily indebted, with few cash reserves; a bad harvest or slump in the commodity market can lead to the loss of the land that he owns or rents. Moreover, as the potential return on land increases through development, there will be more pressure on the smallholder to relinquish his land. Thus foreclosure, abrogation of tenancy, and intimidation likely will result, pushing some small farmers into the wage labor sector. The net result is that as a practical matter the larger farmers and landowners are in a substantially better position to implement Green Revolution technologies. To the extent that this is so, we can expect a widening gap between earnings on the two types of farms, and a significant slippage in the number and size of small farms as peasants are proletarianized or marginalized by changing economic circumstances.

Technology, Inequalities, and Property Relations

The issues of equity and stratification that I am raising here have been much discussed in the development literature, but there the question is usually somewhat different: Do modernization of agriculture and technological innovation all by themselves lead to a worsening of inequalities and the welfare of the rural poor? I suggest that this is not the right question to ask, inasmuch as it emphasizes the technical changes of the Green Revolution rather than the institutional arrangements through which innovation occurs. Defenders of Green Revolution technologies hold that these new techniques confer benefits that are largely neutral across classes, while critics hold that the technologies favor richer farmers. I will make several points on this subject: first, it is the institutional arrangements through which development occurs rather than the technologies themselves that determine the distributive impact of modernization; and second, within the spectrum of available Green Revolution technologies, some favor large farms and some small.[9]

A number of agricultural economists address the question of whether Green Revolution technologies favor large farms over small. There appears to be a rough consensus that the technologies themselves are largely neutral across farm size, and that they do not inherently have the effect of increasing stratification. Thus Robert Herdt (1987) summarizes the experience of the Green Revolution in the Philippines,[10] arguing that there was no clear bias in these technological changes in favor of large farms. Small farms incorporated green technologies as readily as the large farms, there was no tendency for farm size to increase, and real wages for farm labor rose slightly. In a similar vein, Hayami and Ruttan (1985) argue that modern varieties and agricultural modernization do not have the effect of increasing rural inequalities.

But these authors also conclude that the local institutional arrangements—property and political power—decisively influence the distribution of the benefits of innovation. Thus Hayami and Ruttan write: "The potential gains from technical change set in motion both private and bureaucratic efforts to capture the gains from technical change in the form of institutional rents rather than allowing the market to partition the gains among factor owners and consumers. The possibilities for bias in institutional innovations are greatest in societies with highly unequal distribution of economic and political resources" (Hayami and Ruttan 1985, 361). And in his survey of the rural development experience of Mexico, W. Randall Ireson (1987) emphasizes a similar conclusion:

While the findings reported here do support his [Norman Nicholson's (1984)] general contention that Green Revolution technologies by themselves do not increase inequality, the landholding context in which technologies are introduced is found to affect their relative impacts across farm groups. (361)

Most research on Mexico has emphasized an increasing income inequality in the agricultural sector as well as a strong institutional bias in favor of large commercial farms. (352)

The importance of land distribution patterns as a crucial element of agricultural structure must be acknowledged. The data analyzed here clearly indicate the effect of land concentration on increasing income concentration and also the influence of landholding inequality on the different effects of technical change. Perhaps, rather than continuing to debate the distributional consequences of technical change, the development community should pay more attention to the effects of resource concentration on technical change and income concentration. (363)

Finally, in his major study of the rice economy of Asia, Randolph Barker argues that Green Revolution technologies themselves do not create greater inequalities, but that unequal ownership of land and capital leads to greater inequalities of income through technical change (Barker, Herdt, and Rose 1985, 157). Barker comments that the decisive factor determining distribution is the set of property relations and institutional arrangements present:

If ownership of these resources is concentrated in a few hands, then their earnings will likewise be concentrated. . . . The effect of resource ownership on the distribution of earnings is so great that any effect caused by technological change is marginal. . . . That does not say that when incomes are increased because of a technological change, all participants benefit equally. On the contrary, they benefit in proportion to their ownership of resources and the earnings of the resources. . . . The important factor determining who receives the direct income benefits is the ownership of resources. (Barker, Herdt, and Rose 1985, 157)

These observations corroborate the basic point to be argued here. Herdt, Barker, Hayami and Ruttan, and others have shown that modernization and green technologies themselves do not induce inequalities; rather, the inequalities are generated by the institutional arrangements through which these innovations are introduced. Thus new technologies confer benefits and burdens only through the lens of the relations of property and political power that exist in a given country. In this sense the technologies themselves *are* neutral; it is the property relations and political institutions that are the decisive mechanism of distribution.

It is also worth noting that given typical institutional arrangements in many parts of the less developed world—that is, private ownership of land, stratification of landholdings, and credit through private or semiprivate banks—there are sharp differences between different new technological options. Some technological innovations are biased toward large farmers, while others favor small holders' interests, and still others appear to be equally available and beneficial for all strata. New seed varieties are equally available to large and small landholders, while expensive capital equipment and irrigation technology is only available to larger farmers and those with substantial credit available.[11] Thus new agricultural technologies do not form a seamless package of innovations, but rather a differentiated set of options with differential consequences for different classes.[12]

Agrarian Reform

The argument to this point may be summarized in these terms: Quality of life and human development are strongly influenced by household income—and most so at the bottom end of the income distribution. The fundamental determinant of the distribution of income within an economy is the set of property relations through which production occurs. Property relations in the less developed world are typically highly stratified, with a small class owning the majority of wealth (chiefly land). Ownership of wealth confers both high income and substantial political power; so large wealth holders are able to absorb innovations and to influence the political process of planning in a way advantageous to their interests. In most developing economies there is significant stratification of landholding, with consequent stratification of income. In an agrarian economy, land ownership is the primary source of income, so without property reform, it is difficult to see how the lower strata of rural society will be able to improve on their distributive share of income generated by the rural economy.[13]

From this we may draw a conclusion: development that proceeds through existing economic and political institutions will tend to reproduce and perhaps intensify inequalities between classes. This analysis suggests that if we are interested in a process of development that reduces the structure of inequalities, it must be grounded in a set of institutional reforms that redistribute property rights and political powers. In a word, development strategies that aim at reducing inequalities must embody a program of agrarian reform.

What is agrarian reform? It is a process through which property relations and political powers are redistributed in such a way as to favor the interests of the rural poor. Ronald Herring puts the point this way: "Agrarian reforms worthy of the name transform rural society through alterations in the property structure and production relations, redistributing power and privilege" (1983, 11).

The political obstacles to agrarian reform are obvious, both in theory and in history, for as we have already argued, agrarian reform is directly contrary to the economic interests of the politically powerful.[14] Thus agrarian reform appears to presuppose a dramatic increase in the political power and influence of the rural poor. Second, the problem of institutional design—the creation of property arrangements through which efficient, modern agriculture may proceed while serving the ends of equity and welfare—is a knotty one.

The obstacles to a rational and equitable process of agrarian reform are several. First, there is the problem of pre-reform distribution of political power. Existing elites have both the interest and the opportunity to sabotage and defeat fundamental reform. Second, the problem of designing effective and fair institutions is nontrivial and may be expected to require an extended time of experimentation and error. Finally, even with well-designed institutions there will unavoidably be a period of transition that will pose potentially disruptive problems. If property arrangements are to be significantly altered, various players will have counterproductive incentives during the transition. For example, if oxen are soon to be confiscated, then the owner of an ox has no incentive to keep it alive; he may consume it, drive it to death, or in other ways attempt to make use of its value before confiscation. More innocently, as new institutions come into existence it is necessary to rally support from various segments of rural society for them, and this requires raising public confidence in their efficiency, fairness, and stability.

The earliest demand voiced by the rural poor is for fundamental land reform— a "land to the tillers" program. The goal of such a program is to level out land ownership by confiscating the holdings of large landowners and distributing them to the land-poor. The result of such a program in most environments is a system of peasant proprietorship of small plots worked with family labor. Fundamental land reform addresses several of the chief aims of agrarian reform: in particular, it addresses the problem of rural inequality and substantially reduces or destroys the political power and influence of the rural elite.

Fundamental land reform by itself is insufficient, however, if it fails to address problems of efficiency. Small holdings with inadequate access to credit are not a feasible basis for modern high-yield agriculture; but without sustained development in agriculture, it will be impossible to raise either average welfare or the welfare of the least-well-off stratum. Moreover, a peasantry that has achieved the patchwork of smallholdings implied by this system will politically oppose further transformations of the agrarian system.

It is likely, therefore, that rural reform through existing political arrangements will be sharply tilted toward the economic interests of the rural elite (Riedinger 1995). Land reform runs contrary to the most fundamental interests of the rural elite, and this group generally has substantial or even decisive political power. Land reform can only be the outcome of a political process—either through the exercise of state power or through revolutionary action on the part of land-poor peasants. If it is the former, however, the interests of the individuals, coalitions, and organizations involved will play a determining role in the way in which institutional changes are adopted, and the various players have greatly unequal powers. Ronald Herring puts the point this way: "Although land reforms are universally argued for in terms of social justice and economic efficiency, the political reality in South Asian societies is that such reforms are promulgated by ruling elites largely composed of, or structurally or electorally dependent on, agrarian elites" (1983, 3). Herring continues, "Land to the tiller is a direct attack on private property and seems to presuppose an organized and militant peasantry, a revolutionary situation, or some extraordinary concentration of power, perhaps from outside the indigenous political system (as in Japan and Taiwan)" (50). This line of reasoning suggests that a successful policy of land reform requires very exceptional circumstances; in any nation in which the dominant political and economic elite is the landowning class, meaningful land reform appears improbable.[15]

Conclusion

My argument is that in typical circumstances of the less developed world, progress in improving the level of human development of the least well-off— the level of realization of their human capabilities—is unlikely to occur without substantial institutional reform: in particular, redistribution of property rights and political power in favor of previously dispossessed classes (landless, land-poor, share tenants, urban workers, etc.). Absent such fundamental redistribution, the pattern of stratification of measures of quality of life will not change substantially. Thus it is necessary to locate the process of economic development within the broader context of class politics and political power in the developing country.

If we are genuinely committed to realizing human development goals and full realization of human capabilities for the poorest one billion of the earth's population, then substantially greater attention to the distributive institutions within developing societies is needed. And this means that the capability approach needs to reaffirm its pragmatic and intellectual relationship to those voices within development theory that emphasize the centrality of inequalities and the institutions that reproduce them.

NOTES

1. Representative statements of the capability approach include Crocker (1992), Nussbaum (2000), and Sen (1987, 1999).

2. This perspective was welcome to analysts at the World Bank in the 1970s. *World Development Report, 1978* offers this assessment: "Historical experience suggests that the poorer members of the population are unlikely to share equitably in economic growth, mainly because they have less access to the productive assets needed to generate incomes—land, credit, education, and jobs in the modern sector" (World Bank 1978, 8). But the openness to significant pro-poor institutional reform at the World Bank abated in subsequent decades; see Deininger and Binswanger (1999), a recent review of twenty-five years of World Bank thinking on land reform.

3. Another key determinant is the quantity and quality of public goods, such as health care, education, and clean water, that the state is able to provide to poor households. This premise is important but will not be further developed here. It is Sen's primary focus in his discussions of public policy (Drèze and Sen 1989).

4. See Little (2003, chap. 2) for more extensive exposition of these ideas.

5. This framework is very elegantly described by Robert Brenner: "Class structure . . . has two analytically distinct, but historically unified aspects. First, the relations of the direct producers to one another, to their tools and to the land in the immediate process of production—what has been called the 'labour process' or the 'social forces of production.' Secondly, the inherently conflictive relations of property—always guaranteed directly or indirectly, in the last analysis, by force—and by which an unpaid-for part of the product is extracted from the direct producers by a class of non-producers—which might be called the 'property relationship' or the 'surplus' extraction relationship.' It is around the property or surplus extraction relationship that one defines the fundamental classes in a society—the class(es) of direct producers on the one hand and the surplus-extracting, or ruling, class(es) on the other" (1976, 31).

6. Redistributivist perspectives emphasizing the importance of agrarian reform can be found in the research of V. K. Ramachandran and his colleagues (Ramachandran 1991; Ramachandran and Swaminathan 2002, 2005). See also Gillian Hart's writings on agrarian reform in Southeast Asia (Hart, Turton, and White 1989).

7. Land reform is one type of agrarian reform that can significantly improve the distribution of income and well-being in rural societies. The importance of credit reform in poverty alleviation strategies in rural India is emphasized in Ramachandran and Swaminathan (2005).

8. See Ramachandran's (1991) analysis of landless workers in rural India.

9. See Otsuka, Cordova, and David (1992) for a review of some of the interactions of these effects in the Philippines.

10. Herdt's study (1987) is based on an International Rice Research Institute project consisting of a fifteen-year study of two wet rice areas in the Philippines. The project surveys patterns of land tenure, technology, yields, and income distribution, and changes in each of these over the period of under observation (during which time the Green Revolution technologies became available).

11. According to Hayami and Ruttan: "It is critical to recognize that modern technologies are not homogeneous in their effects on agrarian structure. Advances in mechanical technology are usually accompanied by scale economies, resulting in economy in management effort as well as in the use of labor in production. . . . Biological technology, in contrast, is generally embodied in divisible inputs such as improved seed and fertilizer and requires intensive on-the-spot supervisory management decisions. Its effect is to raise the relative efficiency of small family farms and promote a unimodal farm-size distribution" (1985, 332).

12. According to Ireson: "Although the Green Revolution is usually considered to be a package of changes, its different components interact with landholding patterns to produce different effects, some of them contradictory, on income inequality. The political context of farm-level decision making and resource allocation is a third area crucial to understanding the dynamics of technical change" (1987, 363).

13. Riad El-Ghonemy (1990) provides developed arguments concerning the relationship between land reform and poverty alleviation. Benedict Kerkvliet (1990) provides an ethnographic-scale study of these issues in rural Philippines.

14. See Herring's revisiting of land reform in Kerala in his more recent study (1991).

15. Somewhat different analysis is needed for a large and complex nation such as India. In this case there is a much broader range of political powers and interests at work, with a substantial urban sector whose interests may sometimes join with those of the rural poor against the rural elite. See Atul Kohli's careful analysis (1987).

REFERENCES

Adelman, Irma, and Cynthia Taft Morris. 1973. *Economic Growth and Social Equity in Developing Countries*. Stanford: Stanford University Press.

Aschmoneit, Walther H. 1990. Life Quality Index of China. In *Remaking Peasant China: Problems of Rural Development and Institutions at the Start of the 1990s*, ed. J. Delman, C. S. Ostergaard, and F. Christiansen, 204–15. Aarhus, Denmark: Aarhus University Press.

Barker, Randolph, Robert W. Herdt, and Beth Rose. 1985. *The Rice Economy of Asia*. Washington, D.C.: Resources for the Future.

Brenner, Robert. 1976. Agrarian Class Structure and Economic Development in Pre-industrial Europe. *Past and Present* 70 (1): 30–75.

Chenery, Hollis, and Moises Syrquin. 1975. *Patterns of Development, 1950–1970*. Oxford: Oxford University Press.

Crocker, David A. 1992. Functioning and Capability: The Foundations of Sen's and Nussbaum's Development Ethic. *Political Theory* 20 (4): 584–612.

Deininger, Klaus, and Hans Binswanger. 1999. The Evolution of the World Bank's Land Policy: Principles, Experience, and Future Challenges. *World Bank Research Observer* 14 (2): 247–76.

Drèze, Jean, and Amartya Sen. 1989. *Hunger and Public Action*. Oxford: Clarendon Press.

El-Ghonemy, M. Riad. 1990. *The Political Economy of Rural Poverty: The Case for Land Reform*. London: Routledge.

Hart, Gillian Patricia, Andrew Turton, and Benjamin White, eds. 1989. *Agrarian Transformations: Local Processes and the State in Southeast Asia*. Berkeley and Los Angeles: University of California Press.

Hayami, Jujiro, and Vernon W. Ruttan. 1985. *Agricultural Development: An International Perspective*. Baltimore: Johns Hopkins University Press.

Herdt, Robert W. 1987. A Retrospective View of Technological and Other Changes in Philippine Rice Farming, 1965–1982. *Economic Development and Cultural Change* 35 (2): 329–49.

Herring, Ronald J. 1983. *Land to the Tiller: The Political Economy of Agrarian Reform in South Asia*. New Haven: Yale University Press.

———. 1991. From Structural Conflict to Agrarian Stalemate: Agrarian Reforms in South India. *Journal of Asian and African Studies* 26 (3–4): 169–88.

Ireson, W. Randall. 1987. Landholding, Agricultural Modernization, and Income Concentration: A Mexican Example. *Economic Development and Cultural Change* 35 (2): 351–66.

Kerkvliet, Benedict J. 1990. *Everyday Politics in the Philippines: Class and Status Relations in a Central Luzon Village*. Berkeley and Los Angeles: University of California Press.

Kohli, Atul. 1987. *The State and Poverty in India: The Politics of Reform*. Cambridge: Cambridge University Press.

Little, Daniel. 2003. *The Paradox of Wealth and Poverty: Mapping the Ethical Dilemmas of Global Development*. Boulder, Colo.: Westview.

Marx, Karl. 1977. *Capital*. Vol. 1. Trans. Ben Fowkes. New York: Vintage.

Marx, Karl, and Friedrich Engels. 1976. *The German Ideology*. 3rd rev. ed. Moscow: Progress.

Morris, Morris David. 1979. *Measuring the Condition of the World's Poor: The Physical Quality of Life Index*. Pergamon Policy Studies, Overseas Development Council. New York: Pergamon.

Nicholson, Norman. 1984. Landholding, Agricultural Modernization, and Local Institutions in India. *Economic Development and Cultural Change* 35 (3): 569–90.

Nussbaum, Martha Craven. 2000. *Women and Human Development: The Capabilities Approach*. New York: Cambridge University Press.

Otsuka, Keijiro, Violeta Cordova, and Cristina C. David. 1992. Green Revolution, Land Reform, and Household Income Distribution in the Philippines. *Economic Development and Cultural Change* 40 (4): 719–41.

Ramachandran, V. K. 1991. *Wage Labour and Unfreedom in Agriculture*. WIDER Studies in Development Economics. New York: Clarendon Press.

Ramachandran, V. K., and Madhura Swaminathan, eds. 2002. *Agrarian Studies: Essays on Agrarian Relations in Less-Developed Countries*. New Delhi: Tulika Books.

———, eds. 2005. *Financial Liberalization and Rural Credit in India*. New Delhi: Tulika Books.

Riedinger, Jeffrey M. 1995. *Agrarian Reform in the Philippines: Democratic Transitions and Redistributive Reform*. Stanford: Stanford University Press.

Scott, James C. 1985. *Weapons of the Weak: Everyday Forms of Peasant Resistance*. New Haven: Yale University Press.

Sen, Amartya. 1981. *Poverty and Famines: An Essay on Entitlement and Deprivation*. Oxford: Clarendon Press.

———. 1983. *Poor, Relatively Speaking*. Dublin: Economic and Social Research Institute.

———. 1987. *The Standard of Living*. Ed. Geoffrey Hawthorn, with contrib. by John Muellbauer, Ravi Kanbur, Keith Hart, and Bernard Williams. Tanner Lectures on Human Values. Cambridge: Cambridge University Press.

———. 1999. *Development as Freedom*. New York: Knopf.

Taylor, Lance. 1983. *Structuralist Macroeconomics: Applicable Models for the Third World*. New York: Basic Books.

———. 1990. *Socially Relevant Policy Analysis: Structuralist Computable General Equilibrium Models for the Developing World.* Cambridge: MIT Press.

UNDP (United Nations Development Programme). 2000. *Human Development Report, 2000: Human Rights and Human Development.* Oxford: Oxford University Press.

World Bank. 1978. *World Development Report, 1978.* Washington, D.C.: World Bank.

4

Development Ethics Through the Lenses of Caring, Gender, and Human Security

Des Gasper and Thanh-Dam Truong

Globalized Vulnerability

Processes of globalization are diverse in character and have produced contradictory tendencies: integration and differentiation, spread and concentration, inclusion and exclusion, gain and loss. Global concentration of power and authority in trade, finance, and economic policy—the dominance of bodies in Washington, D.C., together with the World Trade Organization and others—has been paralleled by the decline of many weaker economies into structural indebtedness, foreign-imposed economic policy regimes (and their widespread failure), shrinkage of many domestically owned activities, and greatly increased reliance on exports such as drugs, persons, and criminal "services."

Globalization processes offer unprecedented opportunities for those able to take them, including opportunities for more efficient exploitation and crime. They frequently spread inequality within as well as between countries.[1] Forms of exploitation that were largely exiled to the fringes of the world system have revived in the North (see, for example, Ehrenreich and Hochschild 2003), while some countries in the South have restructured their economies and societies such that the sex trade and dependency on women migrants' remittances have become forms of survival both for nation-states and for a growing number of their citizens. Saskia Sassen has called this the feminization of survival: "The sex

The authors may be contacted at gasper@iss.nl or truong@iss.nl.

trade itself has become a development strategy in some areas" (Sassen 2003, 269).[2] A global trade in people has reemerged based on increasingly globalized communications and aspirations, structural economic problems in much of the South and East, and increasing demand yet decreasing local supply in rich locations for some types of labor, particularly of low-cost labor for menial tasks (Sassen 2003).

Many of the most striking examples of these varied processes and transfers are in industrial countries, not least the implosion or decay of parts of the former Soviet bloc and in the work and movements of women (Truong 2003a). The agenda of development ethics on the human costs, options, "trade-offs," and human "write-offs" in socioeconomic development processes, ever more clearly applies not simply to events in a geographically separate South and its relations with a separated North, but to events and relations within the North too. We have a "Global South" everywhere, partly as a migratory consequence of the era of a rich geographically separate North dominating a remote South, and more importantly from endogenous (re-)creation of a South in the North. The term Global South conveys the transnational character of poverty and deprivation, and suggests a convergence of deprivation across geographical boundaries. Pierre Bourdieu wrote of the "sans": those without, the jobless, homeless, paperless. We find pockets of "North" everywhere now as well. The world has become pre-1994 South Africa writ large. To an important extent, the fields of development studies and international political economy now merge (Hettne 1995).

Development ethics' typically strong focus on women grows (for example, Nussbaum and Glover 1995; Sen 1999). Strikingly, many of Narayan and colleagues' *Voices of the Poor* (2000) were women's. Women are characteristically families' "shock absorbers": they care for the ill and infirm, they enter forms of flexible or informal work when family pressures dictate, they are pressured in times of change to embody purported tradition, they give others security and comfort. Their own security and well-being are often in jeopardy, unconsidered, downgraded. Shock absorbers are noticed only when broken. Since the 1990s women have become the majority group in international migration for work, whether voluntarily, by coercion, or through deception (see IOM 2003). But migration and vulnerability are of general relevance, and for the sake of contrast we open with an example that mainly concerns male migrants from economically booming China deployed in an occupation that was dominated earlier by British women (*British Countryside*, 318).

One night in February 2004, twenty-one foreign workers, nearly all of them young Chinese, drowned in Morecambe Bay, northern England. They were harvesting cockles, a profitable shellfish, on the bay's notorious mudflats. Possibly they became "stuck in sucking sands as the tide came in, perhaps [they were] simply swept along in one of the deep channels that can suddenly open up in those sands" (Thompson 2004). Fifteen fellow workers were rescued. Reportedly, some who were stuck or stranded tried to call their families in China by mobile phone to say farewell; they were not familiar with the emergency services telephone number in Britain. According to Xue Xinran, "There are warning signs about 'quicksand and dangerous tides' near where they died, but they would not have understood them. They spoke no English" (2004). Groups of Chinese workers had been saved from the winter sea by lifeboats twice in the previous five weeks.

Subsequent investigations indicated that some of the workers were asylum seekers, others were illegal immigrants who had paid large sums to be smuggled into Britain. All lacked work permits and were controlled by Chinese "gang-masters," who took up to half the income from the cockle sales and supplied the labor to an English boss, who helped obtain the permits for cockle picking. The twenty-one workers lived with twenty others in one small house. They were taken to the sands at any time of day or night, depending on the tides, to reap the unusual temporary abundance of cockles. Local residents and the fishing community in Morecambe Bay had warned for months about the risks.

These events, variously described, attracted much attention in Britain, China, and worldwide. Whatever the exact details of the case, it calls forth questions about work and insecurity in the global market. Are people so reckless or so ignorant, so eager for gain, so desperate, or so misled by recruiters? In fact, no one from the very poorest groups in China can afford transportation and entry to the West; the move leaves many migrants heavily in debt and with families in China to support. Once in Britain they appear willing or forced to risk their physical security in the hope of economic security. Some of the workers who were rescued in February soon returned to work on the mudflats, and two months later, four cockle pickers were rescued after becoming stranded on the same sands.

The risky search for financial gain in a worldwide field of operation is not new. What may be new is the intensity of reporting and reflection, thanks to modern communications technology; and perhaps also new, partly underlying the intensity, is the degree of concern shown in the reporting, with not only outcries at interlopers but in many cases both a lament over the loss and a will to understand. In a piece in London's *Daily Telegraph* (February 7, 2004) immediately after the deaths, Adam Thompson evoked a painting by J. M. W. Turner from the 1840s, an earlier phase of outrage. *Slavers Throwing Overboard the Dead and Dying—Typho[o]n Coming On* depicts the casting of dead and dying slaves into the Atlantic from slave ships to claim insurance by reporting that the slaves were lost in a storm rather than from illness. Turner brought the case memorably to attention, but to an immensely smaller audience than that for modern electronic media.

Later in the nineteenth century, millions of Chinese died in a series of famines. Over ten million died in the North China famine of the late 1870s alone, watched over by an enfeebled imperial government long undermined by Western incursion. In stark contrast, the great North China drought of 1743–44 had been effectively handled by vigorous government action, far more effectively than were comparable famines in Europe in 1740–43 (Davis 2001, 280). Famines of similarly enormous magnitude occurred repeatedly in the late nineteenth and early twentieth centuries in British-ruled India. Its population was as a result virtually stagnant between 1891 and 1921, and indeed stagnant between 1871 and 1921 in many districts (175). Davis notes figures of twenty million excess deaths in India for the 1890s, and ten million excess deaths or more in each of the famines of 1876–79, 1896–97, and 1899–1902 (110–11, 158, 174). As in the Irish famine of the 1840s, British authorities consciously restricted and rejected remedial interventions in the face of weather-related crises. Little or nothing was done to secure access to food for the poorest groups. The famines were recorded and reported in Europe and North America but only as remote and alien events. They received far less attention than the dramatics of war and rebellion. Unlike "the Indian Mutiny" or "the Boxer Rebellion," the famines never entered the popular (or elite) Western memory. Only the insecurity of ruling groups was considered significant. Nowadays with incessant electronic media coverage, deaths in Darfur or Ethiopia may be experienced elsewhere as more manifest, tangible, and urgent. Such events, though, still can be largely ignored, as the loss of millions of lives in the Congo in the past decade testifies. Corpses on a winter night on Morecambe Beach may speak more vividly to northern audiences.[3]

The next section explores some key areas in globalization by using a gender perspective. This takes us beyond the abstracted circuits of economic production and the corresponding categories, and makes us centrally consider reproduction: biological, psychological, and emotional. Otherwise, disjunctions in reasoning at the policy level reinforce and exacerbate dysfunctions in social systems at the local and global level, leading to tragedies at the personal level. A gender perspective may also provide some moral resources for responding to systemic tragedy, in addition to resources for identifying and understanding it. It brings to our attention the centrality of activities and attitudes of care in various settings and forms.

Global changes demand an ethic that honors and protects human dignity as a core value, and that can extend beyond the particular form of governmentality confined by the notions of sovereignty and territorial control. Ethical questions regarding human dignity can no longer be framed within neatly demarcated realms such as the "domestic" (read: self) and the "foreign" (read: distant others). Self and others intertwine in processes of production, reproduction, and consumption. Socialization by foreign au pairs and domestic workers affects children growing up under paid domestic care (Baquedano-López 2002). Withheld wages of commercial sex workers are laundered through international banking systems or invested in real estate and transformed into immobile capital for further accumulation (O'Neill-Richard 1999). The HIV/AIDS pandemic, transmitted through uninformed or uncaring unsafe sex, has caused an intergenerational transfer of burdens to AIDS orphans. Vulnerable children become commodities fed into cross-national trafficking chains (Dottridge 2004). There now exist interconnected systems of vulnerability, for which corresponding systems of human security, care, and responsibility are needed to ensure the protection of human dignity as a core value (Truong 2006).

We then proceed to look at responses in the evolution of thinking in development ethics. The gradual move beyond economism to ideas of human development is being deepened by drawing connections to the human rights tradition and by the growth of a discourse of "human security." This discourse represents a response to human insecurity: economic debacles in Africa, the former Soviet Union, Latin America, and, more briefly, in East Asia, and numerous wars and their effects. Does it provide anything more than new packaging? We suggest yes: human security is a return to the substantive agenda of basic human needs, but better grounded in an ethnography of the risks and pressures, hopes and fears of ordinary lives, rather than only an abstracted accounting of deficiencies or an elevated language of opportunities. An ethic of human security and human development must be grounded not only in rich ethnography but be emotionally and existentially grounded too. These required forms of grounding are mutually supportive.

Next we examine the potential contribution of three diverse bodies of thought to grounding such an ethic of human security and human development: the ancient tradition of Mahayana Buddhism; the current work of philosopher-anthropologist Ananta Giri; and feminist care ethics. The final section summarizes and draws conclusions concerning the trajectory and lessons for development ethics. Its work, especially on human development, has to treat development in a global perspective and to reflect on the content of "human," including through careful attention to both gender and caring.

Globalization Through a Gender Lens

Viewing globalization through the gender lens reveals the persistent obliteration of reproduction, the female sphere, in mainstream debates in international political economy.[4] Susan Strange, a founding mother of the field, helped to redirect its focus from state-based to society-based (Palan 1999). She identified four foundational societal structures—knowledge, security, production, and finance—and argued that state power can be understood as an outcome of the articulation of elements in each structure, independently or in interaction. Reproduction—as a foundation of the human condition that maintains and makes possible the continuity of life and social institutions—remains implicit in her framework. Yet Strange held that the object of study of international political economy is nothing less than the "human condition as it is, or was" (Palan 1999, 126).

To provide a more adequate account of the human condition and address the consequences of an androcentric construction of reality requires what Gillian Youngs calls an act of ontological revision: to get "behind the appearance and examine how differentiated and gendered power constructs the social relations that form that reality" (2004, 77).[5] She delineates three levels of interrogation concerning: (1) why women and gender concerns are subsidiary in high politics and diplomacy; (2) why the male subject position reigns in theorizing, despite its selective apprehension about the human condition; and (3) whether these aspects reflect a deeper cultural current of masculinity itself, a phenomenon of power and consciousness historically formed and structured by the separation of public and private life (77–80).

Following her suggestions, let us look at characteristics of globalization as a historical process—a process that has acquired features distinct from early forms of internationalization. These include *deterritorialization* (the growing range of human activities that take place irrespective of the geographical location of participants), *social interconnectedness* (the ways in which activities in one locality can affect the social world of another), and *velocity* (the accelerated pace of human activity and rate of social change) (Scholte 2000, 2005). Our main questions are: Deterritorialization, social interconnectedness, and velocity relating to whom? To which human activities are we referring?

What do these three key features of globalization mean to those located in the Global South? There is an increasing disparity of interests between those involved in the accelerated and perpetual mobility of capital ("the men" who control the corporate sector, including women in masculine positions of power and authority), and those involved in the daily maintenance of firms, farms, and families ("the women," including men in feminized positions). As Beneria (1999) points out, "Davos Man" provides the archetype of human activity in the mainstream account of globalization, displacing the representation of the quotidian reality shared by the two-thirds of humanity in the Global South. The disparity has brought new boundaries in the global geography of wealth, deprivation, and mobility, and rescaled political and economic relations within and between nations. In this new geography, the nation-state is simultaneously irrelevant to some social activities and omnipresent in others.

Contemporary labor migration regimes illustrate this. Evidence on the licit and illicit involvement of migrant laborers (men, women, boys, and girls) in sectors such as construction, agriculture, textiles, and tourism-related activities, including sexualized entertainment and even begging (ILO 2001), reveals the dynamism in international and regional labor markets. These markets reflect structural changes and forces other than those in the welfare systems of industrialized countries.[6] While labor markets increasingly acquire regional and international ramifications—interconnected by vast networks of labor recruitment using methods stretching from high-tech digital facilities down to personal persuasion at village levels—the legal regimes for labor migration still center around assumptions of territorial integrity and cultural separation and difference.

Industrialized countries report three service sectors with major labor shortages: health and care; education; and information technology (OECD 2002). Shortage in the health and care sectors results from an aging population and the absence of substitutes for human labor. More broadly, we see a huge expansion of markets for personalized services, both in essential and luxury sectors. The proliferation of care services, such as body care, child care, care for the elderly, and the plethora of sexual services, feeds on and into a rapid and globalized transformation in social reproduction. Yet migrant labor in a variety of activities affiliated with the maintenance of human life is considered insignificant—and therefore unmonitored—and is supplied through irregular private means, sometimes with the tacit tolerance of state agents. These supply lines have come to form an area of international migration managed with little human rights protection (Truong 2003b; Chapkis 2003), mostly dominated by human trafficking regimes in which migrants are subject to gross violations of rights by unruly practices of underground organizations (Truong 2003c; Iselin 2002).[7]

Currently, regulatory regimes of migration for work consist of a combination of global, regional, and bilateral regimes. Defined as the movement of natural persons, international migration is a category of trade in services regulated by the WTO General Agreement of Trade in Services Mode 4.[8] This mode covers service suppliers at all skill levels. Government commitments, however, have been largely restricted to the highly skilled male sectors (intra-corporate transfers, business visitors, contract suppliers). There exist isolated bilateral arrangements for labor gaps in formal sectors dominated by women, such as health and care. Some bilateral arrangements also cover sectors that lie at the nebulous junction between formal and informal, such as entertainment and domestic services.[9]

The unwillingness of many governments to commit to regulating the lower strata of the skill ladder reflects a preferential treatment of the male-dominated corporate sphere of work. The desire to protect the integrity of national borders remains entrenched, while the pressing need to protect those living in conflicting frameworks of jurisdiction, stripped of their capacity for control over their destiny, languishes in judicial disharmony. Patterns of "forum shopping" have emerged—choices by trafficking networks of where to operate according to which judicial environment allows them to maximize returns or minimize risks—that constitute a direct challenge to state control (Europol 2000). As argued by Iselin (2002), unless states can create judicial harmony, allow joint investigation, and adopt workable and efficient national and international mechanisms of referencing that protect the human dignity of victims, migrant workers in "feminized" conditions (of submission and obedience) will, irrespective of their gender identity and sector of employment, remain unable to assert themselves as subjects with rights.

In these situations, high velocity as an aspect of globalization fails to apply to the judiciaries, bound as they are by so many considerations derived from history, culture, national identity, and other interests. Despite a formal commitment by states to juridical protection of victims,[10] the slow formation of functioning local institutions to provide this protection has buffeted many undocumented migrant workers into sidelines where they turn to criminal actors for protection—a protection that often transforms into tyranny. The "unpeople," helots or undocumented and bonded migrant workers, do not experience deterritorialization as active agents but as highly dependent subjects. They move through distinct gendered and racialized corridors of the international labor market. They are deployed in stigmatized and risky locations, often with little scope for agency.

By contrast, within the sphere of conventional economic statistics the visibility of migrant workers' contribution is now glaring. Their remittances (as citizens, denizens, or helots) have become a key source in national finances, less volatile than other financial flows and relatively unaffected by financial crises (Ratha 2003). According to the International Office of Migration (IOM 2003), remittances through official channels amounted to $72.3 billion in 2001— double the amount in 1988, implying a growth rate between 5 and 6 percent per year. Since a large number of migrants remit through informal channels, the total amount is much higher. According to the World Bank (2006, ix), remittances from abroad received by developing countries in 2005 were on the order of $167 billion. For many low-income countries, remittances have become two to three times larger than foreign direct investment and far exceed the volume of official development assistance.

The volume of remittances is proportionately more important among the less educated migrants, who have a higher burden of parental and filial duty for the maintenance of the young and the elderly (IOM 2003). But precisely the least protected migrants remit through informal and risky financial channels, for undocumented or temporary migrants cannot open bank accounts. They turn to costly methods offered by private companies who charge between 13 and 20 percent of the amount transferred, or to informal channels where their money is at risk of theft (Ratha 2003). In a pyramid of social relations, new rules provide privileges and protection for workers affiliated with corporate activities but leave the subordinate groups subject to the unruly nature of the global polis, despite their major contribution to the economic security of their nations.

The global economic reforms of the past generation, and current frameworks of analysis and policy negotiation, show great attention to economic productivity and little regard for human and social reproductivity. Norms built into global governance frameworks on liberalization of financial markets and migration have produced, in many contexts, distinct spheres of gendered interests. The transformation of production as a key structure in international political economy has not entailed a transformation of consciousness to address the security and financial concerns of those who are daily engaged in the maintenance of human life and social institutions, without whom the production and financial investment would be impossible.

A reproductive crisis manifests itself in anarchical patterns of unauthorized, illicit, and concealed movements of people across borders in search of work under conditions of high risk to be able to sustain themselves and the livelihoods of those left behind. This crisis, a tragedy for many, has opened up a new space for ethical reflection and for debates on how to foster progressive forces for a more equitable transformation.

Development Ethics: From Economism to Human Development to Human Security

Theories and Practices

As a field, development ethics is a space of analysis and action regarding the trajectory of societies, with special reference to suffering, injustice, and exclusion within societies and between societies on a global scale (see, for example, Gasper 2004 for other characterizations). Its typical focus on humans in their own right, irrespective of location, rather than as abstract functioning factors in an economy, offers the possibility for a politics of social change that accepts human dignity as a priority.

The development ethics field can be seen as the intersection of various streams of practice and traditions of theorizing. Table 1 presents some major bodies of practice in which ethical issues have been perceived and grappled with, and how they intersect with important streams of theorizing, thereby generating many types of thought and action. The matrix shown is a tool to think actively about work in development ethics, not a facsimile portrait. There are of course overlaps between the streams and traditions presented; professional ethics, for example, connects to many other areas but has become a distinct field of theory as part of practical ethics' theorizing and advice in response to real choices. Further, the matrix lacks a time dimension to convey, say, the rise of human rights in policy terms. Other areas of practice, such as consumption or intercultural relations, and of theory, such as consumer theory and critique or cultural theory and critique, could be added. Arguably we could, for example, add environment as a practice column and participatory approaches as both row and column.

In this chapter we stress some sources that are not prominent in past work but whose importance in development ethics is growing: feminist theory and practices in struggles for gender equity, and migration as a social reality from which many ethical questions emanate and are being scrutinized in the same way that emergency relief and intervention have been and continue to be. We will in addition propose to extend beyond disembedded moral philosophy and spirituality and to draw from existentialist thought and ethics of care.

Human Development

Much of the literature in development ethics has arisen in the shaded cells in table 1, where some schools in moral philosophy and social science, including critiques of mainstream economics, address issues arising in socioeconomic

Table 1. Some Sources and Streams in Development Ethics: Examples of the Resulting Work

		Some sources in practice		
		Socioeconomic development policy, programs, projects	Human rights activism and practice	Emergency relief, conflict, and humanitarian intervention	The world of work and corporate responsibility
Some streams in theorizing	Critiques of mainstream economics	Sen and capability approach; Haq and "Human Development"; Grameen Bank	"Rights-based approaches" to development (not led by HR theory)	The entitlements approach to famine and hunger	"Triple bottom line"
	Well-being research	Participatory poverty assessment; Ellerman on building autonomy via assistance	Galtung, Max-Neef et al. on autonomy and participation in one's community	Harrell-Bond on promoting autonomy in relief programs	De Moraes, Carmen, on autonomy in work
	Moral philosophy	Nussbaum's capability approach; O'Neill's approach to justice	Rights of women, children, workers, aged, handicapped, animals	Kantian ethics of obligations; Red Cross	[Western moral philosophy has been largely too abstract to contribute distinctively here]
	Religions	Liberation theology; Buddhist economics; Sarvodaya	Liberation theology; Gandhism; socially engaged Buddhism	Christian relief agencies; Red Crescent	Catholic social thought; Vedantic business ethics; "faith-based . . ."; SEWA
	Humanism	Goulet; Berger; Illich; Max-Neef	Universal Declaration of Human Rights	Oxfam relief; MSF	UN Global Compact
	Human rights theory, jurisprudence	Right to work; basic income; rights of the displaced	Human rights covenants; work on legal constitutions, legislation; judicial activism	Doctrines of (non-) intervention	Labor rights; child labor; UN Protocol on Human Trafficking (2000)
	Professional/practical ethics	Immersion visits; professional guidelines and codes of practice	Work to apply formally avowed rights in practice	Codes of relief ethics; SPHERE standards	Business practice codes; social entrepreneurship
	Feminist theory	Discerning gender-based social injustice; gender audits; unveiling of the care sector	Complementing rights with emphases on virtues and care; demanding rights for invisible workers and subjects in need of care	Rape as a war crime and a component of genocide (UN Resolution, 2008)	Organizing in the informal economy; domestic workers associations

development policies, programs, and projects. This work is diverse, since the schools are diverse—utilitarian, Aristotelian, Kantian, existentialist, and more— but a major thrust is captured by the subtitle of a recent survey: "From Economism to Human Development" (Gasper 2004). The leading single theoretician in such work has probably been Amartya Sen. Of key importance is his association with the inspiring and influential practitioner Mahbub ul Haq, founder of the United Nations Development Programme (UNDP)'s *Human Development Reports* and of the wider human development movement in development analysis and advocacy. The work led by Haq, Sen, and the UNDP can broadly be called the human development approach (HDA). It has achieved, rather rapidly, a significant degree of institutionalization in national, subnational, and international reporting.

Human development (HD) thinking has broadened the range of objectives routinely considered in development debate and planning. Some other aspects of the HD approach are less obvious and require comment; they include both strengths and lacunae. First, Haq led a rejection of partitioned thinking: the analysis of processes and connections only within conventional disciplinary and national boundaries, and thus within the supposedly largely separate containers of national "economies." He emphatically espoused and embodied "joined-up thinking"—transdisciplinary integrative analysis of development—not hobbled by those boundaries. Second, quietly included without much philosophical trumpeting, HDA also takes a step toward joined-up feeling. As in pure utilitarian or human rights philosophy, the field of reference is all humans, irrespective of their locations in the world. Unlike in market-based economics, the field is not reduced to agents with purchasing power, let alone weighted according to their purchasing power. Global ethics then automatically arises as a topic of attention, as we see, for example, in UNDP's work on global public goods.

Third, the focus on individuals does not make HDA neoliberal. Neoliberalism views the human being through a narrow lens, as an individual economic actor who should be placed on a leveled playing field for competition. HDA endorses a broader spectrum of meaning with regard to being human, seeing people as social, cultural, economic, and political subjects. Humanism implies a view of the self as socially embedded and influenced, but not purely socially determined. While HDA requires and employs such a view, it has not offered an extensive elaboration, except, for example, in the contributions of Martha Nussbaum. We discuss this lacuna further below.

Lastly, a number of criticisms have been made of the conceptualization adopted in the UNDP human development work, which is largely based on Sen's capability approach to welfare evaluation (see, for example, Apthorpe

1997; Truong 1997; Cameron and Gasper 2000; Gasper 2002). While seeking to move beyond mainstream economics, Sen and Haq aimed to bring most of its practitioners with them. The capability approach still bears, then, many of the features of economics discourse that other disciplines and audiences can find problematic. For example:

1. The overgeneralized style of the slogan "Development is the expansion of human capabilities" brings a danger that counting can displace thinking. We must ask: Capabilities for which persons? Which capabilities, why, and to what end? Sen's later slogan, "Development as freedom," provokes similar questions (Gasper and Staveren 2003). Nussbaum's work (for example, 2003, 2006) probes deeper here.

2. In contrast to the human rights tradition, HDA did not establish guarantees for individuals despite its serious concern for equity. Nussbaum's work, focused on constitutional anchoring of basic rights, has faced this issue, and the HDA has moved toward an accommodation with work on human rights (UNDP 2000). It remains worried, though, about human rights formulations as absolutist and too focused on the state (for example, CHS 2003, 28).

3. Why should one care about individuals and particular capabilities? HDA presumes rather than builds a motivational basis. So in fact does much of the human rights tradition, but that more readily connects to some motivating factors. A minority of HDA writers such as Nussbaum have attended explicitly to emotions and motivation (see also Sen 2000).

Recent work seeks to reduce these limitations and deepen the human development approach—for example, by clarifying relationships of human development to human rights and to culture (WCCD 1995; UNDP 2004; Gasper 2007)—and to extend it to cover crucial related areas, notably of human security. Haq warned against a possible fossilization of HDA that could be induced by its extraordinarily rapid institutionalization. He urged ongoing criticism and innovation, and himself led the work on human security in the 1993 and 1994 *Human Development Reports*. Subsequently, Sen has been at the forefront of extension and innovation, including as co-chair of the report *Human Security Now* (CHS 2003).

The Lens of Human Security

The newer discourse of "human security" addresses both the question of guarantees for individuals, sometimes in a more flexible and probing way than in most human rights discourse, and the need for a motivational basis, including providing a foundational rationale for human rights in terms of basic capabilities that concern areas of basic need. It thus complements the established but sometimes partly honorific or stultified discourse of human rights (Penz 2001), and complements and extends the discourse of human development in a number of ways (Truong 2005a; Gasper 2005b, 2008b).

Methodologically and in policy outline, the approach appears the same. We see again the insistence on being empirical and tracking real connections between economy, polity, and society, now including the worlds of war, and drawing the implications—in other words, joined-up thinking. For example: "What is needed is not large amounts of additional financial capacity within the state but more efficient integration of social policy objectives into macro-economic and trade-related policy processes" (CHS 2003, 87); and "Costa Rica, Sri Lanka, and the Indian state of Kerala have managed very effective social protection systems on the same budget as other regions that offered no such protections" (89). Haq brought militarism's opportunity costs as well as its direct costs to center stage, and estimates like the following have become commonplace: "The World Bank and the United Nations estimate that if four days' worth of the annual military expenditure worldwide were diverted into education every year, that would provide the funding needed to achieve worldwide primary education by 2015" (CHS 2003, 117–18). Feminist theory goes on to explore militarism's cultural impacts and consequent other effects.

So what, if anything, does the human security discourse add? First, most obviously, it concerns itself with the stability and security of people's capabilities (seen as the real opportunities of achievement that are open to them and that they value), not only their average level. Second, it has a more substantive character: less generalized and abstracted, a language of the concrete needs of concrete individuals. A concern with security starts with a concern for basic, specific goods: securing life, health, dignity, and peace. The very label human security, initiated to draw a contrast with the security of states, makes us think about what is human, what is the humanity that should be secured. It better grounds the existing human development discourse—in the mud, as Manfred Max-Neef would insist—and directs us toward the quotidian, the most vulnerable and their plural systems of protection. Third, this substantive focus on basics gives the discourse a stronger existential charge, a more vivid and touching content, a firmer motivational base. It goes further toward joined-up feeling in addition to joined-up thinking. Thus Penz (2001) diagnoses it as a fuller move in a cosmopolitan direction. In these last two respects it is close in character to Nussbaum's form of human development theory, but with a more limited focus.

Listen to Costa Rican president Rodrigo Carazo Odio, one of the architects of Costa Rica's welfare state: "I knew the Costa Rica of social injustice: a country of people without shoes or teeth, without [a] university, with scarcely half a dozen high schools. . . . It was a Costa Rica without a limit of working hours, in which children also worked as grown ups; . . . [where] life expectancy was barely more than 40 years. I saw the sick ask for hospital attention as charity. . . . Workers had no vacations, no dismissal notice, no severance pay. . . . A Costa Rica without social guarantees" (quoted in Mora 2000, 24).

The country of people without teeth two generations ago now has higher life-expectancy figures than the United States. The Millennium Development Goals are not yet about helping people keep their teeth, as a basic need, but they are in that same spirit.

These evocations from the notion "human security" survive and in fact grow out of the vagueness and pluriformity of the notion in current usage. A variety of meanings are employed and appear legitimate and important. Evocativeness and richness of content are not inherent mistakes in ethical concepts, but they also bring dangers of confusion and drift. We must distinguish, for example, between socioeconomic security and psychological security. The two are not always closely related. Psychological security can be obtained in various ways besides socioeconomic security, some of which are admirable, some undesirable. Psychological security via a belief in a simple, "true" personal identity, typically from membership in some inspiring group, carries dangers and can come at the cost of openness and humanity to those outside the group (see, for example, Glover 2001).

Human Security Now's policy agenda includes attention to the formation of such basic perceptions, and to more cosmopolitan education that can "teach students to reason, to consider ethical claims, to understand and work with such fundamental ideas as human rights, human diversity and interdependence . . . to grasp the reality of human interdependence more directly and more widely . . . [and] instill in the content of education a new emphasis on ethical values—and on public debate and democracy" (CHS 2003, 122). Education concerns adults, not only children, including "the police, the armed forces, private security forces, and others with access to the means of coercive force" (122). It should include gender awareness, conflict management, and opening up of perceptions of identity, to see oneself as having multiple identities (123). The last of the main recommendations is to strengthen activities for "clarifying the need for a global human identity" (141–42).

The Challenges to Development Ethics

Something important has happened within development ethics in the past twenty years, especially at the level of literature and theorizing, even though with much less progress in the worlds of policy, education and action, yet still with some significant achievements—for example, concerning debt, child labor, the greater centrality officially granted to human rights, and so on. Whether the changes outside the world of words are judged encouraging depends on what one takes as the basis for comparison and evaluation. More should have happened, but at least something did.

Why have some favorable moves occurred, and why not more? The move from words to policy action to institutionalized daily practices is an enormous journey. What have not yet occurred are the required gradual paradigm shifts at all levels, from abstract reasoning through to institutions and daily practices. Historically, major change has often been measured in centuries rather than generations (Krznaric 2007). One hopes that velocity and deterritorialization will grow at the same rate in ethics as they have in many other respects, to keep pace with interconnectedness.

The speed of the journey is affected also by the perceptiveness and methods of the travelers, including how well they converse with those with whom they must work and influence. The preoccupation with theory since the 1970s revival of academic political philosophy and substantive ethics, triggered by John Rawls's *A Theory of Justice* (1971), may have brought insufficient explicit attention to motives and feelings. Rawls incorporated moral intuition into his method but did not interrogate and educate it. In the thought experiment used to render plausible his theory of justice, the imaginary "original position," he sought to incorporate intuitions about fairness into the design of the original position and then rely further only on calculations of self-interest. This appears neither a consistent approach nor one that explores sufficiently the emotional building blocks of ethics.

Where do the intuitions about fairness come from? What if they are absent? Jonathan Glover cites Thucydides' account of the negotiations between the militarily dominant Athenians and the city of Melos in the Peloponnesian War. The Athenians, from their position of strength, listened to and rejected every plea the Melians made on grounds of fairness, sympathy, compassion, or rights. They insisted on Melian subordination in place of neutrality, besieged the city, massacred its male inhabitants of military age when it surrendered, and sold the women and children as slaves (Glover 2001, 28–30). Writing at the same time that British imperialism presided with Olympian indifference over mega-famines in India, Nietzsche commended the Athenians' stance to the aspirants to world power in late nineteenth-century Bismarckian Germany. The viewpoint remains widespread, bedecked sometimes in the philosophical vestments of "realism." Even Rawls explicitly limited his theory of justice to relationships within modern Western liberal polities and rejected its application elsewhere, including to relationships between polities. The development ethics implications of his position are both limited and, in a globalized world, obsolescent.

Without a starting point of concern, care, and motivation, development ethics in particular will have little impetus. Both Sen's work on human development and official human rights discourse may rely on motives that they fail to highlight, discuss, and consolidate. A human rights language is anyway insufficient and must be complemented by the acceptance of duties and the presence and practice of "virtues," appropriate ethical attitudes, and skills (O'Neill 1996). These have a base in fundamental human capacities and proclivities for reflection, empathy, and compassion (Truong 2005b). We saw that *Human Security Now* gives substantial attention to education toward a global human identity. We will see too that some authors on human development ethics such as Giri and Nussbaum seek to fill more general lacunae in HDA by drawing from other traditions in moral philosophy, spirituality, and social theory. We will refer in particular to feminist care ethics, a modern strand within the family of those ethics that stress virtues.

Nothing may be more practical than a good theory, but what factors contribute to the perceived power of a theory, especially in social philosophy and public policy? Rawls's theory achieved impact not only through its elaborate reasoning but because it could tap and also tacitly educate widespread ethical intuitions in his chosen audience. Sen's work has achieved similar or greater influence, including far beyond academe, partly because of his adoption of a more morally evocative vocabulary—of entitlements, functionings, capabilities, agency, freedoms, and human development—than typically found in the existing economics of welfare and policy. Drawing from studies of what types of ideas acquire authority and influence in policy-oriented science and successfully bridge the worlds of science and policy, Asunción Lera St. Clair (2006) argues that successful intellectual "boundary objects" in the emergence of ethics in development theory and policy are those that have had a strong ethical "charge" and that connect well to feelings and intuitions. She posits that human security can be an effective boundary object (see also Gasper 2005a).

Work on human security has been with us for over a decade. Arguably, for the work to reach more of the parts that most development ethics has so far failed to influence, it must consciously employ methods with emotional depth such as life narratives and intimate studies of life spheres. In parallel, it and development ethics more broadly must widen their theoretical attention to cover emotions and motivations, as is done in the literature on an ethics of care. In other words, work on human security requires a methodological broadening to add to its broadened scope in terms of themes and sectors.

The Need for Experientially and Emotionally Grounded Ethics

Early modern social theory in Europe emerged during the seventeenth and eighteenth centuries in the transition from an era driven by immense inter-religious European conflicts to a world dominated by economic forces and interstate competition for global prizes. David Hume expressed his relief to live in the eighteenth century instead of its bloody predecessor. He and thinkers like Bernard Mandeville and Adam Smith advocated strong reliance on a market system, as supposedly guided by and in turn fostering more peace- and progress-giving motives, "the Interests," as opposed to the volatile "Passions" that fuel war (Hirschman 1977). Smith argued that if properly channeled, self-interest is the most reliable way to build both prosperity and peace.

But while the passions can be extremely destructive, it would be deeply erroneous to think that all passions are undesirable and dispensable, or that cooperation and mutual help are dispassionate. Smith himself gave enormous weight to the role of "the moral sentiments" that sustain human society, including market functioning. Others took over his analysis of the first world-wide web, the market system, and presumed that only the amoral sentiments, the desires for material gain and personal convenience, were necessary for its effective, indeed socially optimal, operation. Strangely, some of their present-day successors even try to analyze violent conflicts exclusively as dispassionate struggles for gain.

Ananta Giri's remarkable *Conversations and Transformations* (2002) argues persuasively that social ethics requires deeper pictures of self and how selves relate to others; attention to how reasoning, reasonable, compassionate selves are fostered; and empirical study of how committed, sympathetic reasoning can be embodied and sustained in social practices and styles of ethical argumen-tation, notably in the various spheres of civil society. In effect, he considers the social contexts for moral self-development and action. He reflects on the roles of case studies and biographies, noting Gandhi's insight that people impervious to reason may still be susceptible to influence via their capacity for sympathy; or as formulated by Bhikhu Parekh, that unless there is already sym-pathetic attention to a person she will be ignored or downgraded in reasoning.

Giri therefore proposes that development ethics should draw on the tradition of self-cultivation found in "aesthetic ethics," but must also avoid the possible associated narcissism by strengthening its own tradition of facing and responding to suffering others.

Giri argues that Sen's conceptualization of human well-being rests on an inadequate conception of personhood and lacks a dynamic perspective on self-development. "Sympathy," said Sen in mid-career, is when a person's own well-being is affected by the situation of other persons; "commitment" is when a person acts in support of other persons or other causes even though this does not improve her own well-being. Evidently by "well-being" Sen here meant felt well-being, gratification. His definition of the label "sympathy" (feeling with others) as gratification from another person's well-being assumes that this gratification is the only possible sort of feeling-with-others, and implies that nongratification types of feelings toward others require a different name (he chose "commitment"). Giri prefers the ordinary usages, of sympathy as feeling with others and of commitment as dedication to others. Hence, like Adam Smith he stresses that in these senses, sympathy sustains commitment rather than, as for Sen, the two being mutually exclusive categories. Nor are they marginal: mental health requires some degree of orientation to other people.

Sen has famously proposed that democracy prevents famines, in contrast to the malign neglect practiced by the Imperial British authorities in nineteenth-century India or Ireland. Case studies of contemporary India show that while formal political democracy mitigates famine, in reality it does not eliminate it (Banik 2007; Currie 2000). Underlying Sen's hypothesis is an optimistic vision in which democracy increases not only (1) the flow of information, but also (2) the respectful and sympathetic awareness of others, and (3) the willingness to contribute to help them, at least if other relevant people share in doing so ("collective altruism"—Penz 1986, 202–10; Drèze and Sen 2002). Unfortunately, democracy at the national level does not guarantee any of these three, at a national or even subnational level, let alone guarantee respect, sympathy, and solidarity on a global level. Within the United States, as in India, formal democracy coexists continually with the destitution and malnutrition of large groups of people. And at the global level there is not even formal democracy.

Giri brings in a richer picture of human personality than Sen has used, and this leads to a profound critique. He proposes that Sen's capability approach does not focus on personal growth; nor on the ability to be a friend, not an enemy, to oneself; nor on the nature, as opposed to only the idea, of human agency; nor on the development of "a space for criticism of the self-justificatory claims of one's freedom" (Giri 2002, 210). The approach "[does] not embody striving for self-development on the part of the poor . . . [and] lacks an objective of self-actualization or self-realization" or self-extension (230). "Sen is dismayed by the unreasoned identity shifts that are taking place [in India,] but the reasoned deliberation that Sen is looking for requires much more than reason" (239). His ethics remains too much in the mold of Rawls, lacking an adequate psychological basis. Giri contends similarly that Habermas's discourse ethics does not attend to "the preparation of the self that is required to take part in the public sphere" (302), including the arts of listening and openness to "otherness" that are required for true conversation, nor the enriching role of love that Giri illustrates from the years of intense debate between Gandhi and Rabindranath Tagore.

Richard Sennett's recent study of respect (2004) perhaps carries further warnings for Sen's variant of human development theory. At least we must distinguish carefully between types of attitude toward others. In Sennett's view, opportunity and compassion make an unhappy marriage: opportunity brings inequality and "creaming off" of the brightest of the poor(er), while "charity wounds," as Mary Douglas declared, and compassion is anyway undermined by inequality (Douglas 1990, vii). Compassion easily deforms, in circumstances of inequality, into pity and becomes experienced by receivers as contempt. Sennett warns that it is justice, not charity, that is wanting in the world. For the poorer, not only the poorest, compassion condescends, and meritocracy excludes. Building self-respect among the poor by meritocracy is no solution, for this rapidly brings creaming off. The required response to the inevitable inequality of capitalism, suggests Sennett, should not be for the state to (further) promote meritocracy and opportunity, but to guarantee access to basic needs via, for example, a basic income, not via conditional handouts monitored as part of the "audit society" (Power 1997).

Two more warnings arise. First, fulfillment of basic needs ensures opportunity, but a key question is by how many stages of opportunity (opportunity to have an opportunity to have an opportunity . . .) one is removed from centrally important goods. The guarantee is hollow if there are too many stages. A danger exists that the language of providing opportunities can be used to disguise their absence for most people.

Second, basic needs provision requires continuing commitment and is not a substitute for it. In Costa Rica two ex-presidents recently were charged with corruption and a third prudently resided abroad. Tatiana Mora (2000) reports a growing mental distancing of Costa Rica's affluent urban groups from the expanding urban underclass, growing feelings that the poor, while indeed multiply deprived, are in one way or another outside society—weird, contrary, and not susceptible to or deserving of help: "not one of us." Fighting human development deficits requires human development policies and investments that should be cost-effective, plus a conducive macro-environment, economic and political (no waste and no war). But it also centrally requires ethical commitment: recognition of other people as fellow humans.

From the 1991 *Human Development Report*, Mahbub ul Haq highlighted the lack of political commitment, rather than lack of resources, seen in many low-income countries, as shown by how national budgets are allocated (Haq 1999, 178). Haq's legacy, the Millennium Development Goals (MDGs), are a tool in trying to generate political commitment. By focusing on the real basics for "the people without teeth," the MDGs have captured attention, including that of at least some of the mentally distanced elites. In addition they provide a yardstick by which leaders will be judged, and against which, if there is seen to be failure, there could well be reaction. But targets alone are unlikely to be self-fulfilling in this way; also required for MDG implementation is an ethical and perceptual strategy.

Such issues become harder still in international relations. The goodwill that is feasible, even presumable, between family and friends, and to some degree within a local community and to a lesser extent a nation, becomes yet thinner; many nations lack solidarity. Here too Haq and like-minded progressives made important steps by demonstrating how aid budgets are actually allocated and could be reallocated, and by obtaining rich governments' commitment to the MDGs. But such targets are not self-implementing.

The next section therefore looks at caring and its role in moral thought: in a generalized way, in familial and local contexts, and with some reference to authors who discuss what types of extension or supplementation may be possible in the global arena.

The Lens of Caring

We present now three somewhat complementary streams that offer a social treatment of the self and its interface with ethics and politics. First, the ancient Mahayana Buddhist tradition offers a theory of compassion and systemic transformation through the transformation of human consciousness. Second, the work of Ananta Giri links such concerns to those of development ethics, which requires an ethic of development of the self, to enrich the human development approach. Since the historical record suggests the limits to projects of individual improvement, these must be inserted into a project of the construction of civil society—local, national, and global. Third, feminist care ethics offers strong insights that are beginning to be extended to face issues of care beyond the household or local community. We consider the three streams as different manifestations of a shared yearning for the protection of human dignity and the facilitation of human flourishing. In terms of table 1's survey of development ethics, their sources are from the rows for moral philosophy, religions, and feminist theory.

Buddhism

The Buddhist queries any claim to independence embodied in the notion of "to be," seeing it as arrogant. Rather, the Buddhist seeks to honor a diversity of forms of interdependence and "interbeing," meaning the mutual relevance of all life-forms and events in the social world. He does not reject justice as a universal principle but considers it to be subordinate to compassionate understanding (*prajna*). Unlike some of his Kantian or feminist counterparts, the Buddhist subject does not place justice and care in mutual opposition but seeks constitutional balance of the individual self and the social body. He uses meditation techniques as a worldly tool for ego reduction, not as escape (Truong 2005b).

Buddhist thought may be apprehended through the principle of nonduality, backed by the Buddha's deliberations (sutras) on knowledge and spiritual wisdom. The principle derives from a biocentric approach to human life, nature, and the cosmos. Buddhist thought defines humans as organisms that are interlinked with other organisms. The human being differs from other organisms in nature owing to the endowment of mind,[11] the essential quality of which is formed by the recognition of this interdependency and which expresses itself in different forms known as empathy or interbeing (Thich Nhat Hanh 1993). Organically embedded in nature, the individual self is subject to impermanence and the cycle of life, and hence she requires care and is capable of caring as an intuitive response. What may come between self and others are unwholesome minds, not the specific biological traits of the self or the other.

Prajna, or penetrating insight, is the ability to understand nonduality, the interbeing of all forms of life. This insight has the capacity to transform individual and collective memories of trauma and sufferings into a release of compassion. *Prajna* stands for the image of a fountain from which compassion as a nonviolent life force emerges. To tap the fountain requires mind training. This can help achieve a transformative shift of consciousness to attain what are referred to as the four abodes—caring and friendliness (*maitri*), empathy with those who suffer (*karuna*), sympathetic joy for others without envy (*mudita*), and equanimity or constitutional balance (*uppeka*). A change of perception through *prajna* leads to a change of emotional structure (from hostility to caring and friendliness), a change of attitude (from anger to empathy), a change of behavior (from desiring to take to a willingness to give; from readiness to cause grief to willingness to bring joy), and a change away from being diverted by an unwholesome mind toward maintaining the constitutional balance of nonduality. By practicing the four abodes, or virtues, the individual can achieve moral clarity. Moral clarity enables an understanding of interconnectedness as a phenomenon that lies deeper than the societal level, a clarity that facilitates the acceptance of all differences as manifestations of a universal process in which all human beings are parts.

Knowledge produced by a biocentric approach to human life, nature, and the cosmos is neither anthropocentric nor egocentric. It seeks to apprehend the interconnection between human life and other organisms. Wholesome knowledge comprehends this interconnection; unwholesome knowledge perceives myopically. Buddhist ontology provides a vision of human nature embedded in a biocentric worldview. Organically embedded in the universe, mind is capable both of drowning in conceptual errors or liberating itself from them. Liberating the mind leads to the capacity for generosity and appreciation of other persons' universes. The will of mind (determination) in Buddhism is not geared toward power and control, but toward understanding the nature of interconnectedness, the key to releasing empathy and compassion. Ontological security is not derived from the notion of a fixed stable self, whether socially or morally defined. It is derived from the ethical ideal to perceive oneself in relation to others and, indeed, as others (Adams 2002).

Placed in the context of modern theory of care, the Buddhist notion of care for the self may be understood as the fostering, attaining, and maintaining of constitutional balance, with the expectation that care for others then follows based on the moral clarity achieved. The values of care in Buddhism as represented by the four abodes are applicable to anyone in the community, and achieving constitutional balance and moral clarity, in varying degrees of depth, is the responsibility of everyone in the community. Social injustice is seen as a manifestation of a collective psychological failure, a misperception of the self, as well as inability to see interdependence as a reality and to appreciate the immeasurable virtue of the four abodes.

Ananta Giri and a Non-narcissistic Ethics of Self-Development

Giri adds modern social theory to such concerns with perception and mis-perception. He proposes that "development is a field of relationship" among persons. The broadening of concerns in development policy, as seen in Sen's work, "has lacked a parallel effort to deepen it" with reference to agents' motivation and skills (Giri 2002, 200). "The agents of development have not given much attention to developing themselves" (200), their personalities and empathy, or their ability to listen and cooperate. In contrast, as Bill Cooke (1997) has noted, the established caring professions insist on years of training and testing before their junior professionals are given power over clients and patients. Professional ethics are needed to strengthen a sense of servanthood among the powerful and privileged. Ethics must build a committed ethos, not merely proclaim sets of rules. In fact, professional ethics should critique self-concerned, irresponsible, "professional" identities and drop the old model of the professional as master. Giri advocates here a model of service and of existential, not necessarily geo-graphical, pilgrimage.

This step is central: "Without emphasizing self-transformation we cannot adequately address either the problem of distributive justice or institutional well-being" (262), let alone the issue highlighted by Nancy Fraser (1995) of justice as recognition. The work of development agents can be greatly strengthened by, and even requires, extension of the self, including extension of their sympa-thies and ability to "listen for a change" (Hugo Slim's phrase). According to Giri, "Self-development is also equally a challenge for the [intended/purported] beneficiaries of development"; the poor must "become responsible for their destiny" (200). In India, for example, extension of the self is an essential step in bursting the barriers of caste: "Aesthetics of self-cultivation challenges both the poor as well as the rich" (217).

Development of the self leads us toward the agenda of "aesthetic ethics": self-cultivation, self-transformation, and Foucault's "elaboration of one's own life as a personal work of art" fit for admiration by oneself and others. In caring for the self, people can easily be influenced by their feelings of superiority, insecurity, and resentment. An aesthetic ethics has potential for egoism, vanity, and narcissism; and despite its celebration of difference and otherness, "the radical otherness that poverty poses has been deliberately relegated to the background" (Giri 2002, 201). But an aesthetic stance need not be aestheticist; we can have attention to both self and other. Self-fulfillment in fact requires deep and nonrepressive commitments to others. Thus Giri's exemplars are Kierkegaard, Aurobindo, and, interestingly, Adam Smith, rather than Foucault, for they provide a deeper ontology of the self and its potential.

The premise of eighteenth-century Scottish Enlightenment thinking on civil society was that mutual sympathy is a quasi-universal feature in human nature, providing "a basis for human interaction beyond the calculus of pure exchange" (Seligman 1995, 205), but that it needs to be promoted and defended. Thinking of India and elsewhere (and also of universities), Giri extends this notion:

> The challenge before us is to rethink civil society and transcend the primacy of the political [and the fixation on the state] in thinking about it and being part of it. Those who inhabit civil society are not only rights-bearing, juridical beings but are also spiritually integral beings, and unless civil society is animated and enriched by their *sadhana* of self-transformation and the *tapashya* of unconditional ethical obligation of the self to the other and society, then it cannot perform its creative and critical functions. It shall cease to be a reflective space where the logic of money and power of society is shown its proper place and given a transformative direction. (2002, 289)

Civil society should be seen not only as the realm of rights-bearing individuals who organize to discipline the state and the market, but also as the seedbed for the "cultivation of virtues in the lives of individuals" (290). It requires inspiring figures ready to be martyred to "protect the autonomy of civil society and the dignity of individuals" (304). It also requires more routine and widely accessible schools for the virtues. Giri accepts the view of Claus Offe that schemes such as LETS (local trading arrangements that use their own alternative currency) cannot function directly as tools for societal transformation but have valuable roles both in training and in societal damage limitation. They can help build mutual awareness, including awareness that nobody deserves all his advantages (or disadvantages) and that we exist only through others.

Civil society in multicultural nations must become intercultural, "a learning society where different cultures and individuals are open to learning from each other" (Giri 2002, 325). Identity should then be seen, as Paul Ricoeur suggests, as narrative identity: "not only as a matter of *a priori* formulation and categorical determination; it is also an aspect of an unfolding narrative" (Giri 2002, 327), an ongoing identity formation or "identification." Giri's current work extends this focus to the construction of global civil society, with specific reference to the movements for an alternative globalization.

Feminist Ethics of Care

Our third source, feminist care ethics, offers the richest mix of ethnography, social theory, ontology, and moral reflection. It presents a multifold vision of care: first, as a moral orientation, disposition, and emotion; second, as a set of skills and understandings; third, as a social practice found in a variety of significant relations such as mothering, friendship, nursing, and citizenship; and lastly, as a socioeconomic system jointly managed by private and public actors who faces many dangers, including paternalism and corruption (Tronto 1994; Sevenhuijsen 1998). A care system spans, or should span, various sectors, including the traditional caring professions such as nursing, social work, and schooling; humanitarian relief; and the business sectors, in employment regimes and corporate outreach (Razavi 2007).

Different feminist care ethicists bridge the divide between personal and political in different ways. Some claim the existence of a gender structure in morality and argue for the superiority or equivalence of the ethic of care arising from women's social roles as the feminine principle—which they find obliterated in masculine moral deliberations (for example, Gilligan 1982). Others reject this claim as confining women's moral capability to self-erasure and abnegation, and as lacking autonomy of agency (Clement 1996). They seek to revise the notion of autonomy by removing it from abstract reasoning and ideal types, and to develop a social approach to care and autonomy, private and public, as dialectically linked. Noddings (2003), for example, defends the ethic of care as based on personal relationships but draws out important implications for public concerns (such as social supervision of managed care systems like hospitals, day-care centers, and homes for the elderly). To her, caring as a practice requires personal encounters. Therefore, beyond the defense of managed care systems to prevent their deterioration by public decisions, care practices must be guided by situated ethics, requiring reference to contextual details as well as to general principles of forms of caring (Parton 2003; Keller 1996).

Although there is consensus on the definition of the self as socially situated, interpersonally bonded, and sexually and racially embodied, there seems to be no common feminist position on the relation between this self and social change wider than the contexts of industrialized nations. With some exceptions (for example, Ehrenreich and Hochschild 2003; Tronto 2003; Yeates 2004), the care debate misses an international perspective that can show how changing forms of care in one country may affect the social world of care in another—as in the case of migrant workers in paid domestic services, bilateral arrangements for the migration of nurses, health tourism, and outsourcing of health services. Technological innovations, market forces and cultural shifts create massive change in this international arena. An ethic of care should contribute to reining in market behavior and redirecting technological research to serve all humanity, not just specific groups of moneyed humans. Building this contribution requires an enlarged definition of vulnerability and moral orientation to bring out the multifaceted links between security and vulnerability as states of being, and to use care reasoning to shape research and public debates on human develop- ment. For example, compassionate evaluation of merit remains an insufficient force for transformation. Care as a moral orientation for global social justice must understand the sufferings of those who are denied care as not only a dis- crete tragedy of persons and groups but also an outcome of systemic forces that sustain the functioning of care systems for richer others.

To identify the systemic forces that undermine care systems within and between countries and to respond in a holistic manner, the strategy adopted by Sevenhuijsen (1998), Folbre (2001), Tronto (2003), and Williams (2003) may be useful. This approach seeks to integrate the values derived from the ethics of care (attentiveness, responsiveness, and responsibility) into concepts of citizenship: to enrich the concept of citizenship, based on a more holistic notion of the self in which reason, judgment, and care coexist, interrogate one another, and find resolutions to specific and contextual contradictions. To use the values of care as political virtues to interrogate performance in particular contexts may help to alter systems of values and concepts in service of democracy in all dimensions of life.

Connecting Streams

None of the three positions above has as yet strongly developed attention to international relations, but each has potential. Of great interest for this task are also, first, Martha Nussbaum's work, which spans investigation of the emotions, ethical motivations, and practices of care through to an emergent cosmopolitan global ethic for an ever more joined-up world; and the very different but poten- tially complementary work of Onora O'Neill, which locates the role of ethical virtues within a reasoned framework of the duties we owe others in a system of interdependence. Since Nussbaum's and O'Neill's work is widely and intensively discussed, in this chapter we have concentrated on sources that are equally interesting but less considered in development ethics. Feminist ethics in particular appears to be pregnant with ideas relevant for a wider stage.

Aware of the risk of reducing nuanced, rich traditions to a sterilized presentation of similarities and differences, we yet see the merit in comparing diverse traditions for mutual appreciation and possible synthesis. Competing views on human agency, the body, and moral formation of the self may, however, have to be reconciled.

At the most general level, a view shared by the traditions is of the self as an encumbered rather than unencumbered subject, which we can refer to as embedded humanism. Feminist theory on care, vulnerability, and women's agency grounds the notion of autonomy in real-life conditions, as do Sen's and Nussbaum's theories of human capabilities and functionings. Mahayana Buddhist moral theory on compassion and karmic consequences defines the self as organically embedded in nature and the cosmos, and encumbered by the pain of birth, illness, old age, and death. The self is not fully socially determined but is certainly molded by cultural socialization.

Sharing such a view of the self, the traditions then take different routes in reasoning. Each captures something important. "Vertical reasoning"—emphasizing norms, principles for human capabilities, and functionings—is found especially in Nussbaum's work, whose deliberations suggest the position of a legislator and decision maker in the public sphere, where ideas gain their legitimacy, policy options are chosen, and resources are mobilized.

"Horizontal reasoning" stressing historicity, process, and context is characteristic of early feminist writing on ethics of care. The ethical subject in this line of reasoning is the mother and community builder who interrogates the legitimacy of regnant ideas and norms in the public sphere and demands public attention to everyday survival problems and the maintenance of life. "Spiral reasoning," characteristic in Mahayana Buddhism, stresses the chain of causation of suffering and deprivation, starting with a view of the illusion of the self as a uniform entity, and appeals to the use of methods of mind discipline (meditation) to discover diverse levels of interconnectedness (mind-body, self-other, public-private, local-global) and achieve moral clarity for change. Rather than interrogating others, this tradition interrogates the self, the notion of "to be," and the tragedy of the human failure to recognize the significance of interbeing. The Buddhist ethical subject is a healer and adviser on practices of mindful living as a way of healing social systems.

In an era where human relationships have gone transnational, the values of the ethics of care must be applied on a transnational scale to foster a political agency that can extend itself beyond the particular form of governmentality confined by the notions of sovereignty and territorial control. As Sevenhuijsen pointed out, care structures human relationships and makes them possible, and how we can care defines to a great extent how we can give shape to our society. She suggests the term "caring solidarity" to convey the notions of attentiveness, responsiveness, and responsibility to all sorts of situations in which care is required by human beings who are differently situated. She writes: "This 'caring solidarity' offers more potential for understanding the diversity of needs and lifestyles than a solidarity which takes for granted the norms of homogeneity and a 'standard' human subject. In this respect, care marks the difference between policy as control and policy as an enabling activity" (Sevenhuijsen 1998, 147–48).

In Sevenhuijsen's view, the feminist ethics of care, a politics of needs interpretation, and a caring solidarity could be integrated into a reflexive and dialogic form of discourse ethics. Treating ethics as "enabling discourses" may help us to address human rights, human development, and human security issues in a more situated fashion. Such an approach would allow for ethical judgment of experiences and locations in ways that recognize what Sevenhuijsen refers to as "situated rights," and therefore could enable public provision that is derived from the principle of universality of rights yet meets the standards of what is required in a given situation, place, and time. Applied creatively, feminist ethics of care may contribute to resolving contested issues regarding universality, universalism, and particularism, and may contribute to fostering interconnected systems of human security relevant to the quotidian experience of the most vulnerable people.

As the global public domain is stratified, conflictive, and dominated by interests that are hegemonic and defined according to reigning notions of nation-state and communities, building a caring solidarity at this level would inevitably encounter what Yuval-Davis (2003) refers to as the politics of belonging. Drawing from her empirical work on identity politics, she endorses Crowley's concept of belonging as being thicker than that of citizenship, covering not just notions of membership, rights, and duties but also the emotions that such membership evokes. In her view, belonging is where the sociology of emotions interfaces with the sociology of power, where identification and participation collude. For human security to be possible and a caring solidarity to be active, the sense of belonging and the emotions attached to it must be reoriented beyond the particularities of states or communities to foster a spiritual understanding of the human condition that goes beyond the temporal and partial boundaries of communities.

Conclusion: Globalized Sensibility? Globalized Security?

Development ethics as a field of thought focuses both on the overall trajectories of human communities and on the life paths of the individuals who constitute and span those communities. Its agenda increases in urgency in the face of globalization's vast and varied impacts worldwide, which render some groups of people highly vulnerable. Notably, many impacts are on women, who act as "shock absorbers," custodians of the private and reproductive spheres that are downgraded in business calculation and mainstream economics. Our focus has been on the shock absorbers, specifically on those without security.

The fact of such impacts is not new, though some of the modalities may be. In the recurrent "third world holocausts" of the mid-nineteenth to early twentieth centuries, which Mike Davis (2001) has helped to recover from oblivion, tens of millions of poor people perished. They were victims of a historical phase marked, as Sen noted, by (1) the extension globally of market forces and ideologies, backed by direct rule or indirect imperial policing; (2) the related decay of local capacities to assure subsistence in times of need; and (3) the absence as yet of new national capacities to take on these roles. Such capacities grew in the second half of the twentieth century under most postcolonial governments. In late century and at the start of the new millennium we have seen new holocausts as global market forces outstrip, undermine, and bypass national governments; classes of new helots emerge to serve the rich; some national social compacts that existed for assurance of subsistence have declined; and parts of the globe even fall into the abyss, as happened in the Congo and pockets of West Africa.

While some of these holocausts pass unnoticed (by the rich), there are signs of increased global concern within the global electronic village. The tsunami of December 2004 is not the best indicator since, besides its visual drama, many Western tourists were involved. More striking for our purposes is a case like the Morecambe Bay drownings, where Chinese workers in search of better lives ended theirs as throwaway inputs in a European value chain and thus attracted more attention than they ever did in their lifetimes.

We now require, and are unevenly moving toward, a global frame and global ethics comparable to the earlier emergence of national systems of rights and responsibilities. Will this emergent global framework be one where might makes right and the universal principles are those of market (and other) power, or will it be based on principles of universal human dignity and fundamental human rights? (Held 2004; Gasper 2005a).

This chapter has examined the responses in development ethics in relation to these practical and intellectual challenges raised by attention to human security and gender. We proposed that besides elaboration of detached theory or drafting of conventions, more attention is needed to the emotional, perceptual, and existential grounding of ethics. The human development approach (HDA) has a number of gaps to be filled. It has, as a great strength, substantially put aside economics-dominated frameworks and instead attempts joined-up thinking.[12] It remains much weaker with respect to "human." The approach's previous lack of basic guarantees for everyone is being remedied by connection to the human rights stream and in the recent reformulations of human security, but it lacks a sufficient analytical base concerning the nature of personhood, selfhood, identity, and mutual concern, as well as a considered motivational basis for such concern. It implies a humanist view of the self, but many of its exponents have perhaps not realized that it needs to articulate and elaborate such a view, and to consider how compassionate committed selves could emerge. It presumes and conduces to ethical universalism, joined-up feeling, but needs a more emphatic and profound basis for this.[13] We suggested that Sen's picture of the impact of democracy per se is too rosy, and noted Sennett's warning of the incoherence and instability of a system based on opportunity and presumed compassion alone. The less generalized, less abstract focus in the work on human security, on securing basic needs, supports concern and motivation but is still not enough. Its language is at risk of being hijacked by the psychological insecurities of the rich. The poor too can seek psychic security in dismaying ways.

We presented three contrasting but probably complementary exemplars of more profound attention to the self and to caring, as important illustrative sources: from an ancient religion, from a modern anthropologist-philosopher, and from a stream of feminist investigation. All three go beyond the sort of humane economics found in the United Nations mainstream of human development. Buddhism's biocentric vision of nonduality and interbeing questions the concept of self presumed in economics. Ananta Giri argues that self-development is the indispensable partner to notions of human development and societal development, and that civil society must be a nursery of the virtues. Feminist care theorists provide a major synthesis of observation and social, psychological, and ethical theorization. While not offering an evolved, let alone unified, position on international issues, their work suggests that global justice requires a conception of caring, a "caring solidarity," to complement a systemic vision; and that while compassion alone does not suffice, it is indispensable. For dispassionately reasoned global citizenship faces a headier competitor: the politics of group belonging. Global justice may require a countering notion of global belonging such as hinted at in human rights thought or as more grandly essayed by Buddhism.

We conclude that the field of development ethics needs to be deepened in several directions to better serve those adversely affected by processes of globalization:

1. Development ethics should enrich its conception of the human being. Vulnerability and capability are two sides of the same coin of being human. Care connects both sides and should be considered a virtue to be developed for democracy, solidarity, and social justice to be possible.
2. Development ethics should enrich its notions of well-being, including by drawing from the gender-sensitive study of care and routine life maintenance.
3. Bringing in the ethics of care may help to renew and reshape moral responsibility and reciprocity between persons as citizens within a state and between citizens of different states. This reshaping could be guided by the concept of belonging that incorporates notions of membership and community, along with the emotions that these notions evoke. Emphasizing both the interconnected nature of belonging and empathy as a basic human emotion may help redirect the politics of belonging beyond current territorial and temporal social confines.
4. By this and other means, development ethics should respond to the reality that human processes, and persons, have escaped from national containers. An end to the perceptual and therefore moral blindness regarding interstate care provision is called for.

As Hershock points out, "Tragedy lies at the intersection between the positive moral space of what ought to happen and the negative space of what could not happen" (2003, 24). Ethical and other reflection is sorely needed to reduce that negative space.

In arguing for a development ethics with a global perspective, based on rich ethnography and grounded emotionally and existentially, we in effect call for a revival in substantial part of the agenda mapped and pursued by Denis Goulet since the 1960s (see Goulet 1971; Truong 1997, Gasper 2008a).

Such work is needed to complement the "Sen wave" of the last twenty years. Such an enriched and situated development ethics could contribute to the deepening of the body of social knowledge on globalization and the extension of forms of cosmopolitan judgment and political agency.

NOTES

1. The economic advance of large groups in the two population giants, China and India, may bring decline in measures of global interpersonal equality; but at the same time major groups have suffered absolute declines, in many cases into penury, and the income ratios of global top groups (whether in New York or Mumbai) compared to global bottom groups (whether in Mumbai or New York) have grown dramatically.

2. Bales (2003) presents the sex trades in Thailand as integral components of its development model. A "down market" of virtual sex slavery caters to lower-income workers who can now afford to regularly buy sexual services. An enormous "up market" supplies sex for tourists: "Nearly 5 million unaccompanied men visited Thailand in 1996. A significant proportion of these were sex tourists" (219).

3. The tsunami disaster of December 2004 triggered exceptional sympathy and response in Europe, particularly because of the undeserved nature of the disaster and the vigorous help by local authorities and residents. The involvement of large numbers of European tourists combined with the near-universal nature of the event (who has not spent time on a beach? who cannot imagine a wall of water raging in?), and perhaps the post-Christmas lull in other news, combined to generate enormous attention.

4. We consider gender to be a structure in a multilayered social reality, intersected by other structures such as class, ethnicity, religious affinity, and generation. We use a threefold concept of gender: (1) as a property of individuals (male and female); (2) as one principle that defines the boundaries and hierarchies of social organizations; and (3) as a structure in conceptual systems that gives visibility and significance to the public sphere (the male representation), sidelines the private sphere (the female representation), and at certain points obliterates the continuum of interaction between the two.

5. Ontology is used here to mean a perspective concerning what exists, and the position of the "self" in that reality.

6. For example, reports from NGOs working for trafficked children in Africa show that an increase in the use of child labor seems to be correlated with the fall of world prices of commodities such as coffee and cocoa (Truong 2006, 2007).

7. Belser (2005) estimates that global profits made from forced laborers exploited by private enterprises or agents reach $44.3 billion every year, including $31.6 billion from trafficked victims. The largest profits—more than $15 billion—are made from people trafficked and forced to work in industrialized countries.

8. See the WTO trade services Web site at http://www.wto.org/english/tratop_e/serv_e/serv_e.htm.

9. For example, the arrangements between Japan and the Philippines for entertainment, and Hong Kong and the Philippines for domestic services.

10. See the Convention Against Transnational Organized Crime and the protocol on the human rights protection of victims.

11. An introduction to Buddhist theory of mind and its meeting point with the field of psychology is best found in the conversation between His Holiness the Dalai Lama and Howard Culter (1998).

12. The *Journal of Human Development*, founded in 2000, still chose the subtitle *Alternative Economics in Action*. In 2007 it finally replaced this subtitle with *A Multi-disciplinary Journal for People-Centered Development*.

13. Martha Nussbaum's work is an exception in these respects, but plays an outlier role within the HDA (Gasper 2010).

REFERENCES

Adams, Vincanne. 2002. Suffering the Winds of Lhasa: Politicized Bodies, Human Rights, Cultural Difference, and Humanism in Tibet. In *The Anthropology of Globalization: A Reader*, ed. J. Xavier Inda and R. Rosaldo, 381–409. Oxford: Blackwell.

Apthorpe, Raymond. 1997. Human Development Reporting and Social Anthropology. *Social Anthropology* 5 (1): 21–34.

Bales, Kevin. 2003. Because She Looks Like a Child. In *Global Woman: Nannies, Maids, and Sex Workers in the New Economy*, ed. Barbara Ehrenreich and Arlie Russell Hochschild, 207–29. London: Granta Books.

Banik, Dan. 2007. *Starvation and India's Democracy*. London: Routledge.

Baquedano-López, Patricia. 2002. A Stop at the End of the Bus Line: Nannies, Children, and the Language of Care. Working Paper 51, University of California, Berkeley, Center for Working Families. http://wfnetwork.bc.edu/berkeley/papers/51.pdf.

Belser, Patrick. 2005. Forced Labor and Human Trafficking: Estimating the Profits. International Labor Organization/Cornell University School of Industrial and Labor Relations, DigitalCommons@ILR. http://digitalcommons.ilr.cornell.edu/forcedlabor/17.

Beneria, Lourdes. 1999. Globalization, Gender, and the Davos Man. *Feminist Economics* 5 (3): 61–84.

British Countryside in Pictures. n.d. Library ed. London: Odham.

Cameron, John, and Des Gasper. 2000. Amartya Sen on Inequality, Human Well-Being, and Development as Freedom. *Journal of International Development* 12 (7): 985–1045.

Chapkis, Wendy. 2003. Trafficking, Migration, and the Law. *Gender and Society* 17 (6): 923–37.

CHS (Commission on Human Security). 2003. *Human Security Now*. New York: CHS/United Nations. http://www.humansecurity-chs.org/finalreport/index.html.

Clement, Grace. 1996. *Care, Autonomy, and Justice: Feminism and the Ethic of Care*. Boulder, Colo.: Westview.

Cooke, Bill. 1997. From Process Consultation to a Clinical Model of Development Practice. *Public Administration and Development* 17 (3): 325–40.

Currie, Bob. 2000. *The Politics of Hunger in India*. Basingstoke, UK: Macmillan.

Dalai Lama XIV and Howard C. Cutler. 1998. *The Art of Happiness: A Handbook for Living*. New York: Riverhead Books.

Davis, Mike. 2001. *Late Victorian Holocausts: El Niño Famines and the Making of the Third World*. London: Verso.

Dottridge, Mike. 2004. *Kids as Commodities: Child Trafficking and What to Do About It*. Lausanne, Switzerland: Terre des Hommes International Federation.

Douglas, Mary. 1990. No Free Gifts. Foreword to *The Gift*, by Marcel Mauss, trans. W. D. Halls. London: Routledge.

Drèze, Jean, and Amartya Sen. 2002. *India: Development and Participation*. Delhi: Oxford University Press.

Ehrenreich, Barbara, and Arlie Russell Hochschild, eds. 2003. *Global Woman: Nannies, Maids, and Sex Workers in the New Economy*. London: Granta Books.

Europol. 2000. *1999 European Union Organized Crime Situation Report*. File No. 2530-58r2, October 30. The Hague: Europol.

Folbre, Nancy. 2001. *The Invisible Heart: Economics and Family Values*. New York: New Press.

Fraser, Nancy. 1995. From Redistribution to Recognition? Dilemmas of Justice in a "Post-Socialist" Age. *New Left Review*, July–August.

Gasper, Des. 2002. Is Sen's Capability Approach an Adequate Basis for a Theory of Human Development? *Review of Political Economy* 14 (4): 435–61.

———. 2004. *The Ethics of Development: From Economism to Human Development*. Edinburgh: Edinburgh University Press.

———. 2005a. Beyond the International Relations Framework: An Essay in Descriptive Global Ethics. *Journal of Global Ethics* 1 (1): 5–23.

———. 2005b. Securing Humanity: Situating "Human Security" as Concept and Discourse. *Journal of Human Development* 6 (2): 221–46.

———. 2007. Human Rights, Human Needs, Human Development, Human Security: Relationships Between Four International "Human" Discourses. Norwegian Institute of International Affairs. *Forum for Development Studies* 1: 9–43.

———. 2008a. Denis Goulet and the Project of Development Ethics: Choices in Methodology, Focus, and Organization. *Journal of Human Development* 9 (3): 453–74.

———. 2008b. The Idea of Human Security. Working Paper 28/08, GARNET. http://www.garnet-eu.org/fileadmin/documents/working_papers/2808.pdf.

———. 2010. Logos, Pathos, and Ethos in Martha Nussbaum's Capabilities Approach to Human Development. In *Capabilities, Gender, Equality: Toward Fundamental Entitlements*, ed. Flavio Comin and Martha Nussbaum. Cambridge University Press, forthcoming.

Gasper, Des, and Irene van Staveren. 2003. Development as Freedom—and as What Else? *Feminist Economics* 9 (2–3): 137–61.

Gilligan, Carol. 1982. *In a Different Voice*. Cambridge: Harvard University Press.

Giri, Ananta. 2002. *Conversations and Transformations*. Lanham, Md.: Lexington Books.

Glover, Jonathan. 2001. *Humanity: A Moral History of the Twentieth Century*. London: Pimlico.

Goulet, Denis. 1971. *The Cruel Choice: A New Concept in the Theory of Development*. New York: Atheneum.

Haq, Mahbub ul. 1999. *Reflections on Human Development*. Exp. ed. Delhi: Oxford University Press.

Held, David. 2004. *Global Compact: The Social Democratic Alternative to the Washington Consensus*. Cambridge, UK: Polity Press.

Hershock, Peter D. 2003. From Vulnerability to Virtuosity: Buddhist Reflections on Responding to Terrorism and Tragedy. *Journal of Buddhist Ethics* 10: 21–38.

Hettne, Bjorn. 1995. *Development Theory and the Three Worlds*. Harlow, UK: Longman.

Hirschman, Albert. 1977. *The Passions and the Interests: Political Arguments for Capitalism Before Its Triumph*. Princeton: Princeton University Press.

ILO. 2001. *Stopping Forced Labour: A Global Report*. Geneva: ILO.

IOM (International Office for Migration). 2003. Chapter 16, Statistical Section. In *World Migration, 2003*. Geneva: IOM.

Iselin, Brian. 2002. Barriers to Effective Human Trafficking Enforcement in the Mekong Sub-region. Paper presented at the 2nd Regional Conference on Illegal Labour Movements: The Case of Trafficking in Women and Children, November 28–29, Bangkok. http://www.unodc.un.or.th/material/document/10Barriers.pdf.

Keller, Jean. 1996. Care Ethics as a Health Care Ethic. *Contexts: Forum for the Medical Humanities* 4 (4).

Krznaric, Roman. 2007. *How Change Happens: Interdisciplinary Perspectives for Human Development*. Oxfam Research Report. Oxford: Oxfam.

Mora, Tatiana. 2000. Poverty Matters, But to What Extent? Elite Perceptions of Poverty Through the Literary Discourse in Costa Rica. Working Paper 310, Institute of Social Studies, The Hague.

Narayan, Deepa, with Raj Patel, Kai Schafft, Anne Rademacher, and Sarah Koch-Schulte. 2000. *Voices of the Poor: Can Anyone Hear Us?* New York: Oxford University Press.

Noddings, Nel. 2003. *Caring: A Feminine Approach to Ethics and Moral Education.* Berkeley and Los Angeles: University of California Press.

Nussbaum, Martha. 2003. Capabilities as Fundamental Entitlements: Sen and Social Justice. *Feminist Economics* 9 (2–3): 33–60.

———. 2006. Reply: In Defence of Global Political Liberalism. *Development and Change* 37 (4): 1313–28.

Nussbaum, Martha, and Jonathan Glover, eds. 1995. *Women, Culture, and Development: The Capabilities Approach.* Oxford: Clarendon Press.

OECD. 2002. Labour Shortages and the Need for Immigrants: A Review of Recent Studies. Discussion document for the OECD working party on international migration, Paris.

O'Neill, O. 1996. *Towards Justice and Virtue: A Constructive Account of Practical Reasoning.* Cambridge: Cambridge University Press.

O'Neill-Richard, Amy. 1999. *International Trafficking in Women to the United States: A Contemporary Manifestation of Slavery and Organized Crime.* DCI Exceptional Intelligence Analyst Program. Washington, D.C.: Center for the Study of Intelligence.

Palan, Ronen. 1999. Susan Strange, 1923–1998: A Great International Relations Theorist. *Review of International Political Economy* 6 (2): 121–32.

Parton, Nigel. 2003. Rethinking Professional Practice: The Contributions of Social Constructionism and the Feminist Ethics of Care. *British Journal of Social Work* 33 (1): 1–16.

Penz, Peter. 1986. *Consumer Sovereignty and Human Interests.* Cambridge: Cambridge University Press.

———. 2001. The Ethics of Development Assistance and Human Security. In *Ethics and Security in Canadian Foreign Policy*, ed. R. Irwin, 38–55. Vancouver: University of British Columbia Press.

Power, Michael. 1997. *The Audit Society.* Oxford: Oxford University Press.

Ratha, Dilip. 2003. Workers' Remittances: An Important Source of External Development Finance. In *Global Development Finance: Striving for Stability in Development Finance.* Washington, D.C.: World Bank.

Rawls, John. 1971. *A Theory of Justice.* Cambridge: Harvard University Press.

Razavi, Shahra. 2007. The Political and Social Economy of Care in a Development Context: Conceptual Issues, Research Questions, and Policy Options. Gender and Development Programme Paper 3, Code PP-GD-3, United Nations Research Institute for Social Development.

Sassen, Saskia. 2002. Women's Burden: Counter-Geographies of Globalization and the Feminization of Survival. *Nordic Journal of International Law* 71 (2): 255–74.

———. 2003. Global Cities and Survival Circuits. In *Global Woman: Nannies, Maids, and Sex Workers in the New Economy*, ed. Barbara Ehrenreich and Arlie Russell Hochschild, 254–74. London: Granta Books.

Scholte, Jan-Aart. 2000. *Globalization: A Critical Introduction.* Basington, UK: Palgrave Macmillan.

———. 2005. *Globalization: A Critical Introduction.* 2nd ed. London: Palgrave Macmillan.

Sen, Amartya. 1999. *Development as Freedom.* New York: Oxford University Press.

———. 2000. What Difference Can Ethics Make? Speech delivered at the International Meeting on Ethics and Development of the Inter-American Development Bank in collaboration with the Norwegian government, December, Washington, D.C.

Seligman, Adam. 1995. Animadversions upon Civil Society and Civic Virtue in the Last Decade of the Twentieth Century, 200–223. In *Civil Society*, ed. John A. Hall. Cambridge, UK: Polity Press.

Sennett, Richard. 2004. *Respect: The Formation of Character in an Age of Inequality*. London: Penguin.

Sevenhuijsen, Selma. 1998. *Citizenship and the Ethics of Care: Feminist Considerations on Justice, Morality, and Politics*. London: Routledge.

St. Clair, Asunción Lera. 2006. Global Poverty: The Co-production of Knowledge and Politics. *Global Social Policy* 6 (1): 57–77.

Thich Nhat Hanh. 1993. *Interbeing: Fourteen Guidelines for Engaged Buddhists*. Berkeley, Calif.: Parallax.

Thompson, Adam. 2004. Like Turner's Slaves, the Chinese Cocklers Were the Market's Innocent Victims. *Daily Telegraph* (London), February 7.

Tronto, Joan. 1994. *Moral Boundaries: A Political Argument for an Ethic of Care*. New York: Routledge.

———. 2003. Care as the Work of Citizens: A Modest Proposal. Paper presented at the Dialogues on Care Conference, October, Bergen, Norway.

Truong, Thanh-Dam. 1997. Gender and Human Development: A Feminist Perspective. *Gender, Technology, and Development* 1 (3): 349–70.

———. 2003a. Gender, Exploitative Migration, and the Sex Industry: A European Perspective. *Gender, Technology, and Development* 7 (1): 31–51.

———. 2003b. The Human Rights Question in the Global Sex Trade. In *Responding to the Human Rights Deficit: Essays in Honour of Bas de Gaay Fortman*, ed. K. Arts and P. Mihyo, 185–201. London: Kluwer Law International.

———. 2003c. Organized Crime and Human Trafficking. In *Transnational Organized Crime: Myth, Power, and Profit*, ed. E. C. Viano, J. Magallanes, and L. Bridel, 53–72. Durham: Carolina Academic Press.

———. 2005a. Human Security. In *The Essentials of Human Rights*, ed. C. van den Anker and R. Smith, 172–75. London: Hodder and Stoughton.

———. 2005b. Reflections on Human Security: A Buddhist Contribution. In *Bridge or Barriers: Religion, Violence, and Visions for Peace*, ed. J. Busuttil and G. ter Haar, 275–95. Leiden, the Netherlands: Brill.

———. 2006. Governance and Poverty in Sub-Saharan Africa: Rethinking Best Practices in Migration Management. *International Social Science Journal* 58 (190): 697–714.

———. 2007. *Poverty, Gender, and Human Trafficking in Sub-Saharan Africa: Rethinking Best Practices in Migration Management*. Paris: UNESCO.

UNDP (United Nations Development Programme). 2000. *Human Development Report, 2000*. New York: UNDP.

———. 2004. *Human Development Report, 2004*. New York: UNDP.

WCCD (World Commission on Culture and Development). 1995. *Our Creative Diversity*. Paris: WCCD/UNESCO.

Williams, Fiona. 2003. Rethinking Care in Social Policy. Paper presented at the Annual Conference of the Finnish Social Policy Association, October 24, University of Joensuu, Finland.

World Bank. 2006. *Global Economic Prospects: Overview and Global Outlook*. Washington, D.C.: World Bank.

Xue Xinran. 2004. Comment. *Guardian* (London), February 20.

Yeates, Nicola. 2004. Global Care Chains: Critical Reflections and Lines of Inquiry. *International Journal of Feminist Politics* 6 (3): 326–91.

Youngs, Gillian. 2004. Feminist International Relations: A Contradiction in Terms? Or Why Women and Gender Are Essential to Understanding the World "We" Live in. *International Affairs* 80 (1): 75–81.

Yuval-Davis, Nira. 2003. Human Security and the Gendered Politics of Belonging. Paper presented at the Symposium on Justice, Equality, and Dependency in the "Post-Socialist" Condition, March 22, Centre for the Study of Women and Gender, University of Warwick.

A Methodologically Pragmatist Approach to Development Ethics

Asunción Lera St. Clair

Development ethics is useless unless it can be translated into public action. By public action is meant action taken by public authority, as well as actions taken by private agents by having important consequences for the life of the public community. The central question is: How can moral guidelines influence decisions of those who hold power?

—*The Cruel Choice* (Goulet 1971, 335)

There is an increasing awareness of the ethical aspects of development policy and practice among scholars, practitioners, and development agencies. Development ethics today is slowly evolving into a wider field of knowledge studied in universities and research centers, and there is an increasing number of development ethics courses and seminars.[1] A certain interest in the ethical aspects of development is slowly making a breakthrough among practitioners, donors, and multilateral development agencies, including the World Bank.[2] The most influential multilateral agency proposing an ethically grounded

This chapter was previously published in *Journal of Global Ethics* 3, no. 2 (2007): 143–64, and is included here by permission. *Journal of Global Ethics* is published by Taylor and Francis; see http://www.informaworld.com/. The section on methodological pragmatism draws from an unpublished paper written with Andrew Light called "A Pragmatist Methodology for Development Ethics," presented at the American Philosophical Association (APA) meeting in New York, December 1999. I have updated, transformed, and used some parts and insights developed with Light in a way he may not recognize. I thank Andrew Light, David Crocker, Desmond McNeill, and Alf Nilsen, the organizers and the audience at the MSU conference, and two reviewers. Special thanks to Des Gasper. My work in completing this chapter has been inspired by the writings of Denis Goulet, who passed away at the end of 2006, and by my meetings and interactions with him. Correspondence to: University of Bergen, Norway; e-mail: asun.st.clair@sos.uib.no.

view on development is the United Nations Development Programme (UNDP), through its Human Development Report Office and its flagship publication, the *Human Development Reports*. Amartya Sen's capability approach provides the intellectual basis of human development (UNDP 1990–2007; Sen 1999), and there is a fast-growing body of work on this approach, its reformulation in terms of freedom, and the more philosophically grounded version of capabilities elaborated by Martha Nussbaum.[3] In addition, the revamping of human rights by most UN agencies and donors has led to important research on the role that rights may have in redefining development and poverty.[4] Clearly, there is a fast-emerging group of authors working on global justice and global ethics, also touching on development issues.[5]

This chapter focuses on what type of ethical thinking is needed to address the most important challenges posed by international development and development aid. As the opening quote by Goulet rightly argues, development ethics may be useless unless it has a real impact on those with the power to change the way policies are elaborated and implemented. Development ethics needs also to reach out to private actors (including individuals in advanced economies as well as collective private agents). In other words, development ethics must have a policy impact, to change practices and to influence people's perception of what is good development for all, and thus to lead to alternative courses of action. Even though powerful development agents are starting to acknowledge some of the roles that values may have in increasing the effectiveness of development processes, development ethics as a field of knowledge remains marginal among those who have the power and the legitimacy to frame development problems and to guide global development policymaking. The influence of the capability approach and the importance of human development are increasing, no doubt; but among global institutions, they are too often adopted at a superficial level and at the expense of engaged critique on the value conflicts and challenges to neoliberal policies that the actual implementation of such an alternative development view may lead to. Human rights are also being adapted and often distorted and instrumentalized to suit the conceptual frameworks of global institutions responsible for development policy (for example, through connecting rights to more widely acknowledged ideas such as "participation" and "empowerment")—strategies that have failed to deliver results in other areas such as gender equality. Ethical thinking and the role of values in development risk are being instrumentalized and narrowed down to justify ongoing development policies, or to justify appeals for charity toward the very poor (McNeill and St. Clair 2006). Ethical analysis then loses its roles of providing analytical tools and ethical clarification to formulate alternative knowledge for development centered on the equal moral worth of all human beings, and of shifting development from a charity issue to a matter related to questions of global and social justice. Development ethics may miss the opportunity to contribute to the increasingly obvious ethical flaws of neoliberal ideology and to join forces with a growing body of theories and praxis on global justice, challenging the unfairness of a global system that benefits the powerful and ignores or damages the vulnerable.[6]

This chapter argues that one of the main tasks of development ethics is engagement with the knowledge and policies of multilateral institutions—the most powerful actors responsible for framing what is development and what to do to reduce poverty. It suggests that lessons from the field of environmental ethics and sociological perspectives on knowledge are important for achieving such a goal. The chapter argues for a methodologically pragmatist approach for development ethics that focuses on the interplay between facts, values, concepts, and practices. It views development ethics as a hybrid between a public moral-political philosophy and a public conception of social science. Ethical analyses of poverty and development must lead to fundamental changes in the ways knowledge is produced, legitimized, and justified, and to challenge the dominance of global institutions and orthodox economics as the single sources of expert knowledge for development. The last section of the chapter argues that Amartya Sen's version of the capability approach is already methodologically pragmatist, that there are interesting similarities between Sen and John Dewey's thought. But it requires more awareness as to the ways in which the approach may be distorted by multilateral agencies and used to justify policies not consistent with the philosophy of the approach.

Third-Stage Development Ethics: Addressing the Co-production of Knowledge and Politics

Des Gasper argues that writings on development ethics may be divided into three stages (1997a, 2004). The first stage refers to the realization or the experiencing resulting from moral awareness, or an opening and realization that some issues in development may indeed carry ethical consequences, ethical meanings. This first phase, Gasper argues, is more related to experience that raises moral awareness. Second-stage development ethics is the phase where researchers or practitioners (who presumably have already experienced stage one) formulate concepts and ideas to capture, reflect upon, and theorize on ethical issues in development. The second stage can start with descriptions and clarification of values and value choices in relation to development and development aid. Flowing from this conceptual and theory-building phase comes the stage where there is further systematization and assessment of value choices and problems. Third-stage development ethics attempts to address opposing ethical views, the need to compromise and negotiate and apply insights from stage two. This is the stage of application, compromise, and negotiation—the moment of attempting to reach sufficient support in order to influence policymaking. Third-stage development ethics is the "ethics of policy planning and professional practice, devising and negotiating and trying to execute value-sensitive action" (Gasper 2004, xii).

Gasper acknowledges that all three stages are interconnected and that his distinction among the stages has merely analytical purposes. The three stages may best be seen as part of an organic process that moves from experiencing the moral dilemmas and ethical questions posed by development, to the conceptualization and theorizing of such ethical issues, to the negotiation and sorting out of value conflicts and elaboration of policies. I wish, however, to push forward Gasper's analysis and argue for the need to concentrate precisely on the intrinsic linkages between the third stage of negotiation and policymaking for development with experience, moral awareness, and perceptions (stage one) as well as with the elaboration of concepts and theoretical approaches (stage two). This is a more accurate strategy to investigate the way that knowledge and policies are actually produced by global institutions—the most powerful actors in the dominant framing and policymaking for development. Rather than at a third stage, value clarification is established in stage one, primarily, due to the overarching importance given to the cognitive values of economics above any other value, including ethical values.

Organizational cultures and experts in these global institutions tend to be dominated by neoliberal economics, ill-prepared to deal with the complexities of development processes and their impact on people's lives and the environment; and centered around quantitative analyses built upon a narrow informational basis that tends to discount ethical concerns as relevant knowledge.[7] This blindness toward ethical concerns that characterizes neoliberal ideas influences not only the choice of concepts, but the ways concepts are elaborated and the specific meanings attached to what are often complex ideas. Explicit value clarification and value choices, if they occur, often mean the seeking of justifications for already decided knowledge systems, where knowledge and action overlap. These knowledge systems may not be morally acceptable or have any ethical grounding at all. And by the time one reaches the third stage of policy planning and professional practice, alternatives and values have already been sorted out and it is very problematic to have a well-balanced negotiation. Ethically grounded policy proposals may end up being an artificial superimposition of merely rhetorical value claims that may hide the actual value choices made in the early stages. Ethics and development may simply be outright moralizing and patronizing.

I have explored elsewhere some of the processes in which knowledge systems are built within global institutions, in particular, institutions that have taken as their main tasks not only to produce but also to perform basic research on poverty and development. Using insights from social studies of science (STS), I have argued that ideas in development are best viewed as "intellectual boundary objects" and processes of knowledge formulation as boundary work—a combination of strategies and contingencies rather than simply a scientific endeavor (St. Clair 2006b, 2006d). The notion of boundary object, first introduced by Star and Griesemer (1989), refers to objects that serve as interfaces—linkages—between different communities of practice. Boundary objects permit collaboration among diverse partners who view issues from different perspectives, and thus differently, yet permit joint work and collaboration. I have argued that ideas in the multilateral system can be characterized as intellectual boundary objects, as multilateralism is often an arena where ideas ought to serve many users and many purposes, yet provide an interface—a joint space for collaboration. Ideas in the multilateral system are subject to constant negotiation, framing, and reframing, as well as to distortions and misuses. Yet ideas are entangled with political and ideological goals; often political battles are about who names and thus frames social facts. Characterizing ideas as intellectual boundary objects permits us to deepen our look into processes of knowledge production by multilaterals, the ways in which their economic and political power affects the shape of ideas, and the policy proposals that flow from specific interpretations of such ideas. The aim would be to investigate what happens inside the global institutions with the power to set the political and intellectual agendas for development along the same lines that Latour and Woolgar (1986) investigated what happens in the everyday life of a scientific laboratory.[8]

For example, the World Bank is one of the dominant sources of knowledge for development and poverty reduction. Its research capacities, the influence that the Bank's lending role has in developing countries, and the support it draws from the United States and global financial actors endow approaches and ideas endorsed by the Bank with a unique power and influence. The Bank may be said to be a major global governance actor as much as a major global knowledge actor—a transnational expertised state-like institution setting the scene for both global politics and global knowledge (St. Clair 2006d). Knowledge produced or supported by the Bank, however, cannot be said to be objective science elaborated independently from politics and disembodied from wider social worlds. Not only is the Bank's knowledge limited by its diverse principals who often pose conflicting demands on the Bank's researchers, but also the legitimacy of such knowledge is drawn through circular processes between the knowledge the Bank produces and the audiences that legitimize that knowledge. Bank researchers tend to address their claims to a particular set of audiences—on the one hand their principals, and on the other, their most powerful peers, mainstream economists. This has enormous consequences for which knowledge counts as legitimate and credible; how ideas are used, transformed, and distorted; and why alternative views tend to be ignored.

It is very common that the justification, for example, for rejecting the view that health or education may best be conceptualized as human rights instead of as commodities best supplied by the private sector is simply that Bank experts address their knowledge claims to a narrow audience of ideologically bounded elite mainstream economists, who are the same audience that then legitimizes such knowledge claims. Accepting health as a human right would challenge the authority of economists because such a definition points toward sources of evidence well beyond mainstream economic science and to a broader audience than simply mainstream economists. I argue, thus, that the knowledge-based economic policy dominant in many multilaterals is best seen as straddling an uneven territory between science in the making and politics in the making and not as an objective science or truth speaking to power. It is within this messy interface between knowledge and action, knowledge and politics, and institutional cultures and the wider social worlds where we must see the role of ethical values, starting in stage one as defined by Gasper (2004).

Rather than simple social facts waiting to be discovered, poverty and development are complex and ill-structured issues that cannot be fully captured by the cognitive tools of a single discipline nor subjected to standard methods. Knowledge for development is not reached through objective truths or scientific consensus; rather, it tends to be formed by what can be called "fact-surrogates," partial accounts of a complex social problem; or as sociologist Stephen Turner puts it, well-structured parts of an ill-structured and complex whole (Turner 2003). The particular shape of these fact-surrogates is decided by the hierarchies of cognitive and moral values entailed by the audiences that legitimize the knowledge claims of these global institutions. These are often the result of a consensus among certain scientists rather than a scientific consensus (St. Clair 2006b). Awareness of the partially constructed character of knowledge is very important, as it is during this messy construction process that values get chosen and decided upon—some at the expense of others. It is at the very early stages, for example, that concerns for human rights become residual to the values of consumerism and individualism held by mainstream economists. As Alfredo Sfeir-Younis, former senior adviser to the Managing Directors Office at the World Bank, insightfully puts it:

> For the time being, the implementation and realization of human rights remain just a residual of another paradigm: i.e., the present paradigm of economic development. . . . If countries adopt a "human rights based approach to development," human rights values must permeate each and every aspect of a development strategy, so human rights issues do not come as a residual of economic transactions or other possible leading activities. . . . What many human rights activists would like to see is that human rights values must cut at the centre of economic values. (Sfeir-Younis 2003, 45)

Ideas that challenge mainstream ideology are distorted as a result of the pressures to depoliticize and economize them. And ideas that have ethical content are not excluded from such distorting processes. Value conflicts and trade-offs are commonplace in the battlefield of development agencies, and ethical values that challenge hegemonic ideas and pre-established policy goals tend to be distorted or supplanted by cognitive values. In particular, cognitive values such as measurability, simplicity, and efficiency tend to prevail over concerns for global justice or any other ethical principle that challenges the dominance of a market ethic. As politicians also want simple, measurable, and quantifiable data, the cognitive values of neoliberal economics tend to coincide with the cognitive values of policymaking and draw still more power from such overlapping of goals. The widely shared assumption that dominant ideas are value free enables "hidden norms" to move freely and shape knowledge and policy for development and poverty in particular ways.

Thus, I emphasize the need for further methodologically pragmatist analysis for development ethics interlinking the experience, theorizing, and policymaking stages in the processes of constructing knowledge for development. This approach may help to convey that development and global poverty are highly complex social facts, and constructing knowledge about them entails sorting out values—accepting some and rejecting others—from the very early stages of moral awareness and formulating ideas and concepts. From this perspective, the role of a self-conscious methodologically pragmatist development ethics is not only as an interdisciplinary reflection on a public issue, development, but must also evolve into a hybrid between philosophical analysis and social science, addressing the role that not only moral but also nonmoral values have in the formation of knowledge for development and global poverty. Such a truly interdisciplinary endeavor requires not only addressing the value conflicts between cognitive and moral values, the processes that construct discourses of fairness, but also unveiling the fairness or unfairness of certain ethical views. Often we tend to disregard the ethical force of what is the dominant global ethic—the ethic of the market. This global ethic, presupposed by mainstream development economics, not only leads to the economization of all social life, but most importantly, it displaces, diffuses, and prevents actual ethical reflection (Bauman 2000, 2004; McNeill and St. Clair 2006; Patomaki 2006; St. Clair 2006c).

The characterization I propose for a modified version of Gasper's third-stage development ethics flows not only from application of insights from the fields of STS and technology but also from espousing a philosophically pragmatist methodology that points toward viewing values entangled with empirical accounts of reality; toward the back and forth relations that occur between experiences, perceptions, theories, and practices and between knowledge and action. I take such a methodological outlook from the field of environmental ethics, which I argue offers us not only important connections between the tasks ahead for addressing jointly environmental sustainability and global justice but also important methodological lessons for the formulation of a truly inter-disciplinary practical ethics that may influence the decisions of those who hold power, which Goulet defined as the overarching goal of development ethics.

A Pragmatist Methodology for Development Ethics

Many in the field of applied ethics have become aware of the need to avoid the mistakes of other fields, where ethical reflection has run parallel and often totally dissociated from the world of action and from the world of policy. As Gasper (2006) argues, development ethics has always been an interdisciplinary meeting point. This has helped to avoid some of the failures that, for example, led environmental ethics to become disentangled from policy, but the warning against ethical analysis de-linked from practice is now more relevant as global institutions start adopting normative concepts such as human rights and capabilities; and there is an increasing number of scholars producing academic work on ethical reflections about global problems. Andrew Light argues that environmental ethics became a haven of extensionism (Light and Katz 1996; Light 2002). This means that ethical and meta-ethical frameworks from the history of ethics have been extended by environmental ethicists to environmental problems. While there is certainly nothing wrong per se with extensionism in any applied field—it has after all produced some very interesting work in a variety of subfields—a strong argument can be made that there is something wrong with extensionism if it hinders progress in an applied field, especially where that progress can be measured by the influence of the field in question on the critical problems of the day. Environmental issues, like development, must be understood as a cluster of problems in the world that affect people and that demand an ethical response.

The field of environmental ethics is focused, especially in the United States, on whether nature has value independent from human consideration of that value (often considered as a form of intrinsic value) and then a determination of the duties, obligations, or rights that follow from that description of the value of nature. Light argues that the resulting philosophical disagreements between nonanthropocentrists (those supporting such a broadly described view) and weak anthropocentrists (those challenging that view based on claims that nonanthropocentric foundations for natural value are incoherent) fail to take into account the moral intuitions of most people with regard to the value of nature. For example, the nonanthropocentric emphasis on determining a value to nature outside human considerations of that value impedes our ability to discuss ways in which anthropogenic impacts on nature can be understood and meliorated through human intuitions about the value of nature. By focusing on whether nature has or does not have intrinsic value, environmental ethics has produced two unfortunate results: first, it excludes from its discussions the many beneficial ways in which environmental protection can be based on human interests, such as founding policies for environmental protection in the common intuitions of obligations to future generations; and second, the focus on abstract concepts of value theory distracts the field from seeking agreement on all those arguments that could morally motivate people to support environmental policies, no matter where those arguments are grounded. Weak anthropocentrists end up spending more of their time debating the value theories of nonanthropocentrists than trying to forge a consensus on the different reasons that can motivate people to protect nature (Light 2002). In short, environmental ethics is not reaching the public or helping policymakers in their task to articulate policies that make sense for a variety of people and institutions. Environmental ethics today is arguably of interest mainly to other philosophers concerned with abstract debates in value theory.

The pragmatist alternative argues that environmental ethics should break free from these debates and make room for a more public task, at least as part of its mandate. Light's version of this form of pragmatism (which he calls "methodological environmental pragmatism") is not based on the claim that nonanthropocentric notions of the intrinsic value of nature are necessarily wrong (as the weak anthropocentrist would argue) but rather that there is a task for environmental philosophy beyond simply the search for a foundational theory of the nature of natural value.[9] This is the task of translating the agreed upon objectives of the environmental community, which are reached for a myriad of different reasons and schemes of value, to the wider public. Environmental pragmatists of this school of thought agree that nature is valuable for many reasons, and so when we have an agreed upon end we wish to translate to the public we do it for as many philosophically valid reasons as is possible to articulate. The advantage of this view is that it does not necessarily require an engagement with and rejection of nonanthropocentrism. Nonanthropocentrists can certainly embrace such a methodologically pragmatist task without giving up their search for the noninstrumental value to nature. They simply need to agree to sometimes set aside their more purely philosophical concerns for this public task in the service of the broader ends of the environmental community.

In the rest of the chapter I shall argue that there are important analogies between Light's analysis and debates within development ethics among diverse moral categories as well as between competing cognitive values, including discussions about the capability approach. A methodologically pragmatist development ethics should busy itself in addressing the ways in which debates about human development could be furthered by enrichment and interactions with other global normative discourses such as human rights and human security. A focus on human development is important because it offers an ethically built view of development already in place among policymakers, with the capacity to make factual changes. In addition, a methodologically pragmatist development ethics would address not only the risks of extensionism proper of philosophical analysis, but also more clearly and explicitly the risks of extending economic theories to a complex and messy world of practices, and would challenge the presumption that knowledge and actions are separate. If development ethics is about value conscious ways of thinking about and choosing alternative paths and destinations, as Gasper (2004) rightly argues, then it is the role of the development ethicist to address the processes that decide which paths are taken and which ones are not, and why, from the very early stages of knowledge formation. Being knowledgeable and interacting with practitioners and staff from global institutions is thus part of the role of development ethicists.

But development ethics still displays a tendency to center on debates about the differences between universalist and particularist views of the essential qualities of a good human life; or on the degree to which it is important to situate views on rights or capabilities within philosophical traditions; or on whether needs, rights, or capabilities are the best fundamental concept for development ethics. This tendency may lead to an unfruitful philosophical gridlock with few practical consequences. In my opinion, one way to strengthen human development is to seek synergies between global justice approaches and development ethics (St. Clair 2006c). For example, debates as to whether Thomas Pogge's (2002, 2004, 2007) proposal for viewing severe global poverty as a violation of human rights, understood primarily as a violation of liberty rights, is philosophically tenable is distracting the attention of many important thinkers at the expense of offering arguments that may influence powerful actors. Pogge's argument is explicitly strategic, aimed to influence the opinions of those who do not view poverty in any way whatsoever as a question of entitlements and rights, yet who understand the basic language of liberty. At the same time, Pogge's analysis of global poverty draws attention to the unfairness of the institutions that regulate the global economy and situates debates on global poverty and the global institutions responsible for knowledge for development within the macro-framework of globalization. Pogge's work is also important because he is increasingly centering his work on the unreliability of empirical knowledge about poverty and on the relations between moral and political philosophy and mainstream methodological tendencies in both poverty research and development research. And, although he does not explicitly acknowledge it, his analysis shows the intrinsic relations between the empirical, the political, and the normative. For example, Pogge rightly points our attention toward the consequences of the methodological territorialism dominant in poverty research not only on people's moral awareness of poverty but also in leading toward underestimating the actual number of poor people. The assumption that poverty and development are issues bounded by the geographical and political boundaries of the state is one of the leading causes for the blindness people and politicians have toward some of the most fundamental forces producing and perpetuating poverty. In turn, methodological territorialism blinds the citizens of advanced economies from viewing their own entanglement with the poor and thus perpetuates the misguided idea that poverty occurs somewhere else and it is those other countries' problem, not their own. It will be important also to see more engagement and linkages on the side of global justice authors, including Pogge, with capability perspectives and lessons for reformulating and expanding the idea of human development.

Pogge's global perspective complements the capability approach, as it is impossible today to understand development without looking into globalization processes and emerging transnational practices that are affecting the development chances of poor countries. In addition, the emerging consensus on human rights as the leading normative framework for global relations leads toward addressing, to put it broadly, the conflicts raised by the contradictory values of neoliberal economic globalization and the globalization of human rights and capabilities, including conflicts among various rights and capabilities and various groups. A global perspective leads development ethics to focus its attention not only on the ethical context of human development and capabilities but often also on contradictory roles of global institutions. For example, the UNDP acts as an institution defending economic globalization while explicitly defending normative understandings of development as social processes toward the improvement of "all" people's quality of life. Such contradictory roles affect the chances of future strengthening of human development, and the UNDP needs to address these conflicts explicitly.

In addition, a methodologically pragmatist development ethics points toward concerns with mainstream economic development doctrines and may add methodological rigor to the analysis I drew earlier from the application of insights from STS.[10] Clearly, mainstream economic thinking, the main builder of knowledge for development, falls into the same types of dogmatism as the meta-ethical debates illustrated by Light (2004), especially as it works within global institutions. Development economics concentrates often on the application of insights from economic theory to the real world and presumes a linear relation between the arena of politics and the arena of science. The presumed dichotomy in mainstream and development economics between "knowledge" and "action" is one of the main reasons for the persistence of outdated and unhelpful theories. The prevalence of formalized and quantified views may be helpful in providing guidance to policymakers in simple issues, but it is dangerous if used to address highly complex and ill-structured problems, more so if substituted for detailed knowledge of local conditions as it is often the case among experts from global institutions. As Ellerman (2005) rightly argues, "Academic economists and global development bureaucrats have little contact with local realities and thus they tend to be driven by such simplified cartoon models. Exiles who have not participated in the give and take of politics in a country for years if not decades also tend to have cartoon models. It is the combination of power and highly simplified models of complex social realities that is particularly lethal." A particular example of the disassociation between knowledge and action, between abstract theorizing and the real world of action, is the pervasive view that economic growth reduces poverty almost on a one-to-one basis. Such "belief" is more the result of extending economic theory to the real world while ignoring a messy world of practices and social institutions. As Jan Vandermoortele (2002) reminds us, the combination of an income-based definition of poverty together with uncritical faith in the over-arching value of logarithmic regressions leads to the "dangerous" prediction that poverty lessens at the same pace as economic growth rises. Such thinking commits the fallacy of misplaced concreteness, Vandermoortele rightly argues, as averages are abstractions and not real observations. That is, "the fact that the income of the poor rises one-for-one with overall per capita income may be statistically correct, but it is not necessarily true" (2002, 9).

A pragmatist methodology for development ethics focuses our attention on the ways in which economic science's abstract theorizing plays in practice. It is impossible to claim the same "certainty of outcomes" in the messy world of practices as it is often claimed in academic theoretical publications. As I have elaborated elsewhere, in practice there are often massive difficulties in establishing the economic situation of a country (St. Clair 2006b). IMF or World Bank missions are messy and complex fact finding exercises, often leading to uncertain and risky guesses that experts are forced to make due to lack of data or contradictory statistical reports of different ministries in client countries. Numbers often end up being interpreted rather than collected, and such interpretations conform more to particular circumstances experts find themselves immersed in or simply those they are able to get because of their social skills than the result of an accurate application of economic theory. Development and poverty, in the same way as climate change or environmental sustainability, are highly complex and ill-structured problems, far from mere facts easily defined, measured, and planned. Knowledge-based policy recommendations in these arenas are plagued with uncertainties and risks. As Stiglitz vividly argues (2001, 2002), uncertainty and risk are defining characteristics of knowledge-based economic policy.

Most importantly, as illustrated earlier, it is at this level of formation of economic knowledge where values are sorted out—some chosen, some rejected—where the politicization of moral worth occurs. The false belief that economic science provides a true account of reality is perhaps one of the most fundamental reasons for rejecting the role of ethical thinking as valid knowledge for development.[11] Untangling the value problems related to the scientific uncertainties of knowledge for development is, therefore, one of the important tasks for development ethics. This is of particular importance for reclaiming the moral worth of all human beings and for preventing intrinsic values from becoming instrumentalized.

There are further lessons to draw from a pragmatist methodology for development ethics. The focus on competing meta-ethical or meta-economic positions can be wrong-headed for other reasons as well. The connection between ethics and public policy does not consist in simply applying a correct moral theory to a specific situation. In fact, we might not want to live in a world where priorities for development policy were thought to reside only in the extension of moral theories. The assumption of an identifiable scheme of moral knowledge would lead to an intractable state of affairs, where no nego-tiations among competing conceptions of the good or a well-organized society were possible. This would be particularly unfortunate in the case of develop-ment because development policymaking always takes place within a political framework—one in which the parties are always unequal. The last thing that development aid and cooperation need is to become part of an inflexible philo-sophical debate as has happened, for example, in the case of family planning. The history of the debate about abortion shows the dangers in making the moral dimensions of public policies explicit while leaving untouched the role played by cognitive values and values hidden under the veil of scientism. In this regard, Paul Thompson claims that "it is at least arguable that the bitterness and inflexibility of the abortion debate today is due to both sides not only having adopted philosophically incompatible positions, but also having buttressed these positions with moral philosophy that demonizes the other side" (Thompson 1996, 205). A similar inflexibility is already the characteristic of globalization debates. Development ethics must aim to cut through it.

The Capability Approach and Methodological Pragmatism

I wish to contribute to the debate on the capability approach by offering now a brief analysis of the ways in which Sen's capability and freedom approach can be seen as an instance of a methodologically pragmatist development ethic. Development as freedom can be seen as a methodologically pragmatist public philosophy that espouses a theory of valuation but not a theory of value. That some freedoms or capabilities are essential, for Sen, does not mean they follow from a theory of true human nature, nor from a universalist notion of values (neither a universal conception of the validity of all local values nor a general universal conception of value) (Sen 1999, 247). Certainly, Sen's approach rests on a universalist presumption about the value of freedom. But this presumption goes hand in hand with the role that bundles of freedoms and capabilities have in leading people to reach fulfilling lives on their own terms. Sen calls these two roles of freedom (1) the evaluative reason and (2) the effectiveness reason. Evaluative, because it allows for an assessment of how much progress development has made in enhancing people's freedoms. Effective, because free agency—the outcome of many interconnected and interdependent freedoms— is a necessary condition for successful development (Sen 1999, 4). For example, women who have the freedom to work outside their homes enhance their social standing as well as contribute to the prosperity of their families. Working outside the home usually gives women more visibility and voice and less dependency, and enhances their education. This in turn strengthens women's agency and usually makes women more informed, able, and empowered to influence family decisions.

The bridge Sen builds between the economic, political, social, and ethical aspects of development is a public philosophy very much in the sense of the term championed by John Dewey. This is not to say, however, that I am arguing for a form of extensionism with respect to classical American pragmatism, nor that Sen is a pragmatist in the Deweyian sense, but there are nonetheless some interesting similarities between Dewey's and Sen's works. Dewey's social and political philosophy is based on the avoidance of metaphysical and meta-ethical dead ends. Sen and Dewey both try to work out a conception of freedom that does not appeal to ontology or epistemology and that eventually breaks through the distinction between theory and practice by making both of them part of experience. But how did Dewey situate this form of freedom?

First, Dewey argued that we cannot have a priori knowledge of our own nature. As Hilary Putnam (1992) puts it: Dewey's view is that we do not know what our interests and needs are or what we are capable of until we actually engage in politics. A corollary of this view is that there can be no final answer to the question of how we should live, and therefore we should always leave it open to further discussion and experimentation. Dewey also warned us about the risks of inverting the relationship between commodities and the good life, and to look for a proper understanding of the role of economics in human life. In his critique of liberalism, Dewey claimed that the new material possibilities resulting from science and technology had brought material security to many, but this abundance is taken as an end in itself and not as a means to a more fulfilling human life. As Dewey claimed: "The habits of desire and effort that were bred in the age of scarcity do not readily subordinate themselves. . . . Even now when there is a vision of an age of abundance and when the vision is supported by hard facts, it is material security as an end that appeals to most rather than the way of living which this security makes possible" (1998b, vol. 11, 44).

Last, at the core of Dewey's thinking lies a politicized conception of individuality as a social product that emphasizes the interdependence of politics with socioeconomic factors. Individuality, for Dewey, is the result of an ongoing social development process, a development that occurs because we are involved in many social interdependencies. According to Dewey, "Individuality, like community, is a process of growth. It is self-realization, the continuous development of one's potentialities" (1998b, vol. 11, 44). And this social conception of individualism leads Dewey to defend a very particular conception of freedom: "Freedom conceived as power to act in accord to choice depends upon positive and constructive changes in social arrangements" (1998a, vol. 3, 100–101).

Sen's conception of development as freedom is consistent with the Deweyian tradition as well as similar to Dewey's concern with the relationship between "our wealth and our ability to live as we would like" (Sen 1999, 13). Most importantly, Sen emphasizes a view of participation and public scrutiny in accord with Dewey's experiential philosophy. As the world changes, so do our values, and our opinions of institutions and cultural systems from the past. The task of the pragmatist philosopher is never finished, and it is historical, yet its consequences ought to be thrown into the public arena in an open-ended process of debate and deliberation.

These similarities make Dewey's and Sen's views of freedom very close—freedom as the ability to choose our own life. Sen, like Dewey, emphasizes the role of politics as well as of ethics in the assessment of the good life, and the need to bring to light the empirical connections among the social, economic, political, and ethical. Sen offers a view of development based on both the intrinsic and the consequential value of different freedoms, as well as on the constructive role these freedoms play in the genesis of values and priorities in development decisions. Although Sen accepts that freedom is an end in itself, he cannot defend moral absolutes. Sen would probably agree with Dewey that people cannot really know all their capabilities—least of all how they want to live their lives—before they have full political liberties. But achieving those political liberties, according to Sen, depends on a wide variety of conditions and opportunities. Development as freedom has to leave conceptions of the good life open-ended and exposed to a continuous process of democratic inquiry. After all, Sen, like Dewey and John Rawls, would accept the claim that moral theory may sometimes require revision on the basis of empirically received facts that help us understand the demands of morality. In order to be consistent, the capability approach needs to see lists of capabilities as drafts in progress and place most of its normative emphasis, as Crocker rightly identifies, on participatory deliberation (Crocker 2005).

The pragmatist stance of the notion "capability" has helped in its acceptance as the theoretical basis for human development as part of the twin boundary object human development-capability (HD-CA) that functions within the UNDP. What seems to have made the difference is the ways in which certain values are imbued in HD-CA. Intellectual boundary objects that have their philo-sophical underpinnings explicitly elaborated with embodied ethical principles and that take ethical views as their point of departure have proven to be, at least partly, driving forces toward alternative policymaking.[12] This boundary object has demonstrated that an "idea" is able to force the institution to develop and use it toward more democratic knowledge production.

Arguably, this represents the substitution of cognitive values by moral values. Indeed, boundary objects with embodied ethical concerns better survive trade-offs with cognitive values and power pressures. They are also more able to lead institutions toward a learning process and to raise support from different stake-holders (thereby affecting the thresholds of legitimacy and credibility). They may also be able to represent the concerns and needs of nonexperts and vulnerable groups who may not be partners in the processes of knowledge production and policy formulation. But the intellectual boundary object HD-CA still lacks a serious assessment of the ways in which development agencies themselves support poverty-producing forces and are institutional mechanisms preventing the eradication of poverty. As it operates within UNDP, the idea still hides the role of inequalities and compares itself with past policies rather than attempting to create alternative paths of action and change. In particular, HD-CA compares itself to mainstream economics but leaves unanswered perhaps less politically correct questions such as the ways in which over-accumulation (of goods but also perhaps of capabilities) may lead to other people's dispossession, to paraphrase David Harvey (2003). A better intellectual boundary object would compare itself with counterfactuals based on global justice and not only with past or dominant knowledge and policy. Foreseeing the future use of ideas by global institutions, I have proposed that a well-designed boundary object ought to have embodied three main ethical principles: equity, accountability, and deliberative participa-tion (St. Clair 2004a). The embodiment of these three principles may act as a con-veying device, or as obligatory passing points, to place discussions about global justice at the core of debates about development. In other words, intellectual boundary objects embodied with these three ethical principles can act as incentives for better and more stable boundary management and for more salient, legitimate, and credible knowledge. Capability already has some of these norms imbued, clearly the norm of participatory deliberation (Alkire 2002; Crocker 2005, 2006), perhaps less so the equity and accountability norms.

In short, I argue that Sen's capability approach is methodologically pragmatist. Sen's capability and freedom approach reminds us all of something very basic that neoliberals seem to have forgotten: that theoretical freedom is not the same as actual freedom for all. Yet capability theorists need more engagement with the consequences of such a view as well as with the ways in which it is being used and abused by global institutions. It may be important to investigate the degree to which in its intellectual boundary form the HD-CA is leading the whole theory toward too much political correctness by not challenging too frontally the established norms and goals of the UNDP and the development aid bureaucracies in general. Although I cannot address this issue here, it will be important to follow up on the ways in which there is an increasing tendency to relegate Martha Nussbaum's version of capability to second place in debates about human development simply because it lacks that element of correctness that Sen's version captures so well. As much as I favor the deliberation aspect imbued in Sen's version of capability, some issues may not be dealt with properly only by open deliberation, as Nussbaum's body of work rightly argues. As Alkire (2002) has illustrated very well, some notion of basic needs is still imbued within capability. Perhaps ideas that are easily transformed into boundary concepts are also vulnerable to loosing their teeth, to becoming softened versions of their intellectual content, leading the capabilities approach to display, as Gasper puts it, a "cautious" boldness.

The capability approach, in all its versions, could be improved by making much more explicit the ways in which it differs from neoliberal economics or other mainstream economic theories. It will be strengthened by clarifying the degree of acceptance of current capitalist globalization; and the ways in which it may be weakened by needing to be "economics," albeit with its philosophical underpinnings explicit. Finally, capability may be improved by more self-reflection regarding its position toward other disciplines besides philosophical ethics and mainstream economics. Not only are markets not the best way to allocate resources equitably, they may also be the cause of massive inequalities that prevent people's exercise of their political freedoms and lead to powerlessness.[13] These and other basic insights have had extensive treatment in sociology, anthropology, social psychology, and international political economy, and today are being addressed by critical globalization studies.[14]

Concluding Remarks

To conclude, a methodologically pragmatist development ethics may enable philosophers and nonphilosophers to ground each other's views, to enrich analysis and critiques of development, and to reach forward not only by envisioning better futures and attending to how to generate moral awareness for the poor and vulnerable, but also by engaging in formulating institutional changes that may make a difference in practice. Development ethics is already multidisciplinary, but the warning against moralism and against leading debates about the goodness or badness of development and globalization toward unfruitful meta-ethical and meta-theoretical discussions is indeed relevant.

If disembodied from policies and practices, there is a risk that ethics may lead to confusing rather than to clarifying policy debates, whether debates center on competing conceptions of the good, on competing moral categories (for example, capabilities or rights), or on competing economic theories (for example, social choice or behavioral economics). And given that the empirical, political, and normative elements of development debates are entangled, clarifying their moral dimensions may lead disputants to insist on an interpretation of the problems that conforms to their philosophical positions. To avoid falling into moralizing an already polarized debate thus precluding rather than helping political action, development ethics must be necessarily and explicitly both a moral and political philosophy and a hybrid of philosophy and social science, drawing from practitioners' knowledge and practices. Yet a pragmatic form of this dual strategy would remain agnostic with regard to the possibility of absolute moral and scientific knowledge. A pragmatist methodology would focus attention not only on a plurality of values but also on a plurality of possible epistemologies. It leads our attention toward coping with scientific uncertainty and value conflicts and toward unveiling and avoiding the politization of the moral worth of people, actions, and institutions. It is here where the overarching normative value of deep democracy is justified, yet many issues cannot be left to deliberation. The formulation of a methodologically pragmatist approach to development ethics offered here leads our attention toward disentangling false dichotomies such as, for example, the distinction between altruistic and self-interested behavior, or the distinction between knowledge and action and between poverty and development research by global institutions as separate realms of global politics. To the question of what comes first: facts, values, or practices, I wish to answer, "all of the above," as coming to grips with moral conflicts and the sorting of moral responsibilities lies on the interfaces of the three (Busch 2000). In short, a methodologically pragmatist development ethics needs to engage with processes of knowledge formation by global development institutions and to aim at democratizing those by unveiling, pointing, and clarifying value choices, conflicts, and value-laden concepts from the very early stages of knowledge production. Development is a public issue and not a matter to be left only to certain experts. Above all, it is important to retake the meaning of development, to investigate what has happened to it since the end of World War II, and to divest it from all the negative aspects it has accrued, all the bad habits sewn in by those who have tailored its meaning to goals that may not be the best for the common good.

As Dewey rightly argued, philosophy ought to be a critique of prejudices, a "kind of intellectual disrobing. We cannot permanently divest ourselves of the intellectual habits we take on and wear when we assimilate the culture of our own time and place. But intelligent furthering of culture demands that we take some of them off, that we inspect them critically to see what they are made of and what wearing them does to us" (1958, 36). Development ethics can contribute to the undressing and redressing of development debates and to attempts to influence those in power to put ethics first rather than prevent ethical debate. As stated at the opening quote, very similar arguments were offered by the pioneer of development ethics, Denis Goulet. In his landmark study *The Cruel Choice* (1971), he warned of the direct relations between moral awareness, technocratic development aid, and the foregoing of moral evaluation. Development is, as Goulet rightly and insightfully argued, a "cruel choice" plagued with value conflicts that deserve "public" attention and that affect us all, the developed and the developers, the experts and the lay people, the poor and the non-poor. As Gasper insightfully argues, Goulet "called for methodologically sophisticated ethical investigation and debate that are driven by experience, not primarily based in academic philosophy" (2006, 2). A methodologically pragmatist development ethics is an offspring of Goulet's life and work, and a path forward in this interdisciplinary space includes revisiting, updating, and expanding Goulet's insights in a way that it may influence the decisions of those who hold power.

NOTES

1. This chapter does not aim to present the field of development ethics, nor to outline authors and tasks of global ethics or global justice. The term "development ethics" emerged in the late 1950s and 1960s and was formulated as a field of knowledge by Denis Goulet. See a recent collection of papers written from the 1950s until his death (Goulet 2006). Gasper

(2006) offers a summary of the relevance of Goulet's work for current debates on development ethics and development aid. Crocker (1991, 2006), Gasper (1997a, 2004), and St. Clair (2006a) offer introductions to the field. For information on course syllabi and activities on development ethics see http://www.development-ethics.org/.

2. For example, the World Bank has a small department addressing value-related matters, in particular faith-based principles but including also the role of values in development (see Marshall and Keough 2004), and many value-related issues are slowly being taken up by the Bank's key publications, for example, *World Development Report, 2006: Equity and Development* (World Bank 2006). The Inter-American Development Bank has an Initiative on Social Capital, Ethics, and Development (see http://www.iadb.org/etica/index.cfm?language=En& parid=1).

3. For an updated bibliography on Sen's and Nussbaum's work and extensive information on authors, approaches, and courses on the capability approach see the Human Development and Capability Association (HDCA) Web site at http://www.capabilityapproach.com/.

4. See, for example, OHCHR (2005), Osmani (2005), Sen (2005), Sengupta, Negi, and Basu (2005), and Sengupta (2007).

5. Thomas Pogge (2002, 2007), Barry and Pogge (2005), and Follesdal and Pogge (2005) are the most well-known authors working on global justice. Among others, see also Simon Caney (2006), Barry Gills (2007), the special issue of *Journal of Global Ethics* 3, no. 2 (2007), and Commers, Vandekerckhove, and Verlinden (2008). I have addressed the relations between development ethics and global justice in St. Clair (2006c).

6. See, among others, Louise Amoore (2005), Atitlio Boron (2005), Jeremy Brecher (Brecher, Costello, and Smith 2000), Robin Cohen and Shirin Rai (2000), Donatella della Porta et al. (2006), Catherine Eschle and Bice Maiguascha (2005), Susan George (2004), Michael Hardt (2004), Michael Hardt and Antonio Negri (2000), Ray Kiely 2005, Marjorie Mayo (2005), David McNally (2002), and Amory Starr (2005).

7. My critique of economics applies only to neoliberal economics and to the presumption by many development experts that this is the single most important cognitive tool for framing and formulating development policy. Amartya Sen and many human development economists are aiming precisely to formulate alternative economics (as the subtitle of the *Journal of Human Development*, "A Multi-disciplinary Journal for People-Centered Development," states). Many authors are addressing very different types of economic science and the specific shortcomings of neoliberal economics. See, for example, the *Real-World Economics Review* (http://www.paecon.net/). See also, for example, the work of Paul Ekins, Nicholas Georgescu-Roegen, Peter Söderbaum, C. T. Kurien, and Herman Daly, or feminist economists such as Nancy Folbre or Irene van Staveren. For a fine and extensive discussion of values and economics see McCloskey (2006).

8. I cannot expand the notion of intellectual boundary objects in this chapter. I have elaborated it further in St. Clair (2006b), an extensive discussion can be found in St. Clair (2004a), and a working paper is currently under peer review. See also McNeill and St. Clair (2009). For a more general analysis of the role of ideas in the multilateral system see Boas and McNeill (2004).

9. Light distinguishes "methodological environmental pragmatism" from "historical environmental pragmatism," the latter usually indicating a process of extending the work of the traditional pragmatist figures such as Dewey, James, Peirce, etc. to environmental problems (see Light 2004).

10. Although I do not have space to address this in this chapter, I wish to point out that environmental pragmatism may gain much from engaging itself with the ways in which climatologists and environmental scientists in general interpret evidence, the social aspects of such knowledge, and the role played by global institutions responsible for formulating scientific knowledge.

11. The work of Pierre Bourdieu and more recently Mary Douglas are instances of well-known and thorough critiques of the notion that economic science provides a true account of reality.

12. See Gasper (2005) for a discussion on the notion of human security using this framework.

13. If I understand it correctly, this is exactly the main argument of Thomas Pogge in arguing that severe poverty is, de facto, a violation of the liberty rights that can be traced to an unfair system of global economic relations (past and present).

14. See, for example, Appelbaum and Robinson (2005) and Gills (2005).

REFERENCES

Alkire, S. 2002. *Valuing Freedoms: Sen's Capability Approach and Poverty Reduction*. Oxford: Oxford University Press.

Amoore, L., ed. 2005. The *Global Resistance Reader*. London: Routledge.

Appelbaum, R., and W. Robinson, eds. 2005. *Critical Globalization Studies*. London: Routledge.

Barry, B., and T. Pogge. 2005. *Global Institutions and Responsibilities: Achieving Global Justice*. Metaphilosophy Series in Philosophy. London: Blackwell.

Bauman, Z. 2000. *Liquid Modernity*. London: Polity Press.

———. 2004. *Wasted Lives: Modernity and Its Outcasts*. London: Polity Press.

Boas, M., and D. McNeill. 2004. *Global Institutions and Development: Framing the World*. London: Routledge.

Boron, A. 2005. *Empire and Imperialism: A Critical Reading of Michael Hardt and Antonio Negri*. London: Zed Books.

Brecher, J., T. Costello, and B. Smith. 2000. *Globalization from Below: The Power of Solidarity*. Boston: South End.

Busch, L. 2000. *The Eclipse of Morality: Science, State, and the Market*. New York: Aldine de Gruyter.

Caney, S. 2006. *Justice Beyond Borders: A Global Political Theory*. Oxford: Oxford University Press.

Cohen, R., and S. Rai, eds. 2000. *Global Social Movements*. London: Athlone.

Commers, M. R., W. Vandekerckhove, and A. Verlinden, eds. 2008. *Ethics in an Era of Globalization*. Aldershot, UK: Ashgate.

Crocker, D. 1991. Toward Development Ethics. *World Development* 19 (5): 457–83.

———. 2005. Deliberative Participation: The Capabilities Approach and Deliberative Democracy. http://www.publicpolicy.umd.edu/faculty/crocker/Deliberative%20Participation5 -5-04.pdf.

———. 2006. Development Ethics, Globalization, and Stiglitz. In *Globalization, Development, and Democracy: Philosophical Perspectives*, ed. M. Krausz and D. Chatterjee, 122–37. Lanham, Md.: Rowman and Littlefield.

Della Porta, D., Massimiliano Andretta, Lorenzo Mosca, and Herbert Reiter. 2006. *Globalisation from Below: Transnational Activists and Protest Networks*. Minneapolis: University of Minnesota Press.

Dewey, J. 1958. *Experience and Nature*. New York: Dover. Quoted in J. P. Murphy, *Pragmatism: From Peirce to Davidson* (Boulder, Colo.: Westview, 1990), 70.

———. 1998a. *The Later Works, 1925–1953*. Vol. 3. Carbondale: Southern Illinois University Press. Quoted in Gregory F. Pappas, "Dewey's Ethics: Morality as Experience," in *Reading Dewey: Interpretations for a Postmodern Generation*, ed. L. Hickman, 100–101 (Bloomington: Indiana University Press).

———. 1998b. *The Later Works, 1925–1953*. Vol. 11. Carbondale: Southern Illinois University Press. Quoted in John Stuhr, "Dewey's Social and Political Philosophy," in *Reading*

Dewey: Interpretations for a Postmodern Generation, ed. L. Hickman, 82–99 (Bloomington: Indiana University Press, 1998).

Ellerman, D. 2005. Can the World Bank Be Fixed? *Post-Autistic Economics Review* 33 (September): 2–16. http://www.paecon.net/PAEReview/issue33/Ellerman33.htm.

Eschle, C., and B. Maiguascha. 2005. *Critical Theories, International Relations, and "the Anti-Globalisation Movement": The Politics of Global Resistance.* London: Routledge.

Follesdal, A., and T. Pogge. 2005. *Real World Justice: Grounds, Principles, Human Rights, and Social Institutions.* Studies in Global Justice. Berlin, Kluver: Springer Verlag.

Gasper, D. 1997a. Development Ethics—an Emergent Field? A Look at Scope and Structure with Special Reference to the Ethics of Aid. In *Ethics and Development: On Making Moral Choices in Development Cooperation,* ed. C. J. Hammelink, 281–302. Kampfen, the Netherlands: Kok.

———. 1997b. Sen's Capability Approach and Nussbaum's Capability Ethic. *Journal of International Development* 9 (2): 281–302.

———. 2004. *Ethics and Development: From Economism to Human Development.* Edinburgh: Edinburgh University Press.

———. 2005. Securing Humanity: Situating "Human Security" as a Concept and Discourse. *Journal of Human Development* 6 (2): 221–45.

———. 2006. Everything for Sale? Ethics of National and International Development. Special issue of *Ethics and Economics/La revue Éthique et économique* 4, no. 2. Selected papers from the 7th international conference of the International Development Ethics Association, Makerere University, July. http://ethics-economics.net/?lang=fr.

George, S. 2004. *Another World Is Possible, If . . .* London: Verso.

Gills, B. 2005. "Empire" Versus "Cosmopolis": The Clash of Globalizations. *Globalizations* 2 (1): 5–13.

———, ed. 2007. *Global Poverty or Global Justice.* London: Routledge.

Goulet, D. 1971. *The Cruel Choice: A New Concept in the Theory of Development.* New York: Macmillan.

———. 2006. *Development Ethics at Work.* Routledge Studies on Development Economics. London: Routledge.

Hardt, M. 2004. *Multitude.* Harmondsworth, UK: Penguin.

Hardt, M., and A. Negri. 2000. *Empire.* Cambridge: Harvard University Press.

Harvey, D. 2003. *The New Imperialism.* Oxford: Oxford University Press.

Hickman, L. 1998. *Essential Dewey: Pragmatism, Education, Democracy.* Bloomington: Indiana University Press.

Kiely, R. 2005. *The Clash of Globalisations: Neoliberalism, the Third Way, and Anti-globalisation.* Amsterdam: Brill.

Latour, B., and S. Woolgar, S. 1986. *Laboratory Life: The Construction of Scientific Facts.* 2nd ed. Princeton: Princeton University Press.

Light, A. 2002. Taking Environmental Ethics Public. In *Environmental Ethics: What Really Matters? What Really Works?,* ed. D. Schmidtz and E. Willott, 178–87. Oxford: Oxford University Press.

———. 2004. Methodological Pragmatism, Animal Welfare, and Hunting. In *Animal Pragmatism: Rethinking Human Non-human Relations,* ed. E. McKenna and A. Light, 119–39. Bloomington: Indiana University Press.

Light, A., and A. De-Shalit, eds. 2003. *Moral and Political Reasoning in Environmental Practice.* Cambridge: MIT Press.

Light, A., and E. Katz, eds. 1996. *Environmental Pragmatism.* Routledge, London.

Marshall, K., and L. Keough. 2004. *Mind, Heart, and Soul in the Fight Against Poverty.* Washington, D.C.: World Bank.

Mayo, M. 2005. Global *Citizens: Social Movements and the Challenge of Globalisation.* London: Zed Books.

McCloskey, D. N. 2006. *The Bourgeois Virtues: Ethics for an Age of Commerce.* Chicago: University of Chicago Press.

McNally, D. 2002. *Another World Is Possible: Globalization and Anti-capitalism.* Winnipeg: Arbeiter Ring.

McNeill, D., and A. L. St. Clair. 2006. Development Ethics and Human Rights as the Basis for Poverty Reduction: The Case of the World Bank. In *The World Bank and Governance: A Decade of Reform and Reaction,* ed. D. Stone and C. Wright. Routledge/Warwick Studies in Globalization. London: Routledge.

McNeill, D, and A. L. St. Clair. 2009. *Global Poverty, Ethics, and Human Rights: The Role of Multilateral Organisations.* London: Routledge

OHCHR (Office of the High Commissioner for Human Rights). 2005. *Guidelines for a Human Rights Approach to Poverty Reduction Strategies.* Geneva: OHCHR.

Osmani, S. R. 2005. Poverty and Human Rights: Building on the Capability Approach. *Journal of Human Development* 6 (2): 205–19.

Patomaki, H. 2006. Global Justice: A Democratic Perspective. *Globalizations* 3 (2): 99–120.

Pogge, T. 2002. *World Poverty and Human Rights: Cosmopolitan Responsibilities and Reforms.* London: Polity Press.

———. 2004. Assisting the Global Poor. In *The Ethics of Assistance: Morality and the Distant Needy,* ed. D. Chatterjee, 260–88. Cambridge: Cambridge University Press.

———, ed. 2007. *Freedom from Poverty as a Human Right: Who Owes What to the Very Poor?* Oxford: Oxford University Press.

Putnam, H. 1992. *Renewing Philosophy.* Cambridge: Harvard University Press.

Sen, A. K. 1999. *Development as Freedom.* New York: Knopf.

———. 2005. Human Rights and Capabilities. *Journal of Human Development* 6 (2): 151–66.

Sengupta, A. 2007. Poverty Eradication and Human Rights. In *Freedom from Poverty as a Human Right: Who Owes What to the Very Poor?* ed. T. Pogge, 323–44. Oxford: Oxford University Press.

Sengupta, A., A. Negi, and M. Basu. 2005. *Reflections on the Right to Development.* New Delhi: Sage.

Sfeir-Younis, A. 2003. Human Rights and Economic Development: Can They Be Reconciled? A View from the World Bank. In *World Bank, IMF, and Human Rights,* ed. W. van Genugten, P. Hunt, and S. Mathews. Nijmegen, the Netherlands: Wolf Legal.

Star, S. L., and J. R. Griesemer, 1989. Institutional Ecology, Translations, and Boundary Objects: Amateurs and Professionals in Berkeley's Museum of Vertebrate Zoology, 1907–39. *Social Studies of Science* 19 (3): 387–420.

Starr, A. 2005. *Global Revolt: A Guide to the Movements Against Globalization.* London: Zed Books.

St. Clair, A. L. 2004a. Poverty Conceptions in the United Nations Development Programme and the World Bank: Knowledge, Politics, and Ethics. PhD diss., University of Bergen, Norway.

———. 2004b. The Role of Ideas in the United Nations Development Programme. In *Global Institutions and Development: Framing the World,* ed. M. Boas and D. McNeill, 178–92. London: Routledge.

———. 2006a. Development Ethics: Open-Ended and Inclusive Reflections on Global Development. In *Poverty, Politics, and Development: Interdisciplinary Perspectives,* ed. D. Banik, 324–45. Bergen, the Netherlands: Fagbokforlaget.

———. 2006b. Global Poverty: The Co-production of Knowledge and Politics. *Global Social Policy* 6 (1): 57–78.

———. 2006c. Global Poverty: The Merging of Development Ethics and Global Justice. *Globalizations* 3 (2): 139–58.

———. 2006d. The World Bank as a Transnational Expertised Institution. *Global Governance* 12 (1): 77–95.

Stiglitz, J. 2001. Ethics, Economic Advice, and Economic Policy. Inter-American Development Bank Initiative on Ethics, Social Capital, and Development. http://74.125.77.132/search?q=cache:DgeA5HPBlyoJ:www.policyinnovations.org/ideas/policy_library/data/01216+Stiglitz.+Ethics,+Economic+Advice,+and+Economic+Policy.&cd=1&hl=no&ct=clnk&gl=no.

———. 2002. *Globalization and Its Discontents.* New York: Norton.

Thompson, P. 1996. Pragmatism and Policy: The Case of Water. In *Environmental Pragmatism,* ed. A. Light and E. Katz, 187–208. London: Routledge.

Turner, S. 2003. *Liberal Democracy 3.0: Civil Society in an Age of Experts.* London: Sage.

UNDP. 1990–2007. *Human Development Reports.* New York: Oxford University Press.

United Nations Office of the High Commissioner of Human Rights (OHCHR). 2004. *Human Rights and Poverty Reduction: A Conceptual Framework.* New York: United Nations.

Vandermoortele, J. 2002. Are We Really Reducing Global Poverty? Working Paper, United Nations Development Programme Bureau of Development Policy.

World Bank. 2006. *World Development Report, 2006: Equity and Development.* Oxford: Oxford University Press.

6

Social Development, Capabilities, and the Contradictions of (Capitalist) Development

Shelley Feldman

Despite the increasing numbers of sociologists, anthropologists, and women's studies specialists exploring questions related to development and change, including those now working in development institutions, it is curious that so few have contributed to discussions about capability—as approach, method, and evaluative tool (Gasper 2002).[1] Instead, ongoing debate is largely circumscribed by economics and philosophy, a fact that is hardly surprising given that Amartya Sen was the original architect of a capability approach, and both he and Martha Nussbaum are among its key proponents (Sen 1980, 1993; Nussbaum and Sen 1993).[2] Importantly, their contributions have generated sustained academic and policy dialogue extending well beyond their initial framings, focusing on questions of measurement, universalism, and the value of a list of central human capabilities or selection biases in identifying capabilities, deliberative democracy, and freedom. The character of discussion suggests the accepted centrality of the capability approach to some current analyses of development, equity, and gender and social justice. Its partial institutionalization in the formulation of a Human Development Index as a new development indicator also suggests its contemporary salience.

Not unexpectedly, after a period of relative silence about questions of poverty and development, particularly following the debates of the 1970s and their focus on the New International Economic Order and "basic needs," as well as what Gilbert Rist (1997, 205) would call "a toned-down form of IMF proscriptions to maintain the internal and external balance of high-debt countries in the language of structural adjustment with a human face," a discourse of human development based on the capability approach ignited a flurry of (re)thinking about poverty, its intranational and comparative configurations, and the pressure placed on multi- and bilateral aid-dependent recipient countries to meet new standards for development resources. The focus on human development and the theoretical contribution offered by the capability approach creatively connects academic theorizing with strategic policy and program intervention.[3] It also provides the basis for the shift from economic to human development with a commitment to expanding individual choices in ways that enable people to lead lives they value (UNDP 1990, 1997, 2000). Absent from most of these discussions of capability and human development, however, is attention to the concept of development itself, although within the human development framework development is viewed as "a process of enlarging human choices" (UNDP 1990, 10) or, as Sen argued earlier:

> the concept of development is . . . essential to economics in general. Economic problems do, of course, involve logistic issues, and a lot of it is undoubtedly "engineering" of one kind or another. On the other hand, the success of all this has to be judged ultimately in terms of what it does to the lives of human beings. The enhancement of living conditions must clearly be an essential—if not the essential—object of the entire economic exercise and that enhancement is an integral part of the concept of development. . . . The concept of development—whether explicitly put forward or discussed by implication—has to be examined in this broad perspective related to economics in general, rather than only in terms of "development economics" narrowly defined. (1988, 11)[4]

Sen then differentiates the indicators useful for understanding development, highlighting the difference between growth and distribution or market and nonmarket means of well-being. As he concludes: "The assessment of development cannot be a matter only of quantification of the means of achievement. The concept of development has to take note of the actual achievements themselves" (1988, 15). Sen then cautions his readers: "One of the difficulties in adequately characterizing the concept of development arises from the essential role of evaluation in that concept. What is or is not regarded as a case of 'development' depends inescapably on the notion of what things are valuable to promote" (20). Adding this caveat, while clarifying, generates the plausible assumption that development is a state or status of being that can be referenced to a person, collectivity, or national entity. But, even recognizing these cautions associated with the possible meanings of development, the concept itself remains ambiguous.

Greater specificity is offered by other social science literature where (social) development is understood as "a process of planned social change designed to promote the well-being of the population as a whole in conjunction with a dynamic process of economic development" that is understood as progressive and universal (Midgley 1995). This definition shares the basic assumptions of Sen's approach but differs in its suggestion that development be understood as a process rather an endpoint or outcome, although its product too is the securing of well-being and (domestic) equity. Such a contemporary frame is remarkable in echoing U.S. president Harry Truman's inaugural observations: "We must embark on a bold new program for making the benefits of our scientific advances and industrial progress available for the improvement and growth of underdeveloped areas. . . . The old imperialism—exploitation for foreign profit—has no place in our plans. What we envisage is a program of development based on the concepts of democratic fair dealing" (quoted in Esteva 1992, 6).

The broad claims of development have been the focus of debate for the past four decades, but during the past decade development has come under attack by those who challenge its universal claims, its ahistoricity, and its persistent failure to alleviate poverty and global inequality. Postdevelopment thinkers (Ferguson 1994; Escobar 1995; Rahnema and Bawtree 1997; Rist 1997; Gupta 1998; Peet 1999) in particular have taken a strong stand against monism and teleology in the definition of development as only industrialization, economic growth, or social revolution. Despite this, development as practice, project, and goal continues to provide a seductive frame of reference. I situate Sen among those who recognize the historical failure of development but nonetheless are seduced by its promise (Feldman and Gellert 2006).

Recognizing the promise associated with development, the following discussion focuses on the adequacy of Midgley's definition for understanding capabilities and, perhaps more important, for devising interventions to realize the ability of people to be "all they can be." For example, there is little doubt that globalization represents both a new discursive framework for understanding development among and within nation-states, and a new set of practices and foci of intervention.[5] While debates about globalization continue, there is little disagreement that new social relations among peoples and states characterize development at the present juncture. Believers in hyperglobalization, for instance, argue for a withering of the control once held by nation-states, and see in globalization an increasing standardization of cultures and meanings.

In contrast, there are those who argue for significantly less dramatic change in the global political economy but tend to agree on the unprecedented intensity of global relations, new constraints on national autonomy, and recognition of the unevenness of the process. Moreover, there is increased recognition that various resistances, both within national formations and cross-nationally, will continue to shape the kinds of relations that characterize the global community. This is revealed clearly at economic forums such as the 1999 WTO Ministerial Conference in Seattle and the annual Davos World Economic Forums, and in the now annual World Social Forum gatherings, where efforts are organized to challenge the increasing control embedded in the International Monetary Fund, the World Trade Organization, and the World Bank. These countermovements, whether transnationally or locally organized, challenge the assumed autonomy of the nation-state with their rallying cry that "another world is possible."

If there is agreement on this changing face of the development context or in the kinds of autonomy now enjoyed by national states and bureaucratic authorities, then it is difficult to speak generally about the relationship between capabilities and social development because the environment for planned intervention or "engineering" is continually being constituted and reconstituted. As Feldman and Gellert (2006) suggest, even if the definition and goals of development were (universally) agreed on, their institutionalization within particular contexts likely would reflect diverse and complex products and processes.[6] Thus it is important to historicize the concept of development, what we refer to today as the triumph of neoliberalism, and to examine its relationship to what might be considered the (smaller) triumph of human capabilities. Are they constituted relationally, and if so how? To explore the relationship between capabilities and social development requires that we recognize the need to problematize and historicize development as an ongoing and changing social project. I therefore will use the present occasion to query the notion of development and its taken-for-grantedness in debates on capability and development.

To accomplish this task I examine two interrelated issues. First, I offer a brief, and therefore truncated, genealogy of capabilities and then summarize the various meanings of development, social development in particular. Second, I relate the neoliberal commitment to individualism to the salience of the capability framework in securing the premises of neoliberal reform. This section provides the basis for viewing the capability approach as instrumentalist rather than as an alternative to the neoliberal development project, mindful and appreciative, to be sure, of the great advance over economic indices alone that is offered by rethinking relations of inequality in the framework of capability, freedom, and deliberative democracy.

Certainly there is a significant body of research by economic and development sociologists that has been central to debates on human capital formation and the potential of export production, microcredit, and increases in women's education as means to reduce poverty and fertility. Participation in these activities is also viewed as a means to enhance women's bargaining power within the household and in the public sector through increased representation in political decision making. Much of this work is indebted to the contributions of Sen, not only for his role in rethinking famines, cooperative conflicts, and household bargaining, but also for identifying the determinants of the more than one million missing women, corresponding, to be sure, to his understanding of difference, entitlements, and justice (Sen 1990b). As Sen observes, inequality can yield a diagnosis of injustice only through some theory (or theories) of justice (1999, 260). This connection is evident when Sen argues that tolerance of gender inequality is closely related to notions of legitimacy and correctness, and to normative understandings of gender difference.

Demographers, too, are key contributors to discussions of poverty reduction rather than gender equity per se, as they illuminate relationships among women's education, fertility, migration, employment, children's education, and enhancements of women's bargaining power. Moreover, feminist discussions of the differential gender effects of globalization are central to analyses of gender inequality, particularly as they concern social capital formation, credit access, informal employment, and labor market segmentation (Elson 1991, 1992, 1999; Beneria and Feldman 1992; Rai 2002). The women in development, gender and development, and more recent empowerment literature speak directly to the differential and often contradictory consequences of development assistance for women and men (Feldman 1992; Miller and Razavi 1995; Jaquette and Summerfield 2006; Gunewardena and Kingsolver 2007).[7]

But I would like to situate my remarks here on the terrain of historical and comparative sociology and the meanings attendant to development as a social project. Such a focus will highlight the changing character of development interventions as they constitute the political and bureaucratic context in which the challenges posed by the capability approach are enacted. In so doing, I will outline how the commitment to a capability approach presumes a particular economic formation—a nation-state system characterized by uneven development within a global structure of capitalism. I will argue that the approach also presumes the end of history because it takes the liberal assumptions of economic change—modernization, development, and capitalism—as given rather than either open to contestation or an outcome of sustained negotiation over the direction and configuration of the economy. This should not be conflated with a critique of the strong reformist impulse in the capability approach as a means to measure development success or as a way to contest some of the structural effects of prior development initiatives.

Capabilities

In his 1979 Tanner Lecture on Human Values, Sen posed the critical connection between economics and moral philosophy, and recognized "the fundamental diversity of human beings [which] have very deep consequences [that affect] not merely the utilitarian conception of social good, but [also] the Rawlsian conception of equality" (1980, 202). The displacement of commodities and utility with functionings and capabilities was introduced in this work, as was Sen's recognition of "basic capability equality." Basic capability equality is built on a critical engagement with the claims of utilitarian equality, total utility equality, and Rawlsian equality. But Sen is clear: alone or in combination, these suggestive offerings have been insufficient as a framework for building equality. Instead, Sen offers a perspective whose core claim is that development should be evaluated in terms of "the expansion of the 'capabilities' of people to lead the kinds of lives they value—and have reason to value" (1999, 18), with its evaluative claims focused on people's functionings (i.e., their "doings and beings"), on substantive freedoms rather than utilities or primary goods. According to Sen, "Capability is thus a kind of freedom: the substantive freedom to achieve alternative functioning combinations (or, less formally put, the freedom to achieve various lifestyles)" (75).

As Sen outlines, "If the object is to concentrate on the individual's real opportunity to pursue her objectives . . . then account would have to be taken not only of the primary goods the persons respectively hold, but also of the relevant personal characteristics that govern the *conversion* of primary goods into the person's ability to promote her ends" (74). And, as he continues:

> While the combination of a person's functionings reflects her actual *achievements*, the capability set represents the *freedom* to achieve: the alternative functioning combinations from which this person can choose. . . . The evaluative focus of this "capability approach" can be either on the *realized* functioning (what a person is actually able to do) or on the *capability* set of alternatives she has (her real opportunities). The two give different types of information—the former about the things a person does and the latter about the things a person is substantively free to do. (75)

Alkire summarizes the distinction clearly: "We are really interested in what persons are actually able to do or be—that is, in their functionings—not in the pounds of rice they consume" (2005, 6). Goods, in other words, are relevant for the ways in which they allow people to achieve different "doings" or "beings," called functionings. The set of functionings available to a person represents her capability set, where capability is closely related to the idea of opportunity or advantage (Basu and Lopez-Calva 2010). As Sen summarizes it: "The 'capability perspective' involves concentration on freedoms to achieve in general and the capabilities to function in particular" (1995, 266). This perspective, whether in Martha Nussbaum's or Sen's framing, acknowledges a debt to Aristotle: "A good human life would not only require adequate functioning in terms of 'nutrition and growth,' a purely animal feature, but the possibility of exercising choice and practical reason" (Basu and Lopez-Calva 2010; see also Stewart and Deneulin 2002). But this "good human life" depends on providing conditions that facilitate people's ability to lead flourishing lives, as Sen is always sure to emphasize (Stewart and Deneulin 2002).

Basu and Lopez-Calva (2010)[8] note that the distinctiveness of Sen's capability approach is its discord with traditional welfare economics. Walsh (1995) confirms this: "It is important that the non-economist reader be alerted to the fact that Sen's analysis of inequality in terms of capabilities that we require for our most important functionings and the attainment of our goals, together with his critique of utilitarianism, constitute, in their full development in his works, a critique of the whole approach of orthodox economics to questions of human well-being, inequality, and the 'efficiency' or 'optimality' of economic societies" (558). Des Gasper suggestively remarks, borrowing perhaps from Dudley Seers,[9] that this represents the "dethroning [of] economic growth as the centerpiece" of development (2002, 430).

In addition to appreciating Sen's challenge to analyses of well-being that are limited to command over goods and services, Gasper also values Sen's distinction between achievement and freedom. As Sen himself acknowledges, "Primary goods are the *means* to the freedom to achieve, and cannot be taken as indicators of freedoms themselves" (1999, 264).[10] Sen's attention to questions of freedom—both positive freedom and negative freedom, agency freedom and well-being freedom—reveal a debt to Isaiah Berlin (1969), who differentiated freedom in the sense of not being prevented from doing something from the actual ability to do something (Sen 1990a; Crocker 1995, 183; Prendergast 2004), the latter point being central to creating the conditions that enable people to be all they can be. To highlight the value of freedom to Sen's understanding of capabilities, Basu and Lopez-Calva quote T. H. Green: "When we speak of freedom we do not mean merely freedom from restraint or compulsion. . . . When we speak of freedom as something to be so highly prized, we mean a positive power or capacity of doing or enjoying something worth doing or enjoying, and that, too, something that we do or enjoy in common with others" (Green 1900, 371, in Basu and Lopez-Calva 2010, 9). In outlining these definitional distinctions, Basu and Lopez-Calva concur with others who note that because the freedom of one person may depend on the preferences of another, capabilities may be difficult to deploy in evaluating social states or societies. Another difficulty with the capability approach is what Robeyns (2005) outlines as the problems attendant to the selection of capabilities for quality of life measurements. In a thoughtful survey of the approach,[11] she offers the following: the capability approach is a "normative framework for the evaluation and assessment of individual well-being and social arrangements, the design of policies, and proposals about social change in society." Framed within liberal theory, the approach "evaluates policies according to their impact on people's capabilities" and rejects theories that rely exclusively on utility and that exclude nonutility information from moral judgments. As she concludes, the capabilities framework has been institutionalized as a measure of progress and development and a guideline highlighting criteria for reducing poverty, increasing gender equity, and enabling a more just social environment (2005, 93–95).

Importantly, Robeyns also argues that the capability approach differs from instrumentalist approaches, including that of human capital, because rather than focusing on achieving particular outcomes, its goal is to enhance people's opportunities and choices. To realize this goal, both context and normative practices and expectations need to be included in assessment as well as planned intervention. Education is supported, for example, because educated women have been shown to reduce their fertility and increase their productive capacity, thereby enhancing their well-being, agency, and empowerment (Arends-Keunning and Amin 2001). According to the capability approach, these goals are part of a focus on creating conditions that provide people the ability "to lead lives they have reason to value and to enhance the substantive choices they have" (Sen 1997, 1959). Robeyns acknowledges, too, the benefit that declines in fertility offer women, including expanding opportunities beyond their roles as mothers. Thus the approach contributes to changing gender relations and enhancing women's participation choices.

Two points that distinguish the capability approach are especially worthy of comment. First, while human capital approaches indeed take a different relationship to the question of outcomes than do those focused on capabilities, human capital practitioners, too, explore the benefits of increases in education for reducing fertility and improving productive capacity. Yet human capital practitioners do not tie these outcomes, or investments, to enhancing women's substantive choices and opportunities. They neither open a space for deliberative practices that include women, nor do they identify constraints that inhibit realizing capabilities. The approaches are similar, however, in their focus on the individual as the measure of success, an important point to which I will return below.

Perhaps more significant for the current discussion, however, is the way in which the capability approach imagines social development. Practitioners of the capability approach, with their concern for normative choices and outcomes, for instance, may indeed challenge "local" norms in situations where women's employment is in conflict with the norms of purdah and women's public exclusion. But such reforms fail to challenge the broader neoliberal framework where such norms are instantiated. This has the effect of leaving neoliberal assumptions and normativity intact.[12]

By contrast, offering opportunities that depend, for example, on skills rather than literacy training, or on collective or cooperative rather than individual enterprise development, may contribute to securing work, building self-esteem, and enhancing women's bargaining power. It would also be more likely to challenge the mode and direction of the contemporary production paradigm, one that seeks to extend capitalist production relations and individual and autonomous responsibility into all aspects of social life. Moreover, attention to and investments in such alternative institutional arrangements might reignite debates on land reform or the role of multinational capital in transforming extant production regimes, and open up new choices for national planners and decision makers. Said differently, there may be households that can no longer engage in subsistence forms of production as an alternative to large-scale industrial agriculture but that may nonetheless desire to do so.

Yet new investments in agriculture may be discouraged if measures of development success and appropriate parameters of capabilities and functionings are delimited by the frame of neoliberalism. For example, in circumstances where agriculture is privatized and concentrated, there may be a concomitant erosion of the choices people can make and the kinds of investments that are valued. Thus, while the capability approach is indeed more sensitive to context than are human or social capital initiatives, a focus on "getting capabilities right" (as defined within a particular political formation) can elide debate about the constraints imposed by the political economy of market reform.[13] What one might conclude from this is that when the capability approach supports the education of people to enable them to better compete, as well as to seek opportunities and imagine choices and desires in an increasingly internationalized marketplace,[14] it takes the contemporary historical formation as given even as it seeks to reform some of its negative attributes.

This means that when comparing various approaches to development, it would be important to show how project and investment goals are constituted historically and imagined as appropriate to a particular, normative set of desired social relations and practices. Such an accounting would help to explain why goals that enhance opportunities for market participation as individual workers and as members of small families—characteristics of the modern bourgeois, neoliberal social formation—may be given priority over investments in collective or cooperative production relations. It would also help to identify a reformist impulse or limitations of these opportunities for the social whole; and finally, it would reveal such investments to be instrumental in realizing the goals of the dominant paradigm.

In a related vein, Robeyns (2005) responds to the charge that Sen's capability approach is individualistic by distinguishing between ontological and ethical individualism. She argues that ontological individualism is a claim about the nature of human beings that does not depend on contextual or institutional relations to constitute understanding of social life, since social life is merely the aggregation of individuals. Ethical individualism, in contrast, is a position consistent with approaches such as the capability approach since it accounts for the social embeddedness of the individual. Methodological individualism, too, recognizes that individuals are affected by their social worlds. But, as Weber (1968) reminds us, explanation resides in individual actions that are explained through reference to individual intentionality. In his preface to *Development and Freedom* (1999), Sen argues for the place of individual agency in development in this way: "The freedom of agency that we individually have is inescapably qualified and constrained by the social, political, and economic opportunities available to us. There is a deep complementarity between individual agency and social arrangements. It is important to give simultaneous recognition to the centrality of individual freedom and to the force of social influences on the extent and reach of individual freedom. To counter the problems that we face, we have to see individual freedom as a social commitment" (xii). For me, recognizing "deep complementarity" differs from relationality or constitutiveness. Thus I agree with Stewart and Deneulin's charge (2002), as well as that of Evans (2002), that Sen's approach is one based on methodological individualism, even as Sen rejects this in his response to Stewart and Deneulin: "Social influences can stifle the understanding of inequality and muffle the voice of protest. This is one reason why we have to celebrate political activism related to class-based resistance, or anti-racist struggles, or feminist challenges, as an integral part of the process of social justice. . . . Nothing can be more remote from method-ological individualism, with its reliance on detached and separated individuals" (Sen 2002, 81). Despite Sen's acknowledging the importance of collective action and resistance, and his claims of complementarity, on the question of ethical individualism in the capability approach, I agree with his critics and recognize that the debate has yet to be resolved (Evans 2002; Stewart and Deneulin 2002; Sen 2002; Prendergast 2004).

In fact, these epistemological concerns continue to be important for inter-preting the design of policies and programs for change, two areas where Robeyns calls for collaboration across the disciplines—sociology, anthropology, history, and gender and cultural studies—to more fully understand the importance of institutions, collectivities, and context in identifying policies and programs that can contribute to enabling people to be all they can be. Robeyns suggests that division of labor is appealing in terms of substantive expertise, but it is important to recognize that cross-disciplinary inquiry may not escape the problem since epistemological premises are readily shared among disciplines (2005). Thus the solution is not to be found in a call for interdisciplinary research but in sustained reflection on the question of the relationship between structure and agency.

As is evident from this brief discussion, I have taken Sen's template rather uncritically and avoided fully engaging the rich insights offered by Gasper (2002) and others (Robeyns 2005; Deneulin 2005) who question the theoretical status of the capability approach and identify limitations in the framework of what Gasper specifies as Sen's capability approach (as distinct from the capability approach). Outlining the approach, however, should be sufficient to appreciate the importance of continuing to refine the concept of capabilities and freedom in relation to a historicized understanding of development. It should also prove suf-ficient to address a key question before us today: what is the relationship between a capability approach and a "thick" understanding of development?

Social Development

To begin, it is worth recalling the meanings of development. According to the *Oxford English Dictionary*, development is the "gradual advancement through progressive stages, growth from within as in nations proceed in a course of Development, their later manifestations being potentially present in the earliest elements."[15] And, from the same entry, "the bringing out of the latent capa-bilities" of anything, or "the act or process of developing." A number of points are worth emphasizing here. One is that development is understood as a progressive and apparently natural process of change, the latent capabilities of change being present in historical evolution itself. Two, and crucially important for the discussion to follow, development is an act, an intervention, the bringing out of, or the act of developing. This framing puts human agency and relations of intervention centrally in the process of "doing" development as a social project and contextualizes and complicates human development as merely "the process of enlarging people's choices, by expanding human functionings and capabilities" (UNDP 2000, 17).

There is no doubt agreement on development as relations of intervention toward improvement, bringing modernity—in social relations, institutions, and political practices—to the not yet modern. This point is suggestively developed by Ferguson's (1994) identification of a "development industry" that was generated in response to the crises of both development theory and its practices.[16] Let me briefly elaborate this point in an effort to provide a more robust understanding of the concept of development in discussions of capabilities.

What is not included in the *OED*'s definition of development, however, is the role of intervention (contra Sen's use of the term engineering), or what might be called doing development from the outside in. Intervention, in other words, is "bringing to" what others are either dependent on or "should have." Development is, in short, a relation of power, even when recipients desire what is shared. Intervention or the practices of development include the extension of development aid and assistance to others, and its articulation and institutionalization in different sites. What remains largely unaccounted for in this definition is specification of the processes and relations that attend to development; that is, what is transformed or perhaps lost, as well as added, in the institutionalization of particular interventions. To be sure, the literature is replete with examples of agricultural transformation and relations of production in response to the transfer of technology and new farming practices, or the consequences of global culture on consumption and desire, but there is less attention to how the experience of loss relates to people's choices and assessments of economic and social security.[17]

In the current debate on the capability approach, as well, there is limited discussion of the context(s) of these relations and the unequal power that characterize relations of dependence. Yet understanding these contexts and relations of power is crucial for an adequate appreciation of the specificities of reception, and whether and how target groups are mobilized to participate and encouraged to engage in ways that increase their opportunities to realize the kinds of lives that they (should) value. This could be accomplished by modifying institutions and practices in ways that correspond to people's perceived needs, desires, and expectations, or, following debate and deliberation, may be constituted to correspond to people's actual needs, expectations, and desires. At the level of the collective, ignoring the role that power relations and relations of dependence[18] play in assessments of achievements and capabilities can lead to a failure to understand the very constitution of state capacities, institutional and infrastructural resources, and political interests that are crucial for creating a context in which capabilities can be realized.

Attention to these aspects of the development project need not devolve into ideological or political debate, but instead ought to depend on taking into account the changing interests and conditions, such as institutional formations and forms of accumulation and consumption, that condition the choice of intervention and its reception. This suggests that even if one were able to clearly read off "interests" that include boosting production and exports or accessing new markets, "it remains impossible to simply read off actual events from these known interests as if the one were simply an effect of the other" (Ferguson 1994, 16).[19]

Likewise, it would be insufficient to claim that such interests are simply external to the task of creating institutions, providing resources, and changing conditions in ways that may "enable people to be all they can be and do." Said differently, general statements about interests (of agencies, states, elites, and other constituencies or actors) are as problematic as are general calls for constitutional and institutional reform, since the latter also must account for the particular contexts in which such reforms are likely to be incorporated and adopted. If these actions are to help transform capacity and accountability in aid-recipient countries, then Sen's attention to democratic deliberation (even if underspecified) is crucial for its realization, as is attention to the historically specific institutional and cultural relations that shape the complex meanings of a given social reform.

Interestingly, the *OED* definition of development neither marks conjunctural moments of transition in the process of "gradual advancement" nor identifies periods of contestation, such as when the latent potential of a given moment is inhibited from emerging by externalities. This might appear, for example, when a country faces limitations on its autonomy (as in response to aid or debt dependence) in ways that elide historical antecedents and thus constrain choice or opportunity. Nor do such definitions of development (within particular countries) account for transformations that may accompany global shocks or crises, such as the oil crisis of 1973 or the 1989 collapse of the Soviet Union. Yet development as a social project needs to account for how these "supranational" constraints shape functionings and capabilities and, consequently, the capability approach. Such an accounting requires recognition of the historically specific interventions that facilitate and structure the institutional and social relations that constitute the current neoliberal development paradigm.[20] It also requires that we differentiate among development interventions (and their different meanings) because different constellations of power—to set a global agenda and encourage others to accept it—establish not only the context but also the conditions for the kinds of interventions that are assumed to promote development and realize gender equity and freedom.

The Neoliberal Moment

Neoliberalism is a political and economic project whose policies, beginning in the 1970s and gaining prominence since 1980 under Margaret Thatcher and Ronald Reagan, have altered relations between states and citizens. With an emphasis on market competition and the dismantling of the national regulation of economic life in favor of market governance, neoliberalism is associated with altering the character of state regulation, advocating free enterprise in competitive global markets, facilitating the movement of goods and capital unburdened by tariffs and regulations, and promoting the central value of individualism over collective action. In the discourse of globalization, neoliberalism is realized by internationalizing communication, trade, and economic organization in ways that increase the intensity and density of exchange when compared with earlier interstate relations, and is marked by expanding the role of international capital and transnational institutions in providing "economic" goods and services as well as extending new cultural practices.

Built on an ideology that upholds private property, individual rights, legal equality, freedom of choice, and democratic government, neoliberalism as a set of practices and assumptions also views collective structures—unions, socialist and populist movements and organizations, government intervention and regulation—as impediments to market logic. Its practitioners argue that achieving progress and social justice is best realized by furthering free market relations.[21] The underlying premise of neoliberalism as an ideology is one that provides the basis for competitive capitalism while valuing equality of opportunity and opposing ascriptive statuses that restrict individual choice and deny equal access to achieving satisfaction. This is both the context and the challenge within and against which the capability approach is offered. Thus the demand for historical specificity does not challenge Sen's broad concept of development as "the enhancement of living conditions [as] an essential—if not the essential—object of the entire economic exercise" (1988, 11). Rather, it argues that the kinds of interventions offered and the strategies sought for their implementation—however democratically generated—need to be read against the specificities of neoliberalism for the ways it structures meanings and practices.

To be specific, we might presume, at least analytically, that social development, as distinct from the concept of development, refers to that which is not economic—the social (welfare) and institutional sectors that provide the context of social life and individual choice. Most prominently, especially regarding the substantive focus of the capability approach, these sectors include education, health care, and nutrition—those dimensions of development that are the site of both economic policy failures and, consequently, dramatic changes for the poor and excluded.

Often the purview of social science research broadly defined, research on the social dimensions of development responds to mediating, and perhaps seeking to explain, the continued costs of poverty in the context of growth, as well as crises caused by the escalating scale of indebtedness as informal and not yet fully commoditized relations of production are brought more completely into the market. These concerns remain despite improvements on a number of critical social indicators—education levels have improved and fertility rates have declined, but housing and urban squalor, indebtedness, and under-employment remain high. It is in this context that the capability approach can alter how we imagine intervening to improve not only the outcomes of specific policy initiatives but also the means and values associated with them.

This leads to the question: what is the relationship between development as a field of inquiry and social development as a field of intervention? In a creative engagement with critiques of development (Escobar 1995; Ferguson 1994; Mitchell 1999, 2002), John Harriss explores the genealogy of the concept of social capital. He masterfully demonstrates that its transformation and incorporation into development practice "contributes to a hegemonic social science that systematically obscures power, class, and politics" (Harriss 2001, 2). Harriss argues that the robust view of social capital offered by James S. Coleman—a structure of relations among people able to facilitate exchange and build reciprocity and trust in ways that can reduce transaction costs through enhanced communication and information—was refashioned by Robert Putnam, who transformed the meaning of social solidarities into a technical measure of civic engagement and dislodged it as an instrument of power. As a technical measure, the concept lost its analytic robustness and now celebrates "the centrality of the market in development, and the fantasy of the 'free' or self-regulating market economy." As Harriss continues, "The policies of stabilization and adjustment give rise to the kinds of contradiction that are papered over by such weasel words that relegate a symptom—the lack of civic engagement—into a cause" (13). Interestingly, Putnam continues to be viewed as the "high priest" of social capital.

Like social capital, the concept of capabilities confronts challenges in that its analytic bite can be readily transformed in meaning if it becomes a technical tool of measurement that, as Harriss argues, can be used to "suit the interests of global capitalism [by representing] problems that are rooted in differences of power and in class relations as purely [perhaps primarily is a more appropriate word] technical matters that can be resolved outside the political arena" (2001, 3). As Mitchell (1999) reminds us in his analysis of the role of international aid in Egypt, aid and assistance decisions that fall outside of public debate or public scrutiny tend to exclude challenging extant class inequalities (for example, opening to debate land reform). Sen's emphasis on freedom and deliberative democracy as central aspects of the capability approach is extremely suggestive here, even as there remains a need for its further refinement. But to avoid the pitfalls of institutionalizing capabilities in ways that limit it to a technical assessment or measurement tool, it is crucial to remain attentive to the power and political interests that help to constitute its meanings and practices. It also is crucial to recognize the importance of Sen's call for attention to the relationship between capabilities and reform, especially as he elaborates this in his commitment to freedom and deliberation, and as central features of his project.

Conclusion

In this chapter I have argued that efforts to reduce poverty and enhance social and human rights operate within specific historical and social contexts that today are framed by the uneven development of states embedded within a globalized system of production and exchange. I have suggested that the historical status of contemporary state relations within a global complex is consequential not only for revealing patterns of international inequality but also of intranational inequality, and hence is consequential for the ways in which the capability approach can be realized as a strategic challenge to states. I also have suggested that the character of contemporary global and transnational relations contributes to shaping interventions, including development assistance and aid agreements as well as NGO program support and implementation. In other words, efforts to alter individual opportunities and outcomes are effected through state-sponsored initiatives as well as those of civil society, through production-enhancing efforts as well as governance, the latter including but not limited to anticorruption and accountability efforts. Evidence suggests that the contemporary global economy is characterized by increasing income inequality even as efforts at poverty reduction may have slightly reduced absolute poverty within particular contexts. Thus poverty remains an urgent and difficult problem, especially if its reduction is to include enhancing gender equity and human freedom.

Even though considerable discussion has addressed the strategic significance of different development interventions as means for reducing poverty, there has been a relative silence in discussions of capabilities about neoliberalism as a particular—rather than as a logical or inevitable—social form, and a product of economic and political choices that represent specific rather than general interests. Also, while there is debate over appropriate measures to assess crucial aspects and directions of growth and change, what remains largely uncontested within the capability approach is the assumption that development is a linear unfolding process of change toward improvement, rationality, and modernity, the cornerstones of the Enlightenment. Instead, a view of neoliberal reform can be productively engaged as a political project. Failing to do so ignores the particular character of current development practice, leaving the conditions and relations that contribute to its uneven articulation among states within the global economy underspecified, and contributing to the naturalization of the linear progression of change with neoliberalism as its current (and last?) stage.

NOTES

1. To be sure, political scientists, notably Ingrid Robeyns, social demographers (for example, Arends-Keunning and Amin, 2001), and those writing on education (Unterhalter, 2003) and health (Anand and Dolan, 2005) have engaged in debate with economists and philosophers, but, importantly, they do so on the terrain already established by economics and philosophy. See also the special issue of *Studies in Comparative International Development* 37, no. 2 (2002), for a different framing.

2. There is an enormous literature here in journals that include *Journal of Human Development* and special issues of *Feminist Economics, Journal of International Development, Studies in Comparative International Development*, and *Social Science and Medicine*; and, noted in a footnote in Robeyns (2005), four international conferences on the capability approach held since 2001 and the Human Development and Capability Association, launched in September 2004 (http://www.hd-ca.org/).

3. A recent theme exploring poverty focuses on social exclusion.

4. This is a debate between development economics and economics.

5. It is possible to view the globalization debate, within sociology and anthropology at least, as subsuming discussions of development and reframing the debate as one concerned with whether the neoliberal market economy is good for individual well-being, poverty reduction, or social sustainability, or, conversely, as a way to alleviate economic and social insecurity.

6. See Robeyns (2003) on the procedural aspects of constructing a list of CHC.

7. See Rosen (2002) for an analysis of a single industry and its global and contradictory effects on women.

8. Basu and Lopez-Calva (2010) summarize Sen's framework by emphasizing his understanding of the basis of a moral system as that "concerned not just with 'good things,' but with what these good things do to human beings." Second, "goods have an instrumental value in that they allow individuals to 'function,'" which "represents the *state* of a person, a set of things that she manages to do or to be in her life. The capabilities reflect the alternative combination of functionings that a person can achieve, from which the individual will choose one collection. . . . Well-being will be defined as the *quality* of a person's being, based on those functionings the person can indeed choose from" (18).

9. Noted in Stewart and Deneulin (2002, 62).

10. This view of freedom is linked to Sen's understanding of justice and his critique of utilitarianism as an efficiency-oriented approach that concentrates on promoting the maximum sum total of utilities, no matter how unequally that sum total may be distributed. Such an efficiency approach provides a limited basis for justice.

11. The argument made is that the capability approach is a growth industry with discussion and analyses dispersed across an array of journals and texts. Robeyns is clear, however, that there is need for cross-disciplinary work that includes sociology.

12. By employment I include all forms of waged and unwaged labor, but importantly, breaks with normativity are centered on "modern-sector work," and in this sense it supports the neoliberal project of individual autonomy and responsibility while securing a cheap labor force for global production.

13. Stewart and Deneulin make a similar point: "Sen tends to avoid political economy, which results in an apparent (and knowing Sen it can only be apparent) naiveté in his treatment of both democracy . . . and modern capitalism" (2002, 66).

14. I use the term international here to signal the ways in which the unemployment of educated youth within particular countries is often mediated by employment in the global labor market.

15. S. Lucas Secularia, 1862, in *OED* online 2005.

16. The industry includes support for graduate and professional programs to train students in development studies and related foci (for example, NGO management and participatory action research), as well as support for journals and forums to attend to the needs and desires of the development industry.

17. Some postcolonial literature begins to address this; see, for example, Nandy (1983).

18. This is important whether dependencies reflect intrastate, interstate, or other collective (for example, household) structures.

19. This reflects a critique of structural determinism even as one might claim the constitutive relation of structure and agency.

20. Esteva (1992) refers to development as an "incredibly powerful semantic constellation" that guides thought and behavior that is presently associated with growth, maturation, and expansion. See also Escobar (1995), Rist (1997), and Gupta (1998).

21. The current global economic crisis has revealed the limits of this approach.

REFERENCES

Alkire, S. 2005. Why the Capabilities Approach? *Journal of Human Development* 6 (1): 115–33.

Anand, P., and P. Dolan. 2005. Equity, Capabilities, and Health. *Social Science and Medicine* 60 (2): 219–22.

Arends-Keunning, M., and S. Amin. 2001. Women's Capabilities and the Right to Education in Bangladesh. *International Journal of Politics, Culture, and Society* 15 (1): 125–42.

Basu, K., and L. F. Lopez-Calva. 2010. Functionings and Capabilities. In *Handbook of Social Choice and Welfare*, ed. K. Arrow, A. Sen, and K. Suzumura. London: Elsevier, forthcoming.

Beneria, L., and S. Feldman, eds. 1992. *Unequal Burden: Economic Crises, Persistent Poverty, and Women's Work.* Boulder, Colo.: Westview.

Berlin, Isaiah. 1969. *Four Essays on Liberty.* Oxford: Oxford University Press.

Crocker, D. A. 1995. Foundations of Development Ethics. In *Women, Culture, and Development: A Study of Human Capabilities*, ed. M. C. Nussbaum and J. Glover, 153–98. Oxford: Clarendon Press.

Deneulin, S. 2005. Promoting Human Freedoms Under Conditions of Inequalities: A Procedural Framework. *Journal of Human Development* 6 (1): 75–92.

Elson, D. 1991. *Male Bias in the Development Process: An Overview.* New York: Manchester University Press.

———. 1992. Male Bias in Structural Adjustment. In *Women and Adjustment Policies in the Third World*, ed. H. Afshar and C. Dennis, 46–68. New York: St. Martin's.

———. 1999. Labour Markets as Gendered Institutions: Equality, Efficiency, and Empowerment Issues. *World Development* 27 (3): 611–27.

Escobar, A. 1995. *Encountering Development: The Making and Unmaking of the Third World.* Princeton: Princeton University Press.

Esteva, G. 1992. Development. In *The Development Dictionary*, ed. W. Sachs, 6–25. New York: Zed Books.

Evans, P. 2002. Collective Capabilities, Culture, and Amartya Sen's *Development as Freedom*. *Studies in Comparative International Development* 37 (2): 54–60.

Feldman, S. 1992. Crises, Poverty, and Gender Inequality: Current Themes and Issues. In *Unequal Burden: Economic Crises, Persistent Poverty, and Women's Work*, ed. L. Beneria and S. Feldman, 1–25. Boulder, Colo.: Westview.

Feldman, S., and P. Gellert. 2006. The Seductive Quality of Central Human Capabilities: Sociological Insights into Nussbaum and Sen's Disagreement. *Economy and Society* 35 (3): 423–52.

Ferguson, J. 1994. *The Anti-politics Machine: "Development," Depoliticization, and Bureaucratic Power in Lesotho.* Minneapolis: University of Minnesota Press.

Gasper, D. 2002. Is Sen's Capabilities Approach an Adequate Basis for Considering Human Development? *Review of Political Economy* 14 (4): 435–61.

Gunewardena, Nandini, and Ann E. Kingsolver. 2007. *The Gender of Globalization: Women Navigating Cultural and Economic Marginalities.* Santa Fe, N.Mex.: School for Advanced Research Press.

Gupta, A. 1998. *Postcolonial Developments.* Durham: Duke University Press.

Harriss, J. 2001. *Depoliticizing Development: The World Bank and Social Capital.* New Delhi: LeftWord Books.

Jaquette, Jane S., and Gale Summerfield. 2006. *Women and Gender Equity in Development Theory and Practice: Institutions, Resources, and Mobilization.* Durham: Duke University Press.

Midgley, J. 1995. *Social Development: The Developmental Perspective in Social Welfare*. London: Sage.

Miller, C., and S. Razavi. 1995. From WID to GAD: Conceptual Shifts in the Women and Development Discourse. *Contribution to the Fourth World Conference on Women*. Geneva: United Nations Research Institute for Social Development.

Mitchell, T. 1999. Dreamland: The Neoliberalism of Your Desires. *Middle East Report* 210 (Spring): 28–33. Special issue, "Reform or Reaction? Dilemmas of Economic Development in the Middle East."

———. 2002. *Rule of Experts*. Berkeley and Los Angeles: University of California Press.

Nandy, A. 1983. *The Intimate Enemy: Loss and Recovery of Self Under Colonialism*. New Delhi: Oxford University Press.

Nussbaum, M., and A. Sen, eds. 1993. *The Quality of Life*. New Delhi: Oxford University Press.

Peet, R., with E. Hartwick. 1999. *Theories of Development*. New York: Guilford.

Prendergast, R. 2004. Development and Freedom. *Journal of Economic Studies* 31 (1): 39–56.

Rahnema, M., and V. Bawtree, eds. 1997. *The Post-development Reader*. London: Zed Books.

Rai, S. M. 2002. *Gender and the Political Economy of Development: From Nationalism to Globalization*. London: Polity Press.

Rist, G. 1997. *The History of Development: From Western Origins to Global Faith*. New York: Zed Books.

Robeyns, I. 2003. Sen's Capabilities Approach and Gender Inequality: Selecting Relevant Capabilities. *Feminist Economics* 9 (2–3): 61–92.

———. 2005. The Capabilities Approach: A Theoretical Survey. *Journal of Human Development* 6 (1): 93–117.

Rosen, E. I. 2002. *Making Sweatshops: The Globalization of the U.S. Apparel Industry*. Berkeley and Los Angeles: University of California Press.

Sen, A. 1980. Equality of What? In *The Tanner Lectures on Human Values*, ed. S. M. McMurrin, 197–220. Cambridge: Cambridge University Press.

———. 1988. The Concept of Development. In *Handbook of Development Economics*, ed. H. Chenery and T. N. Srinivasan, 1:9–26. Amsterdam: Elsevier.

———. 1990a. Justice: Means Versus Freedoms. *Philosophy and Public Affairs* 19 (2): 111–21.

———. 1990b. More Than 100 Million Women Are Missing. *New York Review of Books*, December 20.

———. 1993. Capability and Well-Being. In *The Quality of Life*, ed. M. Nussbaum and A. Sen, 30–53. New Delhi: Oxford University Press.

———. 1995. Gender Inequality and Theories of Justice. In *Women, Culture, and Development: A Study of Human Capabilities*, ed. M. C. Nussbaum and J. Glover, 259–72. Oxford: Clarendon Press.

———. 1997. Editorial: Human Capital and Human Capability. *World Development* 25 (12): 1959–61.

———. 1999. *Development as Freedom*. New York: Anchor Books.

———. 2002. Response to Commentaries. *Studies in Comparative International Development* 37 (2): 78–86.

Stewart, F., and S. Deneulin. 2002. Amartya Sen's Contribution to Development Thinking. *Studies in Comparative International Development* 37 (2): 61–70.

UNDP. 1990. *Human Development Report, 1990: Concept and Measure of Human Development*. New York: Oxford University Press.

———. 1997. *Human Development Report, 1997: Human Development to Eradicate Poverty*. New York: Oxford University Press.

———. 2000. *Human Development Report, 2000: Human Rights and Human Development*. New York: Oxford University Press.

Unterhalter, E. 2003. The Capabilities Approach and Gendered Education: An Examination of South African Complexities. *Theory and Research in Education* 1 (1): 7–22.

Walsh, V. 1995. Amartya Sen on Inequality, Capabilities, and Needs. *Science and Society* 59 (4): 556–69.

Weber, M. 1968. *Economy and Society: An Outline of Interpretive Sociology.* New York: Bedminster Press.

7

The Struggle for Local Autonomy in a Multiethnic Society: Constructing Alternatives with Indigenous Epistemologies

David Barkin

Development on a human scale, solidarity economies, and collectivism are terms that characterize the highest aspirations of social scientists concerned with the impact of economic progress on human welfare. The present chapter contributes to the philosophical discussion on the capability approach, offering a deliberately contrasting vision of mainstream discussions. While most contributors to this volume are committed to the concept of "theory that can make a difference in practice," as the editors of this volume have insisted, and that "development should be about giving people more choices to realize those things that they believe make them human" (Esquith, in this volume), present-day institutions are being reshaped to thwart this process. Addressing the "development conundrum," we suggest that the fundamental obstacles to human development are related to the inability of individuals and, more significantly, their organizations, to empower themselves. If it is accepted that effective empowerment, both individual and collective, is difficult in today's world, then the absence of serious consideration of power relations in the capability approach explains why even successful distribution of the "goodies" essential for enhancing individual endowments has been unable to raise social

With the collaboration of Dr. Mario Alvizouri, research director, Hospital Civil Miguel Silva, Morelia, Michoacán; professor María de Lourdes Barón León, Centro Regional de Occidente–Universidad Autónoma Chapingo, Morelia, Michoacán; Ing. Carlos A Paillés Bouchez, Centro de Soporte Ecológico Bahias de Huatulco, Costa de Oaxaca; professor María Evelinda Santiago Jiménez, Instituto Tecnológico de Puebla. To contact the authors please write barkin@correo.xoc.uam.mx.

groups and their nations from the morass of globalized impoverishment. In this light, alternative strategies can only succeed if they directly confront the challenges of limiting communities' ability to control their human, natural, and material resources while also enabling them to define the limits of their efforts at self-government, specifying the spheres of local autonomy and contacts with national and international markets so as to avoid an inevitably self-destructive move toward autarchy.[1]

The focus on the moral complexities of development in a global political economy raised in this book forces us to examine critically both the forces that are shaping our institutions and the possibilities to carve out spaces in which people can exercise the freedoms that are the "means to other good things that people value and ought to value" (Esquith, in this volume) Although the capability approach demands that development economics transcend its traditional focus on the maximization of personal welfare, many analysts still do not recognize the importance of confronting both the structural impediments to the exercise of individual freedoms and the institutional mechanisms that systematically confiscate the labor and resources that people devote to production for the market.[2] By not challenging these mechanisms, the capability approach implicitly condones the transfer of these values—in their financial form—to the global centers of economic and political power. In doing so, it fails to stem, much less reverse, the accelerated process of polarization that characterizes today's global economy.

Although the liberal analysis does not countenance such behavior, it rejects the reality perceived by many thinkers in the "Global South" that the multiple processes of monopolization of production, unequal exchange, and proletarian subjugation are inherent features of the free market economy. Their assumption, like many capability approach advocates, is that individual empowerment and competition among atomistic actors, reinforced by official admonitions against the abuse of monopoly power, are adequate foils to the operation of powerful corporations and cartels. Nowhere in this discourse is there a presumption of the imperial exercise of power deliberately limiting the progress of nations, although there is a grudging realization that numerous social groups may find their particular conditions affected by the abuse of power or the exercise of market power by unethical corporations or political actors.

In today's world, the challenge is to move beyond the conflicts that oppress most of the world's population. Many peoples and social groups tied together in cross-cultural alliances have abandoned their efforts to eek out a slightly fairer share of the global pie, to search for institutional mechanisms for redistributive justice. The liberal struggle for distributive justice cannot respond to the essentialist struggle by grassroots groups for "true" justice: the recognition of their right to maintain their autonomy, for self-determination. These demands for self-government and collective self-realization are not defined for single actors, but rather for participants in collective adventures to maintain and advance their opportunities in the multiple planes of human existence.

In this light, the "development conundrum" is not one that can be resolved by simply raising savings rates or promoting local productive ventures; more accumulation has proved to be a treacherous motor for exacerbating inequalities and even disenfranchisement. Addressing the deficiencies in institutional arrangements to enhance human capabilities might seem a laudable strategy for economic progress, generating new capabilities—renewed forces—for overcoming the obstacles to individual achievement and therefore to social development. But this approach relegates the underlying dynamic of accumulation to a secondary role, as if the basic processes of the monopolistic exercise of power in the political area and the operation of markets can be tamed through the well-intentioned creation of institutions peopled by able public servants committed to promoting individual opportunities and enabling the free and equal interplay of social forces.

In place of the struggle to correct historical injustices and carve out "reserves" for nonmainstream activities, many marginal societies are moving to strengthen their traditional activities or forge new alternatives. Rather than always insisting on something new, they are improving on inherited knowledge and productive systems, consulting with sympathetic outsiders to incorporate the latest technological and scientific advances and train their own people to become able innovators and managers. They are cognizant of the need to develop the required knowledge and skills, creating new governance capacities consistent with the demands for negotiating with regional, national, and international institutions. This is no longer simply a struggle to critique the travesties by engaging in new forms of struggle and to resist the worst forms of exploitation characteristic of the existing order.

The responses of many of these societies and grassroots organizations are no longer limited to diverse forms of resistance in the face of increasing intensity of exploitation of people as workers and as guardians of their ecosystems. To understand this new dynamic, it is no longer sufficient to evaluate these developments as the rescue of cultural capital or adaptive management, as some anthropologists might have us analyze the process. Rather, many communities and grassroots organizations are increasingly and directly involved in the deliberate construction of new strategies for the integrated management of political, social, natural, and productive systems. Although these actors frequently involve "traditional" groups, they boldly propose constructing new societies, freed from the tethers of global political control and proletarian subjugation.

These proposals for creating viable alternative strategies require local control of geographic and political space. In the process, they find themselves confronting powerful military and political forces mobilized to defend the emerging globalized order of political and economic control and centralized accumulation. Powerful international armies of repression are engaging local and regional organizations, mobilized to propose and defend new alternatives, along with movements of national liberation. These strategies involve alliances among peoples searching for permissible new responses to the global forces of marginality and exclusion, and they involve the exercise of power on regional and local levels. Individual communities must build coalitions, and ethnic groups must align themselves with comrades from near and far. In contemporary Latin America, these developments are the order of the day.

Generally misunderstood in the United States, the turmoil and upheavals in national politics in Argentina, Bolivia, Brazil, Cuba, Ecuador, Uruguay, and Venezuela are not very distant from the somewhat more localized movements in these same countries and others (e.g., Mexico). These processes of conflict and accommodation are not all violent and certainly are inspiring new waves of political experimentation and innovation. To be effective, however, they must be accompanied by new processes to assure well-being and preserve diverse cultures and their environments, processes that are capable of confronting the serious attacks from institutions and political systems that will not suffer such impudence from subaltern cultures.

The following text is an attempt to present an analytical framework to introduce one facet of this response. The difficult process of integrating present-day epistemologies into traditional organizations and knowledge systems is generating innovative forms of collaboration and production, political consolidation and social collaboration. The experiences briefly mentioned in this chapter offer an attempt to explain why it is necessary to expand beyond the improvement of individual capabilities and the exercise of individual freedoms if societies are to liberate themselves from the globalized straightjackets imposed by international economic integration with its imperatives of "free" trade and markets. The approaches mentioned in the following pages do not deny the importance of individual improvement and self-betterment, nor do they suggest that individuals eschew public programs that offer to assure entitlements to community members. Rather, they suggest the primacy of collective determinations of the worth of their activities and the focus on collective entitlements, assuring the viability of collective processes for individual participation.

Toward a New Rurality

People attempt to develop in direct consonance with their environments and the natural pressures emanating from the ecosystems of which they are a part. This "animistic" formulation of society finds a complex intertwining of human society and culture that contrasts sharply with Judeo-Christian traditions, in which man was given dominion over the beasts, or, to relate to the images evoked by the ancient epic tale of Gilgamesh, man was embroiled in the primordial struggle between kingly civilization and the forests, the source of all evil and brutishness (see Sinclair 1991).

This struggle continues even more ferociously in our day, as "civilized" society imposes its desires on subjected peoples around the globe. Although these desires are no longer limited to taming the primeval forests and its primitive peoples, many still cherish the idea that technology can harness nature for the benefit of those who are knowledgeable enough to master the planetary forces that have historically limited the advance of humankind. This catechism of social control over nature dominates present-day discussions of the role of science and technology in the solution of social and economic problems, and underpins the wellspring of optimism that guides long-term planning to this day.

In this framework of social and technological superiority it is no wonder that "primitive" peoples still living in premodern societies are dismissed as irrelevant in the search for new solutions. Their collective traditions, which often accord great respect to ancestral memories and to elderly keepers of wisdom, are poor substitutes for the gargantuan budgets that can be mustered to collect information and specimens, systematize information, and generate new knowledge. Still, there is now grudging recognition of the importance of these primitives' ability to discover the myriad varieties of flora and fauna that still inhabit their lands, to identify their characteristics, and to unlock their secrets. Modern corporations are even realizing that this information and these secrets are valuable commodities for solving current-day problems or curing newly identified maladies; they have found that if they cannot steal this wisdom (as was the custom in past generations), then it may have to be purchased.

Many scientists now recognize that society has carefully cultivated the accumulation of knowledge of the natural world through the centuries. Scientists in ancient times developed interesting and innovative solutions to complex problems, sometimes guarding them as cherished treasures by encapsulating them in ceremonial cycles controlled by a local nobility, by burying them in magnificent public works, or by entrusting them to a priest-like caste. Later, such knowledge of natural forces and planetary beings was also appreciated by local communities worldwide, codified into religious and lay traditions that were passed on through the ages in sacred texts and by storytellers or keepers of "the word."

In recent times, anthropologists or ethnoscientists of varying specialties have collected this accumulation of vernacular knowledge. Some native practitioners have crossed the social lines, training themselves in Western traditions of scientific discovery and technological development to place their knowledge at the service of other societies. Others have crossed this cultural and political (and socioeconomic?) line only to return again to the comfortable folds of their communities, to inject elements of the "other" into traditional practices. This complex intertwining of cultures and knowledge systems has created concerns about humanity's ability to safeguard all the secrets of the past, as well as the varieties of species that have developed or been cultivated to attend to social and biological needs. These losses, these disappearances, may now threaten our continued existence as we find ourselves exposed to the fury of new plagues, viruses, and bacteria that exact a terrible price on afflicted peoples, or natural phenomena that wreak terrible damage in the natural environments on which we have come to depend.

Many scientists have reacted to these changes by insisting on the need to expand our horizons, to incorporate into our knowledge systems and social practices some of the insights inherited from these premodern sources. This academic work humbly acknowledges our inherited debt to these numerous traditions. A rich body of materials has accumulated to document different understandings about the functioning of the world and ways we might better attend to our own needs and those of the planet without compromising the integrity of either.[3]

In our work in Mexico, we find ourselves collaborating with members of rural communities who are struggling to escape from the dynamics of social and economic marginality.[4] Like their counterparts elsewhere in the world, many of these peoples are descendants of indigenous communities and peasantries who have been systematically impoverished during the process of modernization and international economic integration. During the more than half century since the United States inaugurated its first development program in 1947 (Point IV), the world has become more polarized and more people have been thrust into the columns of the poor even as some of the worst manifestations of poverty, such as low life expectancies and high infant mortality, have been reduced.

The Development Process

Existing models of development are creating poverty among the masses. This process undermines the viability of rural communities, with their rich social and cultural traditions that developed productive systems to assure their basic needs. In rural areas, people often abandon centuries-old traditions of eco-system maintenance because their search for employment forces them to migrate from their communities. Now there is evidence that if successful rural manage-ment strategies are able to assure better living conditions and higher incomes, the rural poor not only will care for the environment but also will undertake those tasks needed to protect their scarce natural resources (see n. 6).

Today's problems have their roots in settlement patterns created during the colonial period (sixteenth to the nineteenth centuries). As the invaders expro-priated the best lands, indigenous populations found themselves relegated to increasingly marginal ecosystems. These areas were frequently very different from their original places of settlement, and the natives were obliged to pay tribute to their conquerors, when they were not enslaved. These changes were not new, however, as commerce and war were common elements in even the most ancient of societies (Bagchi 2005; Wolf 1982). After independence, the indigenous groups continued to be pushed to increasingly inhospitable and fragile areas, just as colonization schemes transferred peasants to the tropical rain forests.

Rural communities in general and indigenous groups in particular con-tinue under increasing pressure. Their living conditions deteriorated as their production systems demanded more from the land; they produced crops for human consumption on their rain-fed lands, developed handicrafts and other artisan products, and raised animals and horticultural products, including hogs, chickens, fruits, and herbs, in their backyards. The most fortunate among them were able to protect their access to other natural resources, such as a lake or river for fishing and to meet their water needs, or a forest for wood and hunting. Over the decades, they accumulated a rich experience in managing these resources, developing sophisticated management systems that gradually were integrated into their customary practices. They continued trading activities among themselves and with others, maintaining and modifying their tradi-tions, adapting them to changing conditions, strengthening their communities and their identity, choosing to protect their most cherished values and practices in each historical moment.

This process is crucial because it incorporates innovation as a permanent part of social practice, a means to maintain and even reinforce tradition by enhancing customary practices with new materials and techniques that assure the continuity of social and productive processes. One recent example is the case of Purhe'pecha women who decorate cloth (unraveling the threads in attractive ways) to make *huanengos*, a traditional blouse open on the sides. They recently modified their techniques to produce blouses and dresses for visitors, because they noted the demand for their skills for decorating Western styles of clothing, without necessarily modifying the way they dress in their own communities.[5]

Nowadays, many indigenous groups are attempting to exert greater control over their natural resources as well as their economic and political life. The communities are acutely aware of the environmental damage that accompanies most development programs and the toll that these efforts impose on peoples and their ecosystems; for lack of alternatives, they find themselves acting as unwilling accomplices in a vicious circle of environmental degradation and immiserating production. As they acquire a greater capacity for self-governance, their social and political organizations have begun to develop strategies to support demands for more local autonomy and productive diversification. Constructing such alternative strategies involves the complex interplay of the traditional and the modern. On the one hand, the accumulated knowledge required to manage local ecosystems is fundamental to identifying the possibilities that available resources offer for addressing basic needs, while also searching for paths to productive diversification that will permit an advantageous interchange with people in other regions of the country or parts of the world. This latter process often requires alliances with other groups who have privileged access to markets and thereby can assure that the products will receive "fair trade" treatment when sold.

Our research program is designed to confront directly the challenges posed by an international economic system that limits opportunities for poorer social groups seeking to assert their capacity for self-governance. Our work is driven by a deliberate search for strategies that will enable the participants to resist the pressures of globalization by creating opportunities for local self-management and production. Increasingly, communities are becoming aware of the limitations of the prevailing economic model, which at best offers the possibility of proletarian employment or, in the majority of cases, informal marginality. The construction of alternative structures for governance, resource management, and production is an urgent task to which they are increasingly turning.

In this chapter we offer a number of examples in which university-based teams were able to identify ways in which they could interact with indigenous groups and other social organizations associated with these communities to help strengthen their collective projects. This experience is based on the idea that people codify their knowledge systems in such a way as to attempt to manage their environments as well as possible and to produce the goods they need for their own well-being.[6] In what follows, we offer examples of how we went about implementing these programs of collaboration, individual cases that illustrate a larger process.

Innovation to Maintain Tradition

For centuries, backyard animal husbandry has been a central element in a diversified strategy for community consolidation in peasant societies around the world. Transnational corporations have systematically undermined this strategy by imposing new technologies that make small-scale family units uncompetitive and unviable. Genetic selection has produced new breeds of poultry and hogs better suited to intensive feeding and factory-like conditions for reproduction and fattening. As a result, they have displaced the traditional breeds (criollos) that are often more efficient in processing household and small-farm waste streams but require more time before they can be marketed. In our search for strategies to promote sustainable regional resource management, we found that communities in the mountains of west-central Mexico were penalized when they fattened their hogs with local avocado waste (which inhibited the production of body fat on the animals), because the butchers in the region paid less for animals without a layer of fat.

A local doctor, one of the contributors to the work on which this chapter is based (Alvizouri), discovered that avocados actually lowered blood-serum cholesterol levels in people and used this finding to develop a treatment for arteriosclerosis. Our team used his experience to develop a diet to produce pork with a low fat content that could be sold at a higher price. By introducing small modifications in traditional diets for backyard animals, backyard hog raising is being encouraged as a complementary and profitable activity to strengthen the regional economy and, especially, the role of women as a new social force, since they are responsible for production in small-scale backyard activities. This project is the result of a systematic search for ways to improve the economy of an indigenous region by focusing on those aspects of the economy that are controlled by women and where productivity can be improved with relative ease.

To implement the project, the authors began working with an umbrella group that encompasses about 350 communities and more than half a million people in west-central Mexico who share a common ethnic heritage (Purhe'pecha, or Tarascan as they were called by the colonial invaders). The research team and the local communities agreed to use nonmarketable waste avocados to lower costs while creating a quality product (pork "lite") for which a premium price could be obtained. Traditional hog raising is still an important activity in local Purhe'pecha communities, and is being reintroduced in more acculturated villages. The initial effort to develop optimal diets for raising hogs with low cholesterol levels proved successful, and the enthusiasm for the new technology exceeded expectations. Now, approximately a decade later, it is clear that the approach has been accepted and the main obstacle to its full implementation will be the need for people from the region to supervise the quality of the diets and the conditions in which the pigs are raised in the backyard stalls.

In retrospect, the proposed innovation is proving relatively easy to implement because the design fit into the existing structure of village life and political organization. Although based on a declining activity (hog raising), the proposed change was clear to all participants, who understood the relationship between diet and animal nutrition. Its commercial logic was also compelling, especially within today's precarious rural economy. Because of the declining presence of men, who must seek work elsewhere, the project has struck a particularly responsive chord by focusing on an activity traditionally managed by women. Further, with growing awareness of the need to improve sanitary conditions as a result of improving channels of information and concern about health, the project also has created an opportunity to open a discussion of environmental issues (e.g., water quality and sewage treatment).

As the production of low-fat pork moved to the implementation stages, we observed a growing demand in other villages to participate in the new industry. From the perspective of sustainable resource management and popular participation, another attractive feature of the program is its limited scale: the volume of production is inherently limited by the supply of waste avocados. It would not be advisable or profitable to use commercial-grade fruit as fodder for the hogs. In this way the authors hope that the communities will avoid the health and environmental problems that are usually associated with large-scale hog raising elsewhere. There is now talk of building a small, certified butchering facility operated by the organization of Purhe'pecha communities, providing an opportunity to raise the quality of meat available in the region while producing the low-fat pork products for the specialized markets that they are developing.[7]

An interesting development emerging from the work on lite pork was the discovery that *verdolaga* (purslane in English) could be fed to hens to produce "enriched omega-3" eggs. Verdolaga was introduced by the Spanish conquistadores and spread widely as a weed in humid conditions. It was later incorporated into the colonial diet as an herb seasoned with a green chili sauce to accompany pork. It turns out, however, that verdolaga is very rich in omega-3 and can be readily incorporated into the diet of laying hens, displacing the fatty omega-6 from their eggs to produce a lower-cholesterol product.

This nutritional innovation in egg-production systems is part of a larger program to install wastewater treatment plants whose effluent would irrigate the plants and service the poultry. For indigenous and peasant groups searching for ways to diversify their economies and consolidate their social and political institutions, while contributing to improved environmental management, this program is a logical follow-up to the hog project in the central highlands. In this instance, the project does not propose to harness prior knowledge to produce enriched eggs, but rather to exploit a tradition of concern for the integrity of ecosystems to introduce a new activity that promises to produce eggs that can be sold at a premium, generating new sources of employment and income for peri-urban communities throughout the country.

These experiences offer a singular window on the development process. Rather than concentrating on individuals and their capacity to participate effectively in regional governance activities, the approach implemented here joins the search for more productive activities with strategies for increased collective capacities to implement programs for sustainable regional resource management. In the process, participants become active promoters of community programs that increase participation and strengthen the authority of local leaders to implement additional programs. The significant feature of this process is the relationship between individual initiatives and collective decision making that sanctions and integrates the activities into the collective strategy for regional progress.

Recuperating Territory, Rehabilitating Forests, Strengthening Traditional Societies

Indigenous societies, pushed into the mountains by successive waves of productive expansion by conquerors, now find themselves heirs to valuable resources in the headwaters of river basins, resources that are required for urban-industrial development throughout the world. One of the most notable aspects of the modernization crisis is the growing shortage of water, caused by demographic growth and the improper management and use of the resource in urban areas (especially for the production of goods and services). Heightened by industrial and domestic wastes callously dumped into local rivers and aquifers, leaving them unsuitable for social use, the shortages are exacerbated by deforestation and the expansion of ranching and agriculture. Many recent proposals for sustainable production are based on individual economic rationality and a liberal development discourse, advancing a "modern" development strategy in which corporations and governments alike do not go beyond a process of "greenwashing" productive proposals.[8] The sustainability discourse is frequently a camouflage for the capitalist rationale and is tinged with a large measure of biocolonialism, a strategy in which indigenous and peasant communities in regions of megadiversity do not participate except as ecological informants and as objects to be rescued. More recently, however, this strategy has also been an inspiration for alternative approaches, based on the local appropriation of these concepts by peoples conscious of the wealth of inherited knowledge that they can bring to bear to ameliorate environmental problems. These alternative discourses and perspectives have been cultivated mostly in the southern countries, in part by theorists, intellectuals, or practitioners working directly with peoples who express their demands in terms of territorial defense, alternative development, autonomy, sustainability, and self-sufficiency.[9] The more successful of these proposals are designed from the local point of view, where the inhabitants become the protagonists of the recovery and preservation of their resources.

The model implemented in our Mexican projects draws on a long history of struggle by different social groups and reflection by Southern thinkers who have promoted alternative approaches to sustainability. The basic tenets of this work are (1) the active participation of the local population in the design and implementation of program plans, generating a capacity for self-management and a recuperation of social institutions and cultural identity; and (2) the rational incorporation of the ecological diversity into a sound program that helps diversify the local economic base.[10] Thus sustainability itself is a complex set of ideas that is understood differently as people assimilate the lessons into their own individual ethos. These ideas emerge from a group of theoretical dicta, which are then translated into practice as each community or group of peoples invents and specifies its own rules for participating in regional strategy, processes that are themselves transformed in the daily practice of coexistence.

From this perspective, then, people—within their own cultures and in interaction with the larger society of which they are a part—constantly experiment with new proposals to strengthen their society and diversify their economy. As they integrate new activities, they design alternatives to avoid becoming economic refugees in the national and international urban centers. They also learn how to contribute to the development of their region without sacrificing their dignity, evaluating new activities as they develop new relationships between their own culture and the other, dominant one. This enables them to avoid joining the low-waged labor force[11]—a transitory opportunity concentrated in a few development poles—so that they can become protagonists of their own sustainable regional development. This vision, and the guarantees it offers, contributes to strengthening community institutions and permits members to avoid the extremes of poverty and ecological degradation that oppress so many. The conflicts between the practitioners and the dispossessed are also reduced, as outsiders are required to recognize that the locals have a prior claim to the territory.

The active participation of the indigenous and rural communities in the reconstruction and preservation of the ecosystems is vital, because history has placed them in the richest centers of biodiversity. Community members understand the cycles for reproduction and conservation, products of cultural development based on a lengthy process of social and ecological interaction. Where some or all of this understanding has been lost, many groups, sensitive to its importance, have demonstrated their willingness to learn about these facets of their lives. For this reason they often assume without compensation the role of "guardians of the forests," which they consider necessary to use their own ecosystems, frequently defined as "national lands" or protected areas. This is a far cry from the commoditization of environmental services that has become a policy derivative of official environmental pacts, like the Kyoto Protocol.

This example involves a proposal by a local NGO to collaborate with indigenous communities dispersed in the Sierra Madre del Sur (a mountain range on the southern Pacific coast of Oaxaca) to attack the accelerated process of deforestation produced by decades of "top-grading" (or creaming). A serious imbalance in the regional hydraulic system was discovered, the product not simply of a lower rate of recharge of the water table but also of excessive withdrawals resulting from new infrastructure installed for a mega-tourist resort being installed in the Bahias de Huatulco. The Centro de Soporte Ecológico proposed an environmental rehabilitation program in which participants would be invited to recover their lifestyles, reinforcing local institutions and diversifying the productive structure. It explicitly rejected the paternalistic and clientelist approach of government programs implemented in Mexico since the 1917 revolution. Instead, it proposed a new management model that incorporates all the stakeholders in the decision-making structure, including the communities themselves, the water users in Huatulco, and the financing agencies. The program was designed with three objectives in mind: (1) to reconstruct and conserve the region's basins and forests, (2) to use the ecosystems in a sustainable manner, and (3) to join the inhabitants of the coast of Oaxaca in their efforts to recover their dignity. The program provides training to implement clean technologies as well as to update traditional techniques as the communities attempt to deal with practical problems on a day-to-day basis. The "productive conservation" proposal involves using the by-products from forest maintenance efforts—branches cut off for pruning, and small trees cut for thinning the forests—rather than cutting the main growth, thus helping to reduce both the problems of people selling trees to the closest buyer and emigration from the region (Barkin and Paillés 2000, 2002).

The reforestation program was designed to diversify the rural economy by introducing alternative productive systems to raise incomes and strengthen local institutions, blending traditional knowledge systems for conservation with modern production techniques. By deliberately planting surplus trees that must be thinned out to allow for a healthy forest, wood is available to be worked into parts for "director" chairs, while branches gleaned from pruning are shaped into parts for tables, desks, and even baseball bats and decorative figures, generating new jobs and income and avoiding the sacrifice of the healthiest trees. The project is aimed at regenerating the forest, and with it, protecting endangered fauna, allowing some portion to be used in traditional settings for local consumption. It also stimulates local ecotourism businesses and allows the regeneration of the agricultural areas in the river basins, using deep-rooted grasses and legumes to improve the land's fertility.[12] If the Centro de Soporte Ecológico had not considered the enormous potential of traditional knowledge in ecosystem management, the project would have encountered greater resistance from the local communities, as is common in most projects designed by official development agencies in central offices.

Water Forever

The Mixtecan peoples are an impoverished group living in a desolate region in north-central Oaxaca and Puebla who have suffered environmental degradation as a result of centuries of overexploitation. Twenty-five years ago a group of university graduates from Mexico City proposed to collaborate with more than one hundred thousand people living in the region to implement an ecosystem rehabilitation program based primarily on water and land management techniques.[13] Since the program began, an ambitious series of projects focusing on the problem of water scarcity have improved conditions in the one-million-hectare region through a program firmly anchored in community mobilization and training. They identified three factors that have caused the water scarcity: population increase, inadequate management of natural resources in the region, and unequal access to water, most especially the overdrawing of water supplies by a small number of people imposing their will over the community through corrupt power structures.

It was clear that deforestation and surface erosion were the main problems to be attacked. Uncontrolled logging resulted from lumber needs for subsistence uses, including firewood and home construction, and more dramatically, illegal cutting for commercial sale. Various land management projects, including dikes, terraces, and dams, seemed to be indicated, but their cost was prohibitive. During local planning meetings it became clear that the community had not lost its rich inherited culture of water management. The discussions led to a proposal to undertake an ambitious program to rebuild areas where ravines and gullies had been carved out by centuries of erosion, and thereby to regenerate the severely damaged watershed. This regeneration process began in the higher reaches with reforestation using native species and small earthen works to slow down the surface water runoff, rebuild soil, retain topsoil that would otherwise be washed away, and increase water infiltration so that it could be channeled to other parts of the region and used for production. A wide variety of techniques were implemented so that people from all the communities could participate despite a lack of heavy equipment. Stone dams were raised to accumulate soil in new areas for cultivation, water holes were emplaced to permit more systematic development of small herds of animals, while cactuses were replanted for their fruits and water-retention qualities as well as to stabilize the terraces. The cumulative effect of the hundreds of these small efforts was to substantially increase the area of arable land under cultivation and to increase the volume of water available for agricultural production, for the animals, and for the communities.

The strategic method adopted by the participants and designers in this project is worthy of analysis in light of the debate around the capability approach framed in this book. During its long gestation period, this method has demonstrated its ability to promote local capabilities far beyond constructing public works and increasing the region's productive potential. The long-term vision and the emphasis on local capacity building for project implementation has transformed the organization into a sort of substitute local government agency with its own management structure, fleet of vehicles and heavy construction equipment, planning and engineering departments, and even a geographic information systems laboratory. By building a tight internal structure and developing constructive and participatory relationships with local political authorities, the group has come to act as a regional development agency with considerable influence in the local public works agenda while assuring the participation of communities in the program's execution.

Its influence derives, in large measure, from the continued participatory local decision-making and governance structure that is overseen by cooperatives in the more than one hundred communities involved in implementing the model. In the process, dozens of young people have been sent to regional technical training schools, received university degrees, and returned to work in local activities. In their search for productive ventures that might generate an ongoing source of employment and income, the group developed its own industrial processes for manufacturing nutritious snacks and other derivatives from amaranth, an ancient (pre-Columbian) grain whose cultivation had been prohibited by the colonial overlords. This experience further consolidated the reputation and capacity of the group to undertake other projects to strengthen local subsistence activities and promote productive diversification.

This experience is particularly illustrative of the approach offered in this analysis because it was designed to be implemented and maintained by the communities rather than by outside contractors. The limited resources available from outside were channeled directly into employment creation and human resource improvement programs; scheduling took into account the program of agricultural activities, thus reducing the pressures for off-season migration from the area. Using local materials and resources also increased its regional impact. Finally, the integration of the local understanding of water works and land management produced an exceptionally effective hydraulic system that is turning out to be reminiscent of the pre-Columbian irrigation works described by archaeologists and admired by the Spanish colonizers. Rather than an imposition by an outside development agency, the approach implemented in the Mixteca offers a way to reaffirm local cultures and consolidate community institutions, which are now extending themselves into the production of traditional and modern agroindustrial products for sale outside the region.

Similar community management projects are springing up throughout Mexico. Community forest management endeavors now encompass more than one-half the nation's wood resources, where local groups are developing their own production programs and complementing the protection programs with ecotourism, artisan production, water bottling, and the sale of environmental services. Most important, these programs exemplify how people are learning to appreciate the value of their inherited cultural traditions and enriching them with techniques and lessons from the current era.

Conclusion

There are numerous other areas in which traditional knowledge is being harnessed to protect communities and their ecosystems. Even in the metropolitan area of Mexico, several projects are taking advantage of local resources to reinforce local economies and political structures. A degraded forest is being rehabilitated as an ecotourism site and nature preserve where tens of thousands of visitors are treated to a unique set of hiking and biking trails and nature talks that inform and entertain; a trout nursery provides an opportunity for diners to select their own specimen for lunch while educating visitors about biological cycles. A pre-Columbian amphibian, the axolotl, has become a charismatic attraction for visitors to the "floating gardens" of Xochimilco, where one local community has abandoned the crass commercialism of the bawdy trips along the canals in favor of a more sedate tour for people attracted by the opportunity to understand how the complex ecosystem is maintained and managed to provide a variegated cornucopia of fruits, vegetables, and small animals that protect the environment and provide for the economic well-being of the people. This example has now been emulated in at least five other communities, and university research programs are reinforcing these local initiatives.

This anecdotal and quite selective recounting of a small selection of local development initiatives cannot do justice to the breadth of activities being undertaken by millions of Mexicans who have deliberately opted for local development strategies that place them on the margin of international economic integration. Rather than adopting the approach suggested by the capabilities framework, involving skill and institution-intensive programs of human resource development, their focus is on strengthening traditional governance organs—such as the communal assemblies, the councils of elders, and selected local officials—to promote production and conservation programs consistent with sustainable resource management strategies and responsive to local needs. In the process, they are also participating in and transforming market relations with the outside world, replacing the passive relationship with commercial intermediaries for active political and economic ties with the burgeoning markets of fair trade organizations and other "niche" marketers to assure privileged access to protect against the international mechanisms of unequal exchange. The communities are assuming the responsibilities generally abrogated by local governments, tasks that the official organs have proved incapable of realizing. In the process they are assuring rising standards of social services and increases in human capabilities that become mutually reinforcing as their value proves itself in the palpable improvements in production and ecosystem health that contribute to community and individual well-being. In this way they are turning the capability approach on its head: assuming the centrality of political and economic power as instruments to create the possibility of developing their capabilities to serve the needs of their peoples and the ecosystems on which they depend.

In our ongoing interactions with the communities, we have systematized this set of experiences into a formulation of a strategy for sustainable regional resource management that is being repeated throughout the country. This involves four basic management principles that encompass the need for moving beyond the confines of individual communities to acknowledge the crucial role of alliances within regions and ecosystems. These relationships are crucial to garner the political and social power required to defend these initiatives against the continual onslaught from political interests and economic groups bent on preventing these separatist movements from eroding centralized power and accumulating productive resources at the expense of international capital. The four basic principles of this strategy are:

Autonomy
Self-sufficiency
Productive diversification
Sustainable resource management

If there is one lesson that can be extracted from the Mexican experience in rescuing traditional knowledge, it is that for tradition to survive it must become a living process, a resource that is constantly renewed to assure its currency and value to those that depend on it for their survival as a people and as a culture. In Mexico, for these numerous groups now composing more than one-quarter of the population, indigenous epistemologies are truly a building block for constructing alternatives to globalization, thus turning into reality a slightly modified version of the slogan of today's marchers: many other worlds are possible.

NOTES

1. Since finishing this chapter, the significance of the concept of autonomy for the strategic approach suggested here has been highlighted by the work of a consortium coordinated by the Viennese Institute of Intercultural Research and Cooperation. Latautonomy (Multicultural Autonomies in Latin America: A Necessary Condition for Sustainable Development

in Latin America) was intended "to establish new social parameters for a convivial civil society through a research of the basic structures of the ongoing autonomy-processes in the indigenous societies of Latin America" (Latautonomy Web page, http://www.latautonomy.org/). See also various books coordinated by Leo Gabriel and Gilberto López y Rivas (e.g., Gabriel 2007; Gabriel and López y Rivas 2008).

2. The importance of this point is emphasized by scholars analyzing the centrality of the structural components required for "righting basic social inequities or correcting ecological imbalances [through] changes in social institutions and practices," as Marianne Hill (2007) so cogently phrased it. See also the special issue of *Maitreyee* 6 (October 2006), dealing with "power as an integral part of social analysis within the human development framework" (1), published by the Human Development and Capability Association.

3. A collection of analytical articles and case studies can be found in Frey (2000). Of course, the World Bank has also produced a considerable body of materials supporting this approach. One of the most prolific writers in this regard is Fikret Berkes; see his collections of essays on the subject or his analytical articles (e.g., Berkes, Colding, and Folke 2000; Berkes and Folke 1998). Another direction in which inquiry has proceeded is work on "post-normal" science developed in numerous texts, such as Funtowicz and Ravetz (1993), Ravetz (1996), and Ravetz and Funtowicz (1999).

4. Much of the analytical work on this approach is emerging under the rubric of "New Rurality." In contrast to its connotation in the orthodox circles of mainstream development organizations in the Organization for Economic Cooperation and Development countries and in the International Labor Organization—where descriptions of "pluriactivity" are used disparagingly to describe rural socioecosystems without a future—in Latin America we use the concept to analyze the creative tendencies of rural peoples to recuperate and reinvigorate waning traditions and debilitated institutions while innovating in the productive spheres. For an introduction to this approach, see Barkin (2000). A more recent formulation by Ploeg (2008) overcomes this dispute by renaming the phenomenon "the new peasantries."

5. Similarly, in another Purhe'pecha community, a women's artisan group has introduced a technological innovation to produce lead-free pottery in response to market demands while continuing to make the traditional styles that use the leaded glazes. More dramatic shifts accompanied the move toward certified organic coffee, a process that involved important changes in production techniques and management practices, allowing Mexican indigenous producers to command substantially higher prices for increasing volumes of coffee exports.

6. This approach is elaborated at greater length in Barkin (1998). A summary of Barkin's book can be found in Harris (2000).

7. For more information on this project, consult Barón and Barkin (2001).

8. For a critical evaluation of these proposals, see Escobar (1995), Leff (1998), and Utting (2002).

9. The experience in the communities on the Oaxaca coast reveals that indigenous people define their lives within a specific territory, but not one limited to the immediate surroundings of their homes. Their territory usually extends from the heights of the mountains to the seashore; that is, they require a space that includes a number of ecosystems for their sustenance and cultural integrity. For further reflection on this problem, see Toledo (2000) and Harris (2000). On a global scale the literature is abundant; for example, see Borrini-Feyerabend and colleagues (2004).

10. See Barabas and Bartolomé (1999), and Regino (1999). See also Barkin (1998), Toledo (2000), and Leff (1998).

11. A note on the role of wage labor in this strategy is in order. Although many members of the communities described in this chapter search for work in the capitalist firms and receive wages, including some who migrate abroad in search of higher incomes, the ability of the community to offer them a refuge, a place to return to where their livelihood and that of their

family is guaranteed, provides a measure of freedom that most workers do not have; the proletarian relationship, with its accompanying process of alienation, depends to a large extent on the lack of alternatives for people who must accept the wage-labor accord or face starvation.

12. The preferred grass is called "vetiver," selected for its ability to stabilize the soils (http://www.vetiver.org/). It can be combined with a very productive native legume (*Mucuna deeringiana*) to fix nitrogen in the soil (http://web.catie.ac.cr/informacion/rmip/rmip57/ht57-a.htm).

13. For a more detailed description of this and other local initiatives for water management in Mexico, see Barkin (2001). Raúl Hernández Garcíadiego and Gisela Herrerías Guerra direct the group responsible for this program, Alternativas y Procesos de Participación Social.

REFERENCES

Bagchi, Amiya Kumar. 2005. *Perilous Passage: Mankind and the Global Ascendancy of Capital.* Lanham, Md.: Rowman and Littlefield.

Barabas, Alicia, and Miguel Bartolomé. 1999. Los protagonistas de las alternativas autonómicas. In *Configuraciones étnicas en Oaxaca: Perspectivas etnográficas para las autonomías,* ed. A. Barabas and M. Bartolomé, 1:15–54. Mexico City: Instituto Nacional Indigenista, Instituto Nacional de Antropología e Historia.

Barkin, David. 1998. *Wealth, Poverty, and Sustainable Development.* Mexico City: Center for Ecology and Development. http://129.3.20.41/eps/dev/papers/0506/0506003.pdf.

———. 2000. Overcoming the Neoliberal Paradigm: Sustainable Popular Development. *Journal of Developing Societies* 16 (1): 163–80.

———, ed. 2001. *Innovaciones Mexicanas en el Manejo del Agua.* Mexico City: Universidad Autónoma Metropolitana.

Barkin, David, and Carlos Paillés. 2000. Water and Forests as Instruments for Sustainable Regional Development. *International Journal of Water* 1 (1): 71–79.

———. 2002. NGO-Community Collaboration for Ecotourism: A Strategy for Sustainable Regional Development in Oaxaca. *Current Issues in Tourism* 5 (3): 245–53.

Barón, Lourdes, and David Barkin. 2001. Innovations in Indigenous Production Systems to Maintain Tradition. In *Interactions Between Agroecosystems and Rural Human Community,* ed. Cornelia Flora, 211–19. Miami: CRC Press.

Berkes, Fikret, and Carl Folke. 1998. *Linking Social and Ecological Systems: Management Practices and Social Mechanisms for Building Resilience.* Cambridge: Cambridge University Press.

Berkes, Fikret, Johan Colding, and Carl Folke. 2000. Rediscovery of Traditional Ecological Knowledge as Adaptive Management. *Ecological Applications* 10 (5): 1251–62.

Borrini-Feyerabend, Grazia, Michel Pimbert, M. Taghi Farvar, Ashish Kothari, and Yves Renard. 2004. *Sharing Power: Learning by Doing in Co-management of Natural Resources Throughout the World.* Gland, Switzerland: International Union for Conservation of Nature.

Escobar, Arturo. 1995. *Encountering Development: The Making and Unmaking of the Third World.* Princeton: Princeton University Press.

Frey, Scott. 2000. *Environment and Society Reader.* Boston: Allyn and Bacon.

Funtowicz, Silvio, and Jerry Ravetz. 1993. Science for the Post-normal Age. *Futures* 25 (7): 739–55.

Gabriel, Leo, ed. 2007. *Latautonomy: Autonomies multiculturelles en Amérique Latine et ailleurs.* Paris: L'Harmattan.

Gabriel, Leo, and Gilberto López y Rivas, eds. 2008. *El Universo Autonómico: Propuesta para una nueva democracia.* Mexico: Plaza y Valdés.

Harris, Jonathan, ed. 2000. *Rethinking Sustainability: Power, Knowledge, and Institutions.* Ann Arbor: University of Michigan Press.

Hill, Marianne. 2007. Confronting Power Through Policy: On the Creation and Spread of Liberating Knowledge. *Journal of Human Development* 8 (2): 259–82.

Leff, Enrique. 1998. *Saber ambiental: Sustentablidad, racionalidad, complejidad, poder.* Mexico: Siglo XXI.

Ploeg, Jan Douwe van der. 2008. *The New Peasantries: Struggles for Autonomy and Sustainability in an Era of Empire and Globalization.* London: Earthscan.

Ravetz, Jerry. 1996. *Scientific Knowledge and Its Social Problems.* New Brunswick, N.J.: Transaction Books.

Ravetz, Jerry, and Silvio Funtowicz. 1999. Post-normal Science: An Insight Now Maturing. *Futures* 31 (7): 641–46.

Regino, Adelfo. 1999. *Los pueblos indígenas: Diversidad negada.* Mexico City: Ediciones Era.

Sinclair, Andrew. 1991. *The Naked Savage.* London: Sinclair-Stevenson.

Toledo, Victor Manuel. 2000. *La paz en Chiapas: Ecología, luchas indígenas y modernidad alternativa.* Mexico City: UNAM y Quinto Sol.

Utting, Peter. 2002. *The Greening of Business in the South: Rhetoric, Practice, and Prospects.* London: Zed Books.

Wolf, Eric. 1982. *Europe and the People Without History.* Berkeley and Los Angeles: University of California Press.

Capabilities, Consequentialism, and Critical Consciousness

Paul B. Thompson

In her contribution to this volume, Shelley Feldman draws from a number of authors who have commented on Amartya Sen's and Martha Nussbaum's capability approach, concluding that although their work has undeniably moderated some of the excesses associated with development theory and practice of years past, it still fails to challenge the neoliberal paradigm of thinking on the general nature and legitimacy of development, and by extension fails to challenge the unequal distribution of power inherent in the modern state system. David Barkin offers us a rich description of how local knowledge has been integrated with specific forms of technical expertise to create projects for human development in Mexico. By implication he suggests that there is a more effective ethic for involving marginalized and oppressed peoples in processes of development than the capability approach, one that might be summarized as "just do it." Both Feldman and Barkin bring a wealth of development experience to their comments on ethics and development.

I bring up these two provocative essays here not because I have experience or training in development theory or practice that I can counterpoise in this conversation. I have neither. Nor do I put myself forward as someone who wants or needs to be heard by development professionals, much less the intended beneficiaries of development activities, or even by interested bystanders and observers of the various intellectual debates on global inequality, sustainability, or distributive justice. I doubt seriously that what I have to say here will prove useful or even amusing to these audiences. My chapter is offered solely in the spirit of dialog across disciplinary traditions. My qualification is that I earned the doctor of philosophy degree in the discipline of philosophy, and that I have been gainfully employed in various university philosophy departments for the past twenty-five years. I do not make this disclaimer from false modesty, for I am not modest and I do not intend to speak falsely. Modesty, however, is part and parcel of what I want to convey. I will not say, as the German romantic poet Novalis said, that philosophy will bake no bread,[1] but Feldman and Barkin have each given us reason to doubt that the capability approach will do much baking.

Their criticisms, both explicit and implied, lead us to ask, "What questions was the capability approach intended to answer?" Feldman has reviewed some of the key questions for the literature of development theory, in which it was becoming clear by the mid-1980s that the paradigm of expanding markets for commoditized trade, as well as the policy injunction for governments and international institutions to remove policy-induced distortions for individuals to participate in these markets, were failing to address the main problems of the poor. These circumstances prompted questions at both the theoretical and policy levels. Theoretically, the capability approach broadens the scope of development economics by showing that satisfaction of preferences calls for much more than maximization of personal welfare, especially including circumstances and outcomes (such as positive freedom for individuals) for which advances in net social welfare are a wholly inadequate substitute. Sen showed that policy choice could be seen as a procedure for economizing the satisfaction of this broadened conception of preference, resulting in a practical reorientation of development toward policies that favor poverty alleviation and local empowerment. But Feldman, whose chapter might be retitled "Two Cheers for Capability," has also argued that the questions for which capability is an answer do not go nearly far enough, while Barkin has shown how very far it is possible to go with an ethic that is much more prosaic.

What did philosophers think that Sen was doing? In the 1970s, analytic ethics was preoccupied with a split between theorists such as R. M. Hare, J. J. C. Smart, and Richard Brandt, on the one hand, all of whom were advocating some form of utilitarian consequentialism; and opponents such as John Rawls, Robert Nozick, and Bernard Williams, all of whom found reasons to reject it. This is the milieu into which Sen inserted himself, and to those familiar with this field the capability approach seemed to be Sen's attempt at an ethical or political theory that would maintain the basic logical structure of consequentialism while resolving conceptual problems and addressing some disturbing results associated with utilitarianism.

Consequentialist ethical theories interpret moral justification or correctness as a function of the value associated with a state of affairs that is brought about as the causal consequence of action or policy. In the classical portrayal of policy analysis, laws, policies, and managerial activities can be characterized as options available to a decision maker. The consequences of selecting any given course of action can be modeled as a causal process. This is where economic science enters the picture. The question of which option to choose depends on the political orientation of the decision maker. This is where philosophy enters the picture.

Prior to Sen's work, the role of philosophy in policy analysis might have been caricatured as follows: A group of theorists committed to a utilitarian/consequentialist approach carried on a debate about the decision rule that should be applied to the predictions that economists make. Should it evaluate each choice on an action-by-action basis, or should it be applied to broad principles of policy guidance? How should it cope with analytic difficulties in aggregating the preferences of affected parties? Are there certain types of consequence that should be given greater weight, such as those relevant to basic needs? Another group of theorists tended to see policy choice largely in terms of the rationale that can be given for establishing and prioritizing rights and privileges. They believed that a rich characterization of the reasons a person might legitimately have for acting one way or another provided insight into this rationale, and thought that the welfare consequences of a given pattern of rights were, at best, of limited relevance. These theorists had their own debates about the relative importance of property rights and individual liberties as compared to social entitlements, dignity, and respect, but all these criteria accord considerably less weight to economic models.

Although there was plenty of disagreement within each of these opposing groups of theorists, the "top-level" philosophical debate between the groups was the one that had to be understood before one could make sense of anything else. It was a debate between utilitarian/consequentialist heirs of Jeremy Bentham and John Stuart Mill and the nonconsequentialist heirs of John Locke and Immanuel Kant. As described by Sen, utilitarianism fleshes out the basic structure of moral justification or policy choice by making a number of key postulates. First, utilitarianism is a form of consequentialism in which value is associated with outcomes through individual subjective preferences. Second, justification consists in economizing on the satisfaction of these preferences, or as the utilitarian maxim has it, doing the greatest good for the greatest number. Third, preference satisfaction is amenable to a procedure of sum ranking. Fourth, the states of affairs in question are specified wholly in terms of their impact on individual welfare or well-being, which is also taken to be the focus of an individual's subjective preferences (Sen 1987).

The capability approach maintains the first three of these postulates in broad outline, at least, while abandoning welfarism in favor of a substantially broadened notion of the outcome or consequence of actions and policy. In one sense, Sen's accomplishment was to drag economics back to the center of the philosophical debate (something that many economists were keen to avoid) by arguing that the philosophers' concerns penetrate into the economic modeling of consequences or outcomes. In another sense, Sen's accomplishment was to dislodge philosophy's confidence in its hegemony over the normative dimension by arguing that it was possible to incorporate many or possibly all of the concerns raised by nonconsequentialists into the economic models being used to predict the causal consequences of policy choice.

In large degree, the substantial philosophical literature on capabilities to which Feldman refers early in her chapter is still preoccupied with the aftermath of that 1970s debate. A symposium on Sen's work published in 2001 finds political philosopher Philip Petit defending Sen against his critics by arguing that Sen's notion of choice requires that preferences are actually effective in bringing about the desired state of affairs, a view that Petit believes brings Sen much more in line with traditionally nonconsequentialist notions of human freedom while maintaining the consequentialist orientations of the theory. In the same symposium, T. M. Scanlon argues that Sen's reform of consequentialism falls short of the mark, mainly because it is still a form of consequentialism and as such, the goodness associated with a state of affairs is the ultimate basis for assessing actions. In contrast, Scanlon argues that the reasons a particular agent has for accepting a moral principle must be considered, and that these reasons will reflect the particular standpoint and circumstances of the person in question. Sen's reply (2001) to these comments indicates that these philosophers have not simply misread his primary intentions.

I might well fulfill my hope of stimulating cross-disciplinary dialog by feigning shock and dismay at the way in which Feldman and Barkin overlook the debate over consequentialism and nonconsequentialism. This philosophical debate is arguably quite tightly connected to the view that economic growth is the sine qua non of development, and especially to the highly reductive versions of this view that the capability approach was intended to correct. As Sen argued in *On Ethics and Economics* (1987), economic theory, and especially welfare economics, of which development economics is a part, are descended from utilitarian moral theory and incorporate many of its presuppositions and assumptions.

Further, economics owes its ascendancy over the other social sciences in part to its ability to rationalize policy choice through comparing the consequences of policy alternatives. It is in virtue of its compatibility with consequentialism that economics has seemed particularly useful to policymakers, who can readily identify with a theoretical perspective that predicts outcomes from each of several policy options.

There is, however, another way to look at the tight connection between contemporary philosophy and contemporary economic theory, and that is the way suggested by Michel Foucault's work on Jeremy Bentham, the father of utilitarianism. In *Discipline and Punish* (1977), Foucault claims that Bentham's panopticon is an archetype for a complex of social institutions and technical infrastructure that configures power relations in the manner distinctive of modern society. The disciplinary practices that permeate modern society produce not only the knowledge model that integrates economics or philosophy as pursued in modern universities, but also the very form of subjectivity that is accepted by both consequentialist and nonconsequentialist ethical theorists alike. This subject acts in the world through the process of choice, by performing certain behaviors from among an extensive repertoire of possibilities on the basis of beliefs and values. Ethical justification for this subject is a matter of demonstrating the conformity of his or her conduct with rational belief (as determined by the scientific disciplines) and rational choice (as disciplined by philosophical argument). This is not to say that every element of choice is rationally determined, for some aspects of feeling or emotion may be wholly arbitrary. What is more, the aspects of the subject's personality open to flexible and nonuniform determination can be expanded further by attending to the historical and cultural dimensions of virtue and community as aspirational values. Yet it is still the choice-making subject who stands at the center of contemporary philosophical ethics as it continues to be practiced in the analytic tradition.

Regardless of whether Foucault hoped to loosen the knots that bind the subject to its discipline, such a loosening is certainly the project of Arturo Escobar in *Encountering Development* (1995). Escobar's hope is that deconstructing the discipline of development will free oppressed peoples from becoming its subjects. Liberated from this discipline, they might express themselves in ways that have little to do with subjects who express preferences through their production and consumption behavior, or who bear rights and exercise entitlements. They might build a small, certified butchering facility and raise low-fat pork, for example, simply because it is a natural extension of traditional practice, given changing conditions, and not as a choice that is subject to evaluation, justification, or disciplinary analysis by experts (see Barkin in this volume). In so doing, indigenous people escape not only the net of disciplinary philosophy and economics, in which the capability approach is entangled, but also the metatheory of Foucault and Escobar. Freed in this way, it seems they have escaped academic philosophy altogether. It is because I have great enthusiasm for their escape that I describe the message in this chapter as one of modesty and humility.

But development professionals may not want to escape academic philosophy so completely. Feldman's complaint that Sen fails to take up the question of power is reminiscent of a complaint that sociologist C. Wright Mills (1964) lodged against philosopher John Dewey in 1942. Dewey had advocated a reflective and self-critical account of political life in which members of any specific community engage in continuing efforts to bring their understanding of political loyalty into accord with ever more comprehensive, even metaphysical, interpretations of community, democracy, and justice. For Dewey, strategic political maneuverings were not central to this task (Flamm 2006). Mills felt that Dewey's pragmatic social philosophy amounted to a formula for rationalizing alienation and accommodation to the existing status quo. In its place he advocated a vision of participatory democracy, later taken up by the New Left, that sees politics as "the art of collectively creating an acceptable pattern of social relations" (Port Huron Statement 1962).

In recounting Mills's criticism of Dewey, Matthew Flamm (2006) writes that liberals who took up this vision have been left with an impoverished view of ethical and political ideals, one that compresses justice, democracy, and community into the single problem of articulating the conditions for political empowerment (26). Are we now to add "development" to this list? Social scientists who have taken up the task of empowerment deploy their analytic tools in skillful accounts of who wins and who loses under a given set of institutional arrangements, but they are unable to entertain the question of which power relations *should* prevail. Flamm endorses an observation made by James Miller to the effect that this reduces politics to a spectator sport (Miller 1994, 85).

I take it that Flamm and Miller are referring to the way that spectator sports encourage a form of boosterism that amounts to simply rooting for one side rather than another. In the present context, Barkin more than Feldman seems to fall prey to this tendency. Perhaps it is obvious that our sympathies should lie with the poor and dispossessed, and that we should cheer on those development projects capable of subverting the well-documented abilities that powerful people have to co-opt development efforts for their own benefit. Here I have two cheers for participatory development, not because I would ever root against it, or even less because I doubt that Barkin has correctly sided with the most worthy competitor, but because this way of politicizing development seems to leave little role for philosophical reflection and critique, for entertaining reasons *why* we should root for the poor and the dispossessed, much less what sort of broad conceptualization of ethical and political norms could underwrite the various political and economic development activities we clump under the heading of development.

For what it is worth, Dewey proffered his conceptions of community and democracy specifically in response to Walter Lippmann's suggestion that alienated individuals might be better off with experts making decisions on their behalf. As Cornell West has argued, Mills's attack on Dewey should be seen as a "creative misreading" of Dewey's central point (West 1989, 126). It is also worth noting that the 2001 paper by Petit cited above was defending the capability approach against critics who had worried that it might amount to a form of rationalization through the systematic creation of preferences that would be satisfied by the existing status quo. Despite the implicit rebuke that philosophizing receives from Feldman and Barkin, concern over existing power distributions is not wholly absent from the philosophical debate.

Regardless of whether grasping the subtleties of the distinction between consequentialist and nonconsequentialist ethical theory is a necessary condition for integrating philosophical ethics and development theory (and I am inclined to think that it is not), philosophers *are* engaged in an attempt to press beyond a simple articulation of values and their subsequent enforcement in the political realm. There are significant substantive and stylistic differences between philosophers such as Dewey and Foucault, on the one hand, and the analytic tradition in which the capability approach has been developed, on the other. Nevertheless, all these philosophers are trying to state and defend conceptualizations of politics, democracy, community, justice, and development in a discourse environment that is open to any similarly motivated critique. Doing so may require a small space for reflection, argument, or even aggressive give and take, and creating that space may require a respite from collectively creating an acceptable pattern of social relations.

I am not suggesting that Feldman or Barkin falls prey to the reductive caricature of liberal politics that I have sketched above, nor am I calling for any retreat from the empowerment of marginalized groups or engagement with indigenous epistemologies in development practice. The modesty with which I began is quite sincere. People in the thick of development work may quite justifiably feel impatient with my entire effort here. Yet if there is to be any productive engagement between the discipline of philosophy and the disciplines of development, philosophers must be permitted scope to explore their worries about questions such as whether a consequence-predicting model of ethical justification can ever hope to articulate the reasons we take a given notion of development to be adequate or inadequate, even if doing so doesn't bake any bread.

NOTE

1. Novalis was the pseudonym for Friedrich Leopold, Baron von Hardenberg (1772–1801), and the full aphorism, "Philosophy can bake no bread, but she can procure for us God, Freedom, and Immortality," is far less modest. See Carlyle (1904, 1–55).

REFERENCES

Carlyle, Thomas. 1904. Novalis (1829). In *Critical and Miscellaneous Essays in Five Volumes*, 2:1–56. New York: Charles Scribner's Sons.

Escobar, Arturo. 1995. *Encountering Development: The Making and Unmaking of the Third World.* Princeton: Princeton University Press.

Flamm, Matthew. 2006. The Demanding Community: Politicization of the Individual After Dewey. *Education and Culture* 22 (1): 35–54.

Foucault, Michel. 1977. *Discipline and Punish: The Birth of the Prison.* Trans. Alan Sheridan. New York: Pantheon.

Miller, James. 1994. *"Democracy Is in the Streets": From Port Huron to the Siege of Chicago.* Cambridge: Harvard University Press.

Mills, C. Wright. 1964. *Sociology and Pragmatism: The Higher Learning in America.* New York: Paine-Whitman.

Petit, Philip. 2001. Symposium on Amartya Sen's Philosophy: 1 Capability and Freedom: A Defense of Sen. *Economics and Philosophy* 17 (1): 1–20.

Port Huron Statement. 1962. http://coursesa.matrix.msu.edu/~hst306/documents/huron.html.

Scanlon, T. M. 2001. Symposium on Amartya Sen's Philosophy: 3 Sen and Consequentialism. *Economics and Philosophy* 17 (1): 39–50.

Sen, Amartya. 1987. *On Ethics and Economics.* Oxford: Basil Blackwell.

———. 2001. Symposium on Amartya Sen's Philosophy: 4 Reply. *Economics and Philosophy* 17 (1): 51–66.

West, Cornell. 1989. *The American Evasion of Philosophy.* Madison: University of Wisconsin Press.

Development and Globalization:
The Ethical Challenges
Nigel Dower

In this chapter I am going to trace the connections between development and globalization, along with the ethical issues raised, rejecting a simplistic "globalization as expansion of the global economy furthers development as growth" model. I will consider the issues under the headings of the globalization of production, the globalization of problems, the globalization of governance, the globalization of community, and the globalization of information. In the course of this exposition a normative conception of development is developed. In the second half, I look at a couple of ethical issues in more detail: first, the theoretical issue of whether the globalization of ethics captures the issues better than the ethics of globalization; and second, the normative issue of whether the key impediment for development for poor countries and the poor people within them is the international normative framework of global governance or the internal normative framework of development itself.

One simplistic model of the relationship is as follows: globalization is an economic process involving increased international investments and trade in goods and services. Development is a process of economic growth. Globalization is the engine of economic growth, so globalization is the engine of development. Since development is desirable for all countries, rich and poor, globalization is desirable and therefore ought to be promoted.

Another somewhat more complex model might be: globalization as described above (the growth of the global economy) may stimulate economic growth overall, but its benefits are not distributed equally or fairly, favoring rich countries and not poor ones, and favoring the better-off in poor countries and not the very poor, who are often trapped in poverty. Further, global economic growth comes generally at the expense of the environment and so does not contribute to sustainable development. So globalization fails to address (or actually exacerbates) extreme poverty and damages the environment, and is therefore a bad thing and to be opposed; hence, the rationale of the anti-globalization rallies of recent years.

Neither of these models is adequate, since both development and globalization are rather more complex ideas than suggested above. Their causal connections are more complex and hence the ethical issues involved are more nuanced. Certainly neither a blanket commendation nor a simple condemnation of globalization is in order.

Some Ethical Issues

Globalization needs first of all to be seen as a multidimensional process. The global economy, which is often thought of as the heart of globalization, is really only one important manifestation of global connectivity. This is more generally about an expansion of awareness, consciousness, or sense of relatedness of people (Spybey 1996). I shall consider issues under the headings of the globalization of production, problems, governance, community, information, and ethics, following and expanding J. A. Scholte's classification (2000).

Production

Clearly the expansion of the global economy is an important part of globalization. At one level it is just a fact, whether we like it or not, and it has various impacts on development. But at another level, normative issues are involved since this expansion is informed by certain normative assumptions that may be contested:

1. The value of the free market both in itself and as the engine of economic growth, both within countries and between countries, usually goes with the values of privatization and of reducing tariffs, subsidies, and protections— one of the chief goals of the World Trade Organization (WTO).
2. Development is an economic process of growth, which is good because growth enables people to have more economic liberty to make choices.

Critics will pick on the values feature of this. First, libertarian values on their own are inadequate both for development and for globalization. There must be side constraints of various kinds: (1) certain things need to be ruled out as unfair or unacceptable, particularly at the international level in terms of, for instance, labor standards or health and safety standards; (2) there needs to be progressive taxation for the provision of welfare, with analogous procedures in place at the global level whereby the wealth created in the global economy is shared to the benefit of the least well-off. These side constraints, though they are in place in varying degrees within many countries, are not generally in place at the global level.

Second, even libertarian values favoring measures such as the reduction of protectionism may be applied unfairly—for example, rich countries that insist on poor countries reducing their subsidies while they keep their own in place! The genuine conditions of a free market do not exist in many poor countries. For example, inequality of power with few or no trade unions in some countries leads to massive exploitation by multinationals.

Third, if development is thought of not merely as economic growth (even fairly distributed economic growth), then economic globalization may undermine other aspects of development—for example, the importance of traditional community and the diversities of culture. There are dangers of homogenization.

In short, economic globalization—unless it is seriously qualified in various ways—marginalizes the poor, destroys the environment, and damages cultures (see, for example, Sachs 1992). I shall return to this key issue in the last part of the chapter.

The challenge economic globalization faces is well put in the following remarks by Amartya Sen:

> The central issue of contention is not globalization itself, nor is it the use of the market as an institution, but the inequity in the overall balance of institutional arrangements—which provide very unequal sharing of the benefits of globalization. The question is not just whether the poor, too, gain something from globalization, but whether they get a fair share and fair opportunity. There is urgent need for reforming institutional arrangements—in addition to national ones—to overcome both the errors of omission and those of commission that tend to give the poor across the world such limited opportunities. Globalization deserves a reasoned defense, but it also needs reform. (2002, 14)

Problems

Many global problems are byproducts of the expansion of the global economy, but it is worth viewing them as a separate aspect of globalization because they cover a wide range—for example, pollution or resource shortages, global warming, expansion of global tourism, the spread of AIDS, and other health hazards facilitated by global transport, Internet fraud, and terrorism.

What is a problem? A problem arises when there is a gap between a current situation and a goal combined with a difficulty in achieving the goal, either because we do not know how to proceed or because, if we do, we meet obstacles to proceeding; a solution is either finding out how to proceed or finding ways of overcoming the obstacles—be these social, political, or motivational.

What makes a problem global? Something might be a global problem because of its *cause* (for example, many actors all over the world), because of its *effects* (actual or threatened bad consequences for many actors all over the world), or because of its *solution* (requiring actions by many actors all over the world). A paradigm might involve all three elements: a problem for all is caused by actors all over the world and requires solutions in the form of actions/changed policies or behaviors from actors all over the world. Global warming is a good example: the gap between what we want (unchanged weather patterns, sea levels to remain as they are, etc.) and where we are (CO_2 emissions very likely to undermine our goals), caused by the actions of billions throughout the world, and requiring a solution in the form of billions of agents changing their customs and habits.[1]

But other types of global problems might be allowed: a global problem in the form of widespread damage but caused by one country, one group, one organization, or even one person, requiring action by a limited number of actors (e.g., a nuclear accident like Chernobyl); or a global problem perceived by one country as a problem but caused by global activities and requiring action by that country and possibly others (e.g., the American perception of global terrorism).

Even where a global problem is caused by actors worldwide and requires solutions by actors worldwide, the two sets of actors may not be identical. If AIDS is a global problem it is because of the effects on those who contract it, but whether they are the chief agents of the solution is debatable: the solution is partly about stemming the disease's spread to others, which may lie in the hands of other agents who learn—or teach—sexual responsibility regarding condoms, and of the doctors and scientists who produce the drugs that can mitigate its effects.

Most global problems require coordinated action. This presupposes a global ethic in two senses: first, the problem is defined as global because human suffering anywhere is regarded as bad (i.e., we have a global ethic that says all human beings matter and matter equally); and second, we have a duty to cooperate in measures that promote the common good.

Among the most morally compelling global problems are world poverty and, to some extent—though a separate issue—the gap between rich and poor countries. Unlike many problems of the environment where the problem is global because it affects us all in a self-interested way, wherever we are, the problem of absolute poverty is different. What makes it global is not its being globally widespread, though of course it is widespread in many parts of the world and there are pockets of it everywhere, but rather its offending our moral conception of what kind of world we want to have, since the gap between reality and the moral goal is extremely great. We need to note here that the problems of poverty and the imbalances between nations are addressed to the extent that they are seen as global moral problems for those with the power to make things change—rich people, rich organizations, and rich governments. The extent to which there has been a globalization of the problem of extreme poverty is a direct function of the extent of our global moral sensibilities and feelings of solidarity; I shall argue below that this does not go far enough.

Governance

Governance is distinct from and broader than government. It is the sum of the various ways we order our public affairs: formal government with coercive powers is one part—though a significant part—of governance (see CGG 1995). How do we order our affairs at a global level? In one sense global governance has been in existence for a very long time. Ever since the world was sufficiently opened up to allow for extensive cooperation or conflict between different countries or nation-states, there have been attempts by states, acting on their own if very powerful or acting in concert, to try to shape how things go globally, to impose a certain conception of "order" onto international relations. The Westphalian system that evolved from the seventeenth century, in which states both factually were the key actors in the world and normatively had the right to do so, can be seen as a form of global governance. On the other hand, what is often now seen as global governance is a further development in which globalization plays a significant role (see, for example, Linklater 1998). For instance, as manifested in the last fifty years or so, the globalization of governance has the following characteristics:

1. The strengthening of international institutions like the United Nations and the spread of international law. Thus to a far higher degree than before many aspects of life within states are fenced in, if not formally constrained

by, the decisions of international bodies and the laws that are passed. Even if states are still the key actors, the limits in place are far more extensive than before.

2. The increasing influence of nonstate actors such as transnational companies, which play an increasing role in determining how the economies within countries fare, for example, in closing down operations in one city and setting them up elsewhere in the world where labor is cheaper. Such organizations also have a powerful lobbying role in international organizations like the World Trade Organization in helping to shape the developing trade rules, pressing for a General Agreement on Trade in Services (GATS), and so forth. These economic actors may not engage in government or in formulating or approving laws, let alone enforcing them, but they certainly contribute to governance in that what they do and promote influences the way things go globally.

3. The development of global civil society—once described by Mary Robinson, no doubt hyperbolically but with a serious point, as the second superpower alongside the United States. Individuals, whether acting through national nongovernmental organizations (NGOs) or international NGOs (INGOs), or acting through more informal groups (such as those formed for political purposes on the Internet), increasingly play their part in influencing global issues. This may be by pressuring their own governments on internal foreign policy issues, by trying to influence foreign governments (through an Amnesty International letter-writing campaign, for instance), or by presenting their views at international forums (for example, environmental pressure groups helping to formulate international environmental law).

The normative aspect of this is significant as well. If the increasing activities of NGOs in global civil society are a fact, it is a fact that most welcome, both because it is an expression, through membership of relevant bodies, of commitment as "global citizens" to play a part in making a better world, and because of the need to correct the "democratic deficit"—the fact that due to the increasing influence of supranational international institutions (like the United Nations and the European Union) and the powerful influence of transnational companies, in many countries neither governments nor their citizens feel that they control many of the factors crucial to determining their life prospects.

This is particularly so for developing countries, and one of the challenges raised here is how to empower poor countries in international forums where decisions affecting them are made. This is partly a matter of global civil society making sure these voices are properly heard, and partly a matter of empowering people in civil society within poor countries themselves.

It is worth noting in passing that globalization and development are in important respects parallel phenomena. They are processes that their defenders see as moving toward a better state of affairs for human beings, and that their critics see as making things go worse; and they are both to some extent under the control of agents such as governments, international institutions, or large companies. The idea of a process being controlled is more explicit with development than with globalization, but we need to see that any interest in globalization as a multifaceted process that could go in various directions according to our normative priorities is premised on the idea that it is subject, at least to some extent, to human control. Indeed, globalization can be seen as development at a global level, and this thought should remind us that the unit of development is not a fixed datum—it does not have to be the nation-state, and often our focus may be on subnational or supranational levels.

Community

The above discussion about global civil society leads to the next dimension of globalization—the globalization of community. This of course overlaps with governance but is much broader. In many ways this gets to the heart of globalization since it is concerned with the fact that people increasingly feel globally connected. They are conscious of global relationships, and in many ways, in Scholte's phrase, there is a "deterritorialisation of social space" (2000, 45–50). Scholte also speaks of the development of particularist and cosmopolitan solidarities. Particularist solidarities link people from similar groups all over the world (such as indigenous groups, women's groups, etc.), and cosmopolitan solidarities link people who share certain global concerns (such as environmental issues).

In addition to these communities, there may also be developing wider communities of people who sense that they share certain common values, such as human rights, the values of the Earth Charter (2000), or the shared values of a particular church. There is also widespread consensus of people working in NGO movements concerned with development, environment, and peace, though they may differ on particulars and issues of effective means, and there are the shared values of the international relations community or indeed the shared libertarian values of people who do business with each other across the world.

If we mean by community a group of people who are united in sharing certain moral values about what is good or right, then clearly there are emerging many communities of shared ethical values, some overlapping with one another, some in conflict. We cannot say that there is a single global ethical community. On the other hand, we do not need more than some "overlapping consensus" (Rawls 1993, 147–48) for there to be community or society, and it may be that we can talk of emerging global community in the singular, in the sense that we belong to one planet with common vulnerabilities and common fates, and we have somehow to coexist with one another even if our values in many ways differ significantly.

The relevance of this to development is as follows. Regardless of whether there is a single global community, as part of globalization there is certainly an increasing sense among many people that we do share a common global ethic, that we have common but differentiated responsibility across borders, as the Rio Declaration puts it (United Nations, 1992, principle 8), or as the Earth Charter puts it, that with increased power and knowledge comes increased responsibility (Earth Charter 2000, preamble).

The increasing acceptance of this global ethical perspective should in principle be good news for the prospects of development, particularly for poor people in poor countries. The governments of rich countries are, arguably, more likely to give more aid to poor countries and pursue fair trade with them if their citizens see themselves as part of a global community and want, through their own actions and through what they advocate, changed priorities in foreign policy. Whatever cosmopolitan idealists like me may think governments ought to do, the reality is that governments will not act much ahead of—or indeed behind—their electorates in terms of moral priorities, and possibly should not, given the nature of democratic mandate.

Second, I said above that the adoption of a global perspective should in principle favor the poor, but this is an overstatement. This is because to the extent that the communities of shared values include the communities of business and international diplomacy, *and* to the extant that these communities are dominated by the kinds of global ethics that hitherto have dominated, then severe restrictions are in place that hinder the prospects of developing countries. I shall return to this key issue below but briefly remark here that if the values of the relatively unregulated global free market, as well as the internationalist values in international relations theory that legitimate the promotion of national self-interest, remain dominant among those with power, then the prospects for development for poorer countries are limited.

Third, the globalization of community allows for the development of transnational solidarities between different groups in development, often the marginalized, such as minorities, indigenous people, or other groups that are oppressed or whose traditional values are otherwise undermined by modern "progress." Globalization is not merely about homogenization (though it often is, of course) but also about an increased sense of the importance of local differences—a process that has been called "glocalization" (Robertson 1995, 25–44). The point is that the grassroots defense of a traditional conception of development can be strengthened by knowledge of and communication with others who share similar struggles.

Information

The globalization of information (what Scholte calls knowledge) really covers the massive spread of ideas, knowledge, images, sounds, symbols, and so on across the world. This partly covers the phenomenon of McDonaldization or Cocacolarization of the world, contributing to the homogenization of the conceptions of the "good life." But it also has important, serious aspects as well, such as the spread of scientific knowledge, serious academic reflection, and ethical values. While the spread of images and ideas of the good life raises for many thinkers serious doubts because of the wish to preserve cultural diversity in development, the other two areas are more positive in their implications. The sharing of information, particularly information associated with the development of technologies, is actually an important factor in development, and the nature of such transfers raises interesting ethical questions concerning the financial basis on which they are made. On the other hand, ethical values are among the ideas that get transmitted across the world, and this fact helps both with the constitution of global community (or the various communities that collectively make up global community) and the acceptance of a global ethic of some kind.

Further Issues

The Globalization of Ethics

First I want to examine the questions: What exactly is the globalization of ethics? and What is the relevance of the answer to development?

These questions need to be distinguished from the question, What is the ethics of globalization? The latter is—like the ethics of anything—the ethical examination of globalization and its various aspects. It involves the application of ethical values—themselves not a function of globalization—to these issues. These values may be based on a person's religion, theology, philosophy, and worldview derived from various sources. This is an important area of inquiry, and some of the issues germane to it have already been raised in this chapter. A good example of this approach is Singer's 2002 book *One World: The Ethics of Globalization.*

This approach does rest on an important presupposition that some thinkers might question. If globalization is to be subject to ethical assessment (favorable or unfavorable), it must to some extent be capable of change by human intention. Ethics presupposes choice, and therefore if globalization is to be ethically assessed, the assessor must believe it is not an inevitable process that we can do nothing about. The fact that globalization has so many dimensions, as indicated above, strongly favors the view that we can modify its direction if enough of us feel it should be changed. Whether it could be stopped altogether is another matter.

The globalization of ethics, however, comes from a rather different starting point. The assumption here is that ethics is itself the subject matter of globalization rather than the other way round. Just as the globalization of production is about changes in the global economy, and the globalization of governance is about emerging new forms of governance, so the globalization of ethics is about the ways globalization has affected ethics. This is a fascinating question, though it is not often asked.[2]

The globalization of ethics might mean any one of six things (and maybe more):

1. The globalization of ethics is the process whereby the subject matter of ethics as a recognized area of inquiry has come to include global issues and problems. Ethics has become globalized in the sense that an important part of its domain has become global. Ethics becomes or comes to include global ethics. In addition to issues in personal morality and lifestyle and issues in social and political philosophy as applied to the state and society within it, ethics focuses on issues like world poverty, foreign intervention, immigration, international trade rules, debt relief for poor countries, global environmental problems, and so forth. Supporting this factual claim about an area of ethical discourse are these three further claims.

2. The globalization of ethics means that many individuals who did not think about ethics as global ethics come to think of ethics as global ethics: their ethical horizons are expanded because of exposure to what happens in the world through the media.

3. The globalization of ethics may be a process in which many thinkers who may always have accepted that ethics was global in principle now come to see that many of its important issues are in fact global issues. Global ethics in principle becomes global ethics in practice.

4. The globalization of ethics may be, in addition to (1) to (3) and partly as a consequence of them, the process whereby ethics as reflective inquiry comes to involve modified conceptions of ethics itself—not merely the extension of preexisting sets of values to a wider field, but a new understanding of things like responsibility (cf. Jonas 1985), community (Thompson 1992), relationships, "care," and neighborhood (CGG 1995). None of these ideas can mean quite the same thing at a global level as at a local level or even at a national level. Is there, for instance, a quite new sense to global ethics itself, not as a set of beliefs held by an individual but as a shared public social reality? This leads to two further, more specific theses.

5. The globalization of ethics may be a process whereby communities with a "shared ethic" as a kind of social reality come into existence, with membership spread across the world. We noted earlier the development of such communities of shared values. What is being proposed here is an ethic in a new sense—not the sense of a set of values held by a thinker that are for that thinker global in application, but a global ethic as a public social reality—public because it is shared in the strong sense of not just being identical but perceived to be shared by its members. This I shall call the communitarian conception of a global ethic.

6. The globalization of ethics may go further than (4) and be the process whereby certain values come to be accepted by all or almost all people across the world. Globalization either makes explicit commonalities already in existence or it creates this shared universal ethic.

What should we make of these claims, both in themselves and for their relevance to development? The first three claims clearly identify a trend, and are to be welcomed as some of the more positive features of globalization and for their implications for development. The fourth claim about the changing character of ethical concepts, given their global scope, is certainly important to developing the right framework in which people accept their global responsibilities. The fifth claim, that there are emerging various global ethics associated with emerging communities, is at best ambiguous, at worst dangerous, and bad news for development, depending on how the claims are interpreted. The sixth claim, about a single global ethic universally accepted, would, if true, be good news for development since presumably it would include the perspectives of the poor. Unfortunately it is not true, so let us put this one aside first.

It is a claim about something that does not or does not yet exist—though undoubtedly enthusiasts for global ethics think that globalization is either disclosing or producing a global ethic agreed on by sufficiently large numbers to count as global in this sense. Consider the Declaration Toward a Global Ethic of the Parliament of the World's Religions (Küng and Kuschel 1993) and the "global civic ethic" proposed by the Commission on Global Governance (CGG 1995). Whether globalization will eventually produce such an outcome is hard to tell. But if the search for a viable global ethic depends on universal or near-universal consensus, then we have a long time to wait. I shall argue that the validity of a global ethic does not, however, depend on such consensus.

The first three can be taken together. Since from my point of view it is right to see an ethic as global and explicitly so, it can only be a good thing that globalization is leading to more people accepting a global ethic who did not before, to more people turning their global ethic held on principle into an active exercise, and to greater acceptance that ethics as a subject is global as well as social and personal. One way of putting this point is to note that the globalization of ethics has made the ethics of globalization an important part of ethics discourse! Having said that the extension is a good thing, I have to add that much depends on the global ethic that is adopted—not all global ethics will have same benign consequences for development.

From the point of view of development, however, this general trend is to be welcomed. This is not merely because development issues gain from an explicit discourse that tries to find general ethical principles underlying proper development, but more importantly because the acceptance of a global ethic will lead to looking at the whole issue of international responsibilities of individuals, states, and business companies. Indeed, if global ethics has two dimensions—an assertion of universal values and an assertion of trans-societal responsibilities (Dower 1998)—then the globalization of ethics can be seen as the increasing acceptance of the latter, at least for those who already see ethics as implicitly universal. I shall return to this issue again toward the end of the chapter.

The fourth aspect of the globalization of ethics—the development of new conceptions of community, responsibility, and so forth—is potentially important for development, as noted earlier, in that it shakes up limiting prejudices about what morality is about. It could, however, be problematic for development if it either were intended to question that at a fundamental level the core ethical values were permanent, thus opening the way to relativism, or if it led to the dangers of the communitarian conception in the fifth sense.

What shall we make, then, of this sense of a global ethic as an ethic shared by global communities? Is it a good thing that such communities are forming, since ethical action is more likely to be effective if it is embedded in solidarities of various kinds? The difficulty, of course, is that these communities that share values may not have the same values, and they may have values that from one's own point of view are to be rejected or questioned. The so-called Washington Consensus in this sense involved a community of like-minded development thinkers, but their vision of development was one-sided. The community of international diplomats shares certain values about the rights of nations in the international society of states, but for a full-blown cosmopolitan these are inadequate and in a way part of the problem we have in trying to move toward a more just world, as explained more fully below. Of course, if a community has the *right* values, then the fact that these values are embedded in shared practices and mutual support is all to the good.

But the communitarian position is more worrying if a further conclusion is drawn from the fact that there are multiple global ethics associated with different communities: since the validity of an ethic depends on its being accepted by a community of actors who share the ethic, they are just that—a number of different global ethics, none of which is better than any other. The alternative interpretation of this would be to say: Given that there is no single global ethic in sense (6), the idea of a global ethic has no application. A genuine global ethic would be one that is accepted by all, since the alternative would be a "global ethic" imposed on others or applied to others who do not accept it, and this would be unacceptable. So all claimed global ethics are in fact based on error.

This claim that there are multiple equally valid global ethics or none at all, if right, would have dire consequences for development. It would undermine all serious attempts to set out a general account of the character of a development ethic, such as Sen's capability ethic (1999) or O'Neill's Kantian ethic (1989), or attempts to justify development in terms of the progressive realization of human rights. To accept such a universal ethic is not to deny that there may be significant differences in the detailed ways development is pursued. Faithfulness to cultural tradition may well be an important consequence of one of the universal values in development—that people live in accordance with their cultural values and traditions. But the acceptance of diversity within a common framework is a very different story from one in which values are relative to particular cultures or in which a global ethic is denied altogether.

It would also undermine any serious attempt to construct a principled ethical framework for understanding global and international relations. If the validity of an ethical value depends on its being accepted by a community of actors who share that value, there would be no Archimedean point from which to critique the behavior of states or transnational companies, *if* their behavior were based on the global ethic internally accepted by their own community.

We need to get back to some set of first principles for determining a global ethic, and then accept that the globalization of ethics in senses (1) to (3) merely makes it more likely that this ethic will be accepted. And if communities develop, for example, in the development of NGOs with the appropriate shared values, then that fact can help with the realization of the values in question.

This general point can be illustrated by the case of global citizenship. The idea of global citizenship, particularly that of a universal community with a universal ethic, has nothing to do with globalization and indeed goes back to the thinking of the Stoics in the ancient world; the idea was born out of reflection of the general nature of "man" (see, for example, Heater 2002; Dower 2003). But if we look at the modern world we can see how advanced communications and the emergence of global civil society have given a particular social and political expression to global citizenship, and thus made it more likely that people will take up the perspective that has always been available to human beings once they acquired the capacity to think rationally about the general conditions of human nature.

Could Globalization Be a Good Thing for Development?

This leads into my second, more extended issue: Could globalization be a good thing for development? I would rather ask this question than, Is globalization a good thing for development? As things are, the answer to the latter question would have to be on balance "no." For all the many aspects of globalization other than the development of the global economy, such as evolving global communities, strengthening global civil society, and what is called "globalization from below" (Falk 1995, 101), the general effect of the global economy is not good for the world's poor. As Pogge (2002) forcefully argues, the general effects of the global economy are that the socioeconomic rights of millions are simply not being met when they could easily be accommodated if the rules of the system were different—which they could be. Though many may reject capitalism outright (see, for example, Nielsen 2003), it is undoubtedly the case that it could work to much greater advantage for the poor if the types of constraints, taxation regimes, welfare provisions, and other distributive measures, like provision of education and health care for those without the capacity to pay for them— *which are generally taken as read in a rich country*—were applied to international relations. These I take it are the possibilities Sen had in mind in his remarks, quoted above, about the challenge for globalization; likewise, Jonathon Porritt (2005) has argued for the reform of capitalism "as if the world mattered."

There are, of course, many determinants of how well development proceeds in a country and how well a poor person can benefit from it, and these have to do with physical conditions, levels of skill, access to clean water, road infrastructure, and so forth, but arguably among the determining conditions are the ethical assumptions and priorities that guide what agents do. These might be aid agencies working in the field or government agencies in the country in question working with poor people, with certain assumptions about what the good is or what well-being is that development is meant to deliver. It might be governments or businesses pursuing certain general priorities in regard to development because they have a certain conception of what development ought to be. It might be key figures in the governments of other countries and in international institutions who, in addition to views about what the ends and means of development ought to be, have a normative view about the right ordering of international relations (e.g., about what countries ought to do vis-à-vis other countries).

SPHERES OF DEVELOPMENT ETHICS

Development ethics can be divided up in a number of different ways—for example, as Gasper does into case studies, policy formation, and theorizing (2003, xii)—but for my purposes here I want to divide it into the following three sets of questions:

1. What conception of the good should inform development? Here we have the rich and fertile ground of much discussion in development ethics, with such theories as Sen's and Nussbaum's capability approach (see Nussbaum 2000; and Crocker 1991, for example) and O'Neill's Kantian approach (1989) vying with one another, but also presenting themselves as considerably richer than more conventional accounts of the normative basis of development in terms of increasing wealth as the provider of choice or preference satisfaction.
2. What norms should determine the social, political, and economic relations in a society? Which most appropriately deliver the ends of development in the form of well-being? Here we have debates about libertarianism versus Rawlsian distribution and other theories of distributive justice, as well as issues to do with appropriate forms of democracy and participation.
3. What norms should inform the international framework within which countries pursue their development? Here we have debates about the ethical

basis of aid, trade, investment and debt relief, the normative standing of international bodies that deliver aid or support development like the World Bank and the International Monetary Fund, and so on.

Some may doubt that the third question should be considered part of development ethics since it is really an ethical examination of international relations or global relations between people, not of development itself as a process going on inside a given state. But if we accept what I said earlier about the parallels between globalization and development, this distinction may not be so obvious. Development discourse has application where policies can affect how things go for large numbers of people. "International development" can be taken to refer to this dimension. In any case, if the general socioeconomic framework in a country is seen as a means toward the goal of human well-being, exactly the same can be said of the international framework; it is itself another large means to development, including poverty reduction, or it can be a large impediment instead.

The ethical assumptions that underlie the international framework arguably are as crucial to poverty relief as any other ethical determinants. The two main normative obstacles are libertarianism at the global level and nationalism. Unless these are challenged and modified as the ethical ground rules of international relations and the global economy, the conditions of poor countries and the conditions of the very poor within them will remain for a long time. There may of course be some successes through general trickle-down processes, but without a large-scale turnaround, large-scale change will not happen. Yet such change is perfectly possible. It requires simply an ethical metanoia or a changing of ethical priorities.

LIBERTARIANISM AT THE GLOBAL LEVEL

As Sen argues in *Development as Freedom* (1999), we need to distinguish between the basic truth that the freedom to enter the market and buy and sell goods and services is an important constituent of human freedom and well-being—it is an end of development, not merely a means to many other good results—and what is often advocated by economic libertarians, namely an unrestrained and unregulated free market (Sen 1999, chap. 1). For the latter fails to recognize that a person's real or substantive freedom is not the same as his formal freedom (i.e., the fact that there is no law preventing him from entering the market). Substantive freedom, however, like what Rawls calls the worth of liberty (1971, 204), requires many background conditions to enable people to acquire and exercise the relevant freedoms—sufficient material resources, sufficient education, access to health care, a non-oppressive social environment, and so on.

The value of a free market is to be seen in contrast to older practices like guilds, where only certain people could sell certain goods or enter certain professions. It is not to be seen as a license to do *anything*. Restrictions, for instance, on what I may do with dangerous waste, on how little I may pay a worker, on accounting practices, on how much of my money is free from taxation or used to finance public goods and welfare provision, are not unwanted invasions of my economic liberty: they are the framework within which my valuable freedom is exercised, which is needed so that other people can properly enjoy their economic freedom, their other freedoms, and other aspects of their well-being.

There is battle enough to get this perception of the value of economic freedom accepted within economically advanced countries, but my main point is that if anything like it were accepted as the basis of the international free market, we would have a revolution in the way the free market operates. Far more attention would be paid to labor and environmental standards, and far more attention would be paid to creating a genuinely level playing field (e.g., in getting the rich countries to remove their subsidies if poor countries are expected to do so as well). But moving to a level playing field in which the same trade rules are applied consistently for all countries, while a step in the right direction, is hardly enough.

Michael Northcott, speaking at a conference in 2004, likened the level playing field to a chess match between himself and chess champion Boris Spassky: both played by the same rules but Spassky won, and would do so even if he had several pieces removed at the beginning. The analogy is imperfect, of course, since in chess if one person wins, the other must lose, and in free market transactions there may be (as Adam Smith supposed) win-win outcomes. But as we know, the reality is often otherwise, particularly in North-South economic relations, and the analogy of the chess game is apt: the power imbalances are often too great to overcome.

So we need to go further. For example, the profits after tax from international trade and investment go to shareholders who are mainly in rich countries, but more to the point the tax itself generally gets collected by the countries where the companies are registered. Isn't it about time we reconceptualized this? If the profits of international investment are to be taxed, shouldn't the tax be collected for the benefit of the countries involved, or collectively put into an international fund to be used, as inland revenue money is used, to finance education, health, pension and unemployment benefits, and so on? This idea is, of course, a variation on a theme that has been explored by others before, such as the Tobin Tax (Patomaki 2001) or Pogge's Resource Tax (2002). If that idea is too radical, what about the less radical (though still radical enough) idea proposed many years ago by Barbara Ward, that international aid be reconceptualized as "international income tax"?

NATIONALISM

Thinking through the implications of this leads to my next general point about the second level of values that dominate at the moment but need challenging—the nationalist norms. By nationalism here I do not mean a nasty-minded negativity toward other countries and cultures, but rather an assumption, which has a long history in international relations, that the primary duty of governments is to defend the national interest, and that they should do so as long as it respects the sovereignty of other countries (see, for example, Bull 1977; Beitz 1979; Dower 1998). The idea of a tax suggested above used to benefit people worldwide would only be acceptable if we adopted a more cosmopolitan attitude and asked the question, What ought governments do to facilitate the real reduction of world poverty?

Even if we did not go so far as to support some form of international income tax, governments might come to see that not only do we need to have more generous and better aid, we also need to overhaul the whole way the international economy functions—since as it stands we give in aid with one hand but in effect take rather more with the other hand in our general economic relations. The same can of course be said about debt servicing of poor countries: if we really meant business with our aid, we would cancel the debt whose servicing more than cancels out the aid in many cases.

The moral is this: just as the Latin adage says that if you want peace prepare for war, so we might say—and I may add more truthfully—if you want the alleviation of world poverty, prepare for a new normative basis for international relations![3]

Conclusion

If I am right that a major determination of how poor countries fare and how far poor people can escape from their poverty is the international normative regime, and that major changes in this regime—by moving to a less libertarian understanding of global economic relations and a more cosmopolitan basis for foreign policy—could transform the former situation, *could* globalization help with this?

Despite actual current trends, I believe it could, though it may well not do so. Someone once said that I was a factual pessimist and moral optimist. I am the latter because I believe that we can change things for the better—hence the point of all the moral argument in this chapter! Globalization is not a remorseless juggernaut; it is a process we can push in one direction or another. In many ways the processes of globalization are already loosening the shackles of the nationalist paradigm, as more and more people are entering wider communities of concern and flexing their global citizenship muscles. There is also hope that as time goes on we can humanize the libertarian paradigm of the global free market and recognize that the real freedom of all people requires a world ordered by rather different ground rules from those prevalent today.

NOTES

1. For different senses of a global problem, see also Holland (2000, 1).

2. For a related idea of "ethics under globalization," see Commers, Vandekerckhove, and Verlinden (2008).

3. This is not to deny that problems within developing countries—such as corruption and inefficiency—also need to be addressed as impediments to genuine development.

REFERENCES

Beitz, C. R. 1979. *Political Theory and International Relations.* Princeton: Princeton University Press.

Bull, H. 1977. *The Anarchical Society.* London: Macmillan.

Commers, R., W. Vandekerckhove, and A. Verlinden. 2008. Introduction to *Ethics in an Era of Globalization*, ed. R. Commers, W. Vandekerckhove, and A. Verlinden, 1–10. Aldershot, UK: Ashgate.

CGG (Commission on Global Governance). 1995. *Our Global Neighborhood.* Oxford: Oxford University Press.

Crocker, D. A. 1991. Towards Development Ethics. *World Development* 19 (5): 457–83.

Dower, N. 1998. *World Ethics: The New Agenda.* Edinburgh: Edinburgh University Press.

———. 2003. *Introduction to Global Citizenship.* Edinburgh: Edinburgh University Press.

Earth Charter. 2000. http://www.earthcharter.org/.

Falk, R. 1995. *On Humane Governance: Toward a New Global Politics.* Cambridge, UK: Polity Press.

Gasper, D. 2003. *The Ethics of Development.* Edinburgh: Edinburgh University Press.

Heater, D. 2002. *World Citizenship: Cosmopolitan Thinking and Its Opponents.* London: Continuum.

Holland, A. 2000. Sustainable Development: The Contested Visions. In *Global Sustainable Development in the 21st Century*, ed. K. Lee, A. Holland, and D. McNeill, 1–8. Edinburgh: Edinburgh University Press.

Jonas, H. 1985. *The Imperative of Responsibility: In Search of an Ethics for the Technological Age.* Chicago: University of Chicago Press.

Küng, H., and K.-J. Kuschel. 1993. *A Global Ethic: The Declaration of the Parliament of the World's Religions.* London: SCM Press.

Linklater, A. 1998. *The Transformation of Political Community: Ethical Foundations of the Post-Westphalian Era.* Cambridge, UK: Polity Press.

Nielsen, K. 2003. *Globalization and Justice.* New York: Humanity Books.

Nussbaum, M. 2000. *Women and Human Development: The Capabilities Approach.* Cambridge: Cambridge University Press.

O'Neill, O. 1989. *Faces of Hunger.* London: Allen and Unwin.

Patomaki, H. 2001. *Democratizing Globalization: The Leverage of the Tobin Tax.* London: Zed Books.

Pogge, T. 2002. *World Poverty and Human Rights: Cosmopolitan Responsibilities and Reforms.* Cambridge, UK: Polity Press.

Porritt, J. 2005. *Capitalism as if the World Mattered.* London: Earthscan.

Rawls, J. 1971. *A Theory of Justice.* Oxford: Oxford University Press.

———. 1993. *Political Liberalism.* New York: Columbia University Press.

Robertson, R. 1995. Glocalization: Time-Space and Homogeneity-Heterogeneity. In *Global Modernities*, ed. M. Featherstone, S. Lash, and R. Robertson, 25–44. London: Sage.

Sachs, W., ed. 1992. *The Development Dictionary.* London: Zed Books.

Scholte, J. A. 2000. *Globalization: A Critical Introduction.* Basingstoke, UK: Palgrave.

Sen, A. 1999. *Development as Freedom.* Oxford: Oxford University Press.

———. 2002. How to Judge Globalism. *American Prospect* 13 (1): 1–14.

Singer, P. 2002. *One World: The Ethics of Globalization.* New Haven: Yale University Press.

Spybey, T. 1996. *Globalization and World Society.* Cambridge, UK: Polity Press.

Thompson, J. 1992. *Justice and World Order.* London: Routledge.

United Nations. 1992. *Rio Declaration.* New York: United Nations.

Contributors

Sabina Alkire directs the Oxford Poverty and Human Development Initiative (OPHI) at the University of Oxford, which is developing a multidimensional framework for poverty reduction drawing on approaches such as the capability approach initiated by Amartya Sen. She is also a research associate at the Global Equity Initiative at Harvard University. Her publications include *Valuing Freedoms: Sen's Capabilities Approach and Poverty Reduction* (Oxford University Press, 2005) as well as articles in philosophy and economics. Previously she has worked for the Commission on Human Security, the World Bank, Oxfam, and the Asia Foundation in Pakistan. She holds a D.Phil. in economics from Magdalen College, Oxford.

David Barkin is Professor of Economics at the Xochimilco Campus of the Universidad Autónoma Metropolitana in Mexico City. He received his doctorate in economics from Yale University and was awarded the National Prize in Political Economics in 1979 for his analysis of inflation in Mexico. He is a member of the Mexican Academy of Sciences and the National Research Council. In 1974 he was a founding member of the Ecodevelopment Center. His most recent books include *Wealth, Poverty, and Sustainable Development* (Centro de Ecología y Desarrollo, 1998) and *Innovaciones Mexicanas en el Manejo del Agua* (Mexican innovations in water management) (Centro de Ecología y Desarrollo, 2001). He is interested in the process of unequal development that creates profound imbalances throughout society and promotes environmental degradation. His recent research focuses on the implementation of alternative strategies for the sustainable management of resources. Much of his work is conducted in collaboration with local communities and regional citizens' groups.

Nigel Dower is Senior Lecturer in Philosophy at the University of Aberdeen. His main research interests are in the fields of ethics/philosophy of development, environment, and international relations. Much of his research work has stemmed from his involvement in the 1970s in several organizations campaigning for a more just and peaceful world, and through membership in the

World Development Movement and the United Nations Association (he is still chair of the Aberdeen branch of UNA). More recently his work has focused on the challenge of globalization, especially its implications for our understanding of global civil society; on the relevance of the Earth Charter; and on the widening but contested understanding of security. He is the author of *World Poverty Challenge and Response* (Ebor, 1983), *World Ethics: The New Agenda* (Edinburgh University Press, 1998), and *An Introduction to Global Citizenship* (Edinburgh University Press, 2003); and he has edited *Ethics and Environmental Responsibility* (Gower, 1989) and (with John Williams) *Global Citizenship: A Critical Reader* (Edinburgh University Press, 2002).

Stephen L. Esquith is Professor in the Department of Philosophy at Michigan State University and Dean of the Residential College in the Arts and Humanities there. He is the author of *Intimacy and Spectacle* (Cornell University Press, 1994), a critique of classical and modern liberal political philosophy, and has written on the rule of law, the problem of democratic political education, mass violence and reconciliation, and moral and political responsibility. He has been involved in numerous civic engagement projects in the public schools, and also was a Fulbright Lecturer in Poland at the Adam Mickiewicz University in Poznan in 1990–91 and in Mali at the University of Bamako in 2005–6. He leads a study abroad program in Mali on ethics and development, and his book *The Political Responsibilities of Everyday Bystanders* is being published by Pennsylvania State University Press.

Shelley Feldman is a professor in the Department of Development Sociology and Director of the Feminist, Gender, and Sexuality Studies Program at Cornell University, and a visiting professor in the Sociology Department and the Fernand Braudel Center at Binghamton University. As a feminist scholar and critic of developmentalist analyses, her research explores state formation, displacement and dislocation, and economic and social reorganization, including a transforming agrarian structure. She is the author of "Social Regulation in the Time of War: Constituting the Current Crisis" (2007), "Bengali State and Nation Making: Partition and Displacement Revisited" (2003), "Paradoxes of Institutionalization: The Depoliticisation of Bangladeshi NGOs" (2003), "Intersecting and Contesting Positions: Postcolonialism Feminism and World Systems Theory" (2001), and "Exploring Theories of Patriarchy: A Perspective from Contemporary Bangladesh" (2001). Her current research focuses on state formation in East Pakistan and on militarism in the United States.

Des Gasper works at the Institute of Social Studies in The Hague, the Netherlands. He studied economics, development, and policy analysis at the Universities of Cambridge and East Anglia, and then worked in southern Africa through the 1980s. His research interests are development theory and development ethics; public policy analysis, including policy argumentation, evaluation, and "logical framework analysis"; methodologies of policy analysis; and southern Africa. He is the author most recently of *The Ethics of Development: From Economism to Human Development* (Edinburgh University Press, 2004).

Fred Gifford is Professor and Associate Chair in the Department of Philosophy, Faculty Associate in the Center for Ethics and Humanities in the Life Sciences, and Director of the graduate specialization in ethics and development at Michigan State University. His research and teaching interests include the philosophy of science and ethics, especially topics at their intersection. These include ethical issues concerning agricultural biotechnology and "bioprospecting" for drug development. His recent work has focused on ethical and methodological issues in clinical trials and research more generally, and this has taken him recently to questions of the ethics of research in developing nations. He developed and has taught six times a study abroad program, "Ethics and History of Development and Health Care in Costa Rica," which explores bioethics and health care justice as well as ethical issues concerning environment and development.

Daniel Little is Chancellor of the University of Michigan–Dearborn. He serves as Professor of Philosophy at UM-Dearborn, Faculty Associate at the Inter-University Consortium for Political and Social Research (ICPSR) within the Institute for Social Research at the University of Michigan–Ann Arbor, and Center Associate, Center for Chinese Studies, University of Michigan–Ann Arbor. The most recent of his several books is *The Paradox of Wealth and Poverty: Mapping the Ethical Dilemmas of Global Development* (Westview, 2003), a discussion of some of the normative issues raised by processes of economic development in the developing world.

A. Allan Schmid is University Distinguished Professor Emeritus in the Department of Agricultural Economics at Michigan State University and the author of numerous articles and books, including *Property, Power, and Public Choice* (Praeger, 1987) and *Conflict and Cooperation* (Blackwell, 2004). He teaches institutional and behavioral economics at the graduate level and community economics/environmental economics and policy analysis to undergraduates.

His research includes environmental policy and land use, law and economics, public choice, benefit-cost analysis, intellectual property in biotechnology, and institutional transformations in eastern Europe and developing countries. His professional interests include collective action in agriculture and natural resources, institutional and behavioral economics theory, agricultural groundwater pollution, policy and sustainable agriculture, benefit-cost analysis methods, agricultural interest groups and the free rider problem, law and economics of biotechnology, the transformation of formerly socialist economies in Africa and eastern Europe, rural-urban population settlement patterns and economic development, local government fiscal impact of population growth, social capital, and experimental economics.

Asunción Lera St. Clair is Associate Professor in the Department of Sociology at the University of Bergen. Her work has focused on ethical and normative problems related to poverty and development. In particular, she has applied analytical tools from the field of social studies of science to the interface between scientific knowledge on poverty, politics, and ethics among multilateral development agencies. Her current work relates to the problems posed by expertise and responsibilities for the eradication of poverty, and broadly to the tensions arising between economic neoliberal globalization and the globalization of human rights. She is also currently Secretary of the International Development Ethics Association (IDEA, http://www.development-ethics.org/).

Paul B. Thompson holds the W. K. Kellogg Chair in Agriculture, Food, and Community Ethics at Michigan State University, with appointments in the Departments of Philosophy; Agricultural Economics; and Community, Agriculture, Recreation, and Resource Studies. He is the author of *The Spirit of the Soil: Agriculture and Environmental Ethics* (Routledge, 1994), *The Ethics of Aid and Trade: U.S. Food Policy, Foreign Competition, and the Social Contract* (Cambridge University Press, 1992), and *Food Biotechnology in Ethical Perspective* (Springer, 2007); and co-editor of *The Agrarian Roots of Pragmatism* (Vanderbilt University Press, 2000). He has served on many national and international committees on agricultural biotechnology and contributed to the National Research Council report *The Environmental Effects of Transgenic Plants*.

Thanh-Dam Truong is Associate Professor in Women/Gender and Development Studies at the Institute of Social Studies, The Hague, the Netherlands. She received her Ph.D. in social sciences from the University of Amsterdam in 1988. She specializes in gender and international political economy with an empirical focus on international migration, human trafficking, and sex tourism, and has extensive experience in Africa and East and Southeast Asia. She has contributed to the debates on human development, human rights, and human security through the lens of gender practices in policymaking in Asia and Africa. Her current research also includes how Buddhist epistemology may contribute to a dialogic transformation.

Index